# WEB DESIGN: VIDEO SITES

Ed. Julius Wiedemann

TASCHEN

HONG KONG KÖLN LONDON LOS ANGELES MADRID PARIS TOKYO

# CONTENTS

FOREWORD

# Foreword

Nicholas Mir Chaikin

About twelve years ago I assisted in the production of a live video webcast of a Valentine's Day night at the Crazy Horse, a well-known Parisian cabaret. The postage-stamp video was sadly in the middle of a lovely little size of much ado about nothing. The moves and curves of the famous Crazy Horse dancers were lost to the sites' visitors. Nothing to see here, move along. As we all know, the experience nowadays would be vastly different.

We are familiar with buzzwords such as "ubiquitous", "convergence" and "user-driven", and while they now feel ancient (in terms of internet time) they have also proven their pertinence amongst today's key criteria — their values have come true. We have not just YouTube and Dailymotion to thank, or to blame, but the entire cloud of the internets. People are using video everywhere, because they can and because it is easy to do so, because it's a form we understand and can easily master, and because it can help enrich a web experience.

And while the web moves to the forefront of grander and grander campaign and communication strategies, so have the budgets and tools to capture eyes, ears, and clicks. Those of us in the web agency business have found that we are spending more time with film production agencies and script-writers while clients are expecting us to know how to make movies.

Advertisers keep asking for "viral" and see the rapid-fire-millions of eyeballs that throwing a girl through a basketball hoop or a funny kitty can attract on YouTube. Increasingly the I-don't-know-what-I'm-doing aesthetic of your average YouTube video is what web creators are instructed to dream up — hoping to win the random viral jackpot. Will public tastes truly integrate the user-driven home-made aesthetic as our only requirement for filmic entertainment? I do not think so. Production values are not dead! Indeed the inverse could occur as traditional broadcast resolutions look rather flimsy on high-resolution monitors. Furthermore, the roles of directors and camera-persons are not in peril. The casting directors will probably not have to give up their couches, and storytelling will still require the input of professional storytellers.

American-born **Nicholas Mir Chaikin** moved from New York to Paris about a decade ago where he founded the design and interactive agency **Spill**. Spill has specialised in identity and digital communication since 1995, and has been internationally recognised for the elegance, purity, and quality of its work, gathering numerous awards and press coverage from all over the world. **<www.spill.net>**

www.minijet.fr

SMIRTING FILMS: THE COWBOY BREAK TIME BIKINI WONDER FEMME FATALE

CHEZ PIERRE

Smirt-Club

miniJet

</>

miniJet

DE-
SIGN

THE
MINIJET

PASSER
AU
FRANÇAIS

FUN-
CTION

BUY
ONE!

SMIRTING
???

S.T. Dupont

WRITE
TO
US

HIS-
TORY

ACTIVATE YOUR
GUARANTEE

SMIRT
WITH
US

DOWN-
LOAD

CREDITS

# Vorwort

## Nicholas Mir Chaikin

Vor etwa 12 Jahren assistierte ich am Abend des Valentinstages bei der Produktion eines Live-Video-Webcasts im berühmten Pariser Kabarett *Crazy Horse*. Doch das war vertane Zeit: Das Mini-Video im Briefmarken-Format ging irgendwo auf einer schön gestalteten Internetseite unter. Die Tanzbewegungen und Kurven der berühmten *Crazy Horse*-Tänzerinnen waren für den Besucher der Seite fast nicht zu erkennen. Wenn es auf einer Website nichts Interessantes zu sehen gibt, klickt man einfach weiter. Wie wir alle wissen, hat sich mittlerweile sehr viel getan.

Wir sind alle mit Schlagwörtern wie „allgegenwärtig", „Konvergenz" und „Nutzerfreundlichkeit" vertraut. Auch wenn diese Konzepte heute in Zeiten des Internets veraltet zu sein scheinen, haben sie dennoch nicht an Bedeutung verloren – ganz im Gegenteil, sie haben sich bewährt. Das ist nicht nur der Verdienst von YouTube und Dailymotion, sondern des gesamten Internets. Videos gelten überall und immer. Das liegt daran, dass sie einfach herzustellen sind, eine leicht zu verstehende Kommunikationsform darstellen und nicht zuletzt daran, dass sie dazu beitragen, den Besuch im Internet zu bereichern.

Für das Internet werden immer größere Werbekampagnen und aufwendigere Kommunikationsmethoden ersonnen, immer größere Budgets zur Verfügung gestellt und Tools entwickelt, um unsere Augen und Ohren zu beeindrucken und so viele Mausklicks wie möglich anzuziehen. In den Internetagenturen arbeiten wir immer häufiger mit Filmproduktionsfirmen und Drehbuchautoren zusammen, während die Kunden von uns erwarten, dass wir genau wissen, wie man Filme macht.

Werbeagenturen verlangen nach „viralen" Inhalten und haben dabei im Hinterkopf, wie Millionen von Internet-User zusehen, wenn auf YouTube ein Mädchen durch einen Basketballkorb geworfen wird oder eine Katze ihre Streiche spielt. Genau diese spontane „Ich-weiß-nicht-genau-was-ich-tue"-Ästhetik des durchschnittlichen YouTube-Videos ist es, die der Kunde von den kreativen Köpfen der Internetagenturen verlangt und dabei hofft, dass auch seine Seite von Millionen Usern angeklickt wird. Wird das Publikum wirklich die provisorische Ästhetik selbstgebastelter Videos als Maßstab für die Filmunterhaltung ansetzen? Das glaube ich nicht. Die altbewährten Werte der Film- und Videoproduktion gelten immer noch! Tatsächlich wird die Entwicklung entgegengesetzt verlaufen, da die Bildqualität traditionell produzierter Videos auf hoch auflösenden Monitoren mittlerweile zu wünschen übrig lässt. Zudem sind die Rollen von Regisseur und Kameraleuten immer noch eindeutig verteilt. Die Casting-Agenturen müssen also nicht um ihre Existenz fürchten, und das Geschichtenerzählen verlangt immer noch nach der geistigen Arbeit professioneller Geschichtenerzähler.

Der in den USA geborene **Nicholas Mir Chaikin** zog vor etwa zehn Jahren von New York nach Paris, wo er die Design- und Internetagentur **Spill** gründete. Spill spezialisiert sich seit 1995 auf die Bereiche Corporate Identity und digitale Kommunikation. Ihre international bekannten, in der Presse ausführlich besprochenen Arbeiten erhielten zahlreiche Preise und zeichnen sich durch Eleganz und Purismus aus. **<www.spill.net>**

www.minijet.fr

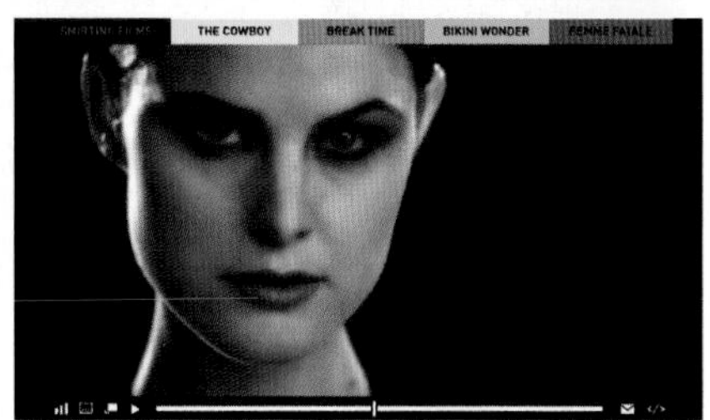

FOREWORD

## Préface

Nicholas Mir Chaikin

Il y a douze ans, j'ai assisté à la production d'un webcast vidéo en direct d'une soirée de la Saint Valentin au Crazy Horse, le fameux cabaret parisien. La fenêtre format timbre-poste de la vidéo trônait tristement au milieu d'un charmant petit site web qui faisait beaucoup de bruit pour rien. Les visiteurs du site ne pouvaient distinguer ni les mouvements ni les courbes des célèbres danseuses du Crazy Horse. Circulez, il n'y a rien à voir. Comme nous le savons tous, aujourd'hui l'expérience aurait été bien différente.

Les termes « universalité », « convergence » et « orientation utilisateur » nous sont familiers, et bien qu'ils semblent maintenant aussi vieux qu'Internet, ils se sont aussi révélés significatifs à l'aune des critères contemporains : les valeurs qu'ils représentent sont aujourd'hui une réalité. Ce n'est pas seulement YouTube et DailyMotion qu'il faut remercier, ou blâmer, mais tout le nuage des internets. Les gens utilisent la vidéo partout, parce que c'est possible et parce que c'est facile, parce que c'est un format que l'on comprend et maîtrise sans peine, et parce que la vidéo peut enrichir l'expérience des utilisateurs du web.

La sphère Internet héberge des campagnes et des stratégies de communication de plus en plus grande envergure, et nous avons accès aux budgets et aux outils qui nous permettent de capter les regards, les attentions et les clics de souris. Nous, les acteurs du secteur des agences web, passons de plus en plus de temps avec les agences de production de film et les scénaristes, et les clients nous demandent de savoir faire des films.

Les annonceurs demandent encore et toujours du « viral » et voient les millions d'yeux qu'une vidéo montrant une fille passant à travers un panier de basket ou un petit chat amusant peut attirer instantanément sur YouTube. De plus en plus souvent, on demande aux créateurs du web de reproduire l'esthétique aléatoire de celui que ne sait pas ce qu'il fait, si courante dans les vidéos de YouTube, en espérant décrocher le jackpot des campagnes virales. Les goûts du public se fixeront-ils sur l'esthétique orientée utilisateur « fait maison » comme unique critère du divertissement audiovisuel ? Je ne le pense pas. La production professionnelle n'est pas morte ! C'est d'ailleurs l'inverse qui pourrait se produire, car la résolution de la télévision traditionnelle est bien peu convaincante sur les moniteurs haute définition. Les rôles de réalisateur et de caméraman ne sont pas non plus en danger de disparition. Les directeurs de casting n'auront sans doute pas besoin de quitter leurs canapés, et une bonne narration nécessitera toujours le savoir-faire des conteurs d'histoires professionnels.

**Nicholas Mir Chaikin** est né aux États-Unis. Il a déménagé de New York à Paris il y a une dizaine d'années et y a créé **Spill**, une agence de design interactif. Elle est spécialisée dans l'identité et la communication numérique depuis 1995, et a été reconnue internationalement pour l'élégance, la pureté et la qualité de son travail. Elle a reçu de nombreuses récompenses et la presse du monde entier lui a consacré des articles. **<www.spill.net>**

www.minijet.fr

## Introduction

Leo Prestes

Bob Garfield, a columnist for *Advertising Age*, was recently at a digital communication event in Brazil. During the talk he gave there, he mentioned the first music video shown on North American MTV, *"Video Killed the Radio Star"* by Buggles, and pointed out its irony, almost thirty years later. Today, MTV has actually cut videos from its schedule, choosing instead to focus on reality shows and entertainment programmes. Garfield stressed the reason behind this: *"Online video killed the MTV Star"*. The ease with which we can now watch music videos on YouTube — from dinosaurs like Buggles, digitalised from a musty old VHS tape, to OK Go, a band which hit the market through one of its videos appearing directly on YouTube — has left the famous channel with no alternative.

Yet this, perhaps, won't be enough to solve the problems MTV and all the other mass-audience channels are now encountering. After all, the day is not far off when reality shows, news programmes, and even live events like football matches and concerts, will be just as common on computer screens as they now are on television.

Until then, however, they will have to put up with the cascading releases of the entertainment industry, which insists on ignoring the power of online videos. Nevertheless, certain media do exist which make use of "online" and "offline" modes intelligently and in a complementary way. The TV series *Heroes* is a good example. It doesn't just put episodes online for people to watch, or simply finish TV shows with the dull "see more at our site". *Heroes* is interactive, from the very moment the scripts are created, as a way of enhancing the episodes, getting to know the audience, creating extra content and, above all, attracting sponsors.

All this information keeps *Heroes* on its toes, makes trends more apparent and sets up references enabling us to produce stronger and sounder PowerPoints and Keynotes; it is also less dependent on tired old phrases like "power to the consumer", "content is king" and "collaborative content". What, however, can be done within an agency so that all these changes come out in our favour, and the next big web video has our name on it?

The question which immediately springs to mind is "should the online video really be produced in a more amateur way than the traditional one?" Does public interest grow when it realises that there is no professional team at work behind the scenes? Or has demand for this kind of video only assumed its current proportions because there was less investment in the digital area, and it was the only possible way of producing innovative scripts?

As the band gets broader still, faster computers and tools are appearing with the result that videos can be included within site graphics (have you seen AgencyNet's quitdoingit.com?) and video mash-ups can be put together with various APIs (check out takethisdance.com and see what I'm talking about). It's possible that the amateur video fashion will die out. In fact, many brands have already realised, in the most disappointing of ways, that for each Coke + Mentos that burst upon the web, there are another 1000 videos just as anonymous as the one of the graduation ceremony of somebody's first cousin twice-removed.

Campaigns like "create your own advert", which followed the same logic as the Doritos 2006 "Crash the Superbowl" campaign, have sprung up around the world in the same fashion, even if they haven't always had the same success as the original. In their anxiety to turn viral, many clients and agencies have forgotten

www.nbc.com/Heroes

that, before making a video, you need to produce a conceptual universe which gives the consumer a good reason to get his camera out of the cupboard. The explosion of virals with no real content to spread may end up condemning the format and leading brands to turn, once again, to professionals.

This possibility sends another doubt echoing down agency corridors: should agencies contract producers to make the videos or should they invest in their own infrastructures? Major digital agencies, such as R/GA and AgencyNet, have their own studios and, even as I write, my agency, W3Haus, is setting up its own. At first glance, this might seem slightly contradictory for those communication companies who have grown precisely because their way of working differs from the overblown and obsolete formulae of traditional advertising. It's nonetheless true that, in an area where financial support is still far from ideal, where the return from the public is immediate, and where reactions to everything that comes out have a decisive effect on what will be done the following day, maybe the presence of a producer in the next room is the best way of responding to client needs.

These, however, are questions and answers that have only proved to be valid at this precise moment. And they may not even outlast the time it takes for this text to be produced and published in a book. Every day, new evaluation parameters appear for our work — and even YouTube started, some time ago, to reveal the origin of its accesses. A new channel showing videos turns up every day. Some weeks ago, I received a link for qik.com, where it's possible to transmit live from a mobile phone and interact with visitors to the site. Have you considered the possibilities this technology offers in a football match, a show or a women's toilet?

New and more precise ways of segmenting audiences and personalising messages for particular spectators are appearing all the time. With each passing day, predictions like the one in the Buggles song become more and more ephemeral and disposable. The formats change, wiping each other out and creating new demands from the general public. The only safe alternative in the midst of all these changes is to follow them closely and interpret them constantly, identifying and evaluating the innovative ideas. That's why books like this don't run the slightest risk of being shot down by the latest trend.

**Leo Prestes** was born in Porto Alegre, Brazil. He's now 30 and has worked in communication since he was 19. Today, Leo is responsible for the creation and planning of **W3Haus**, a bustling digital agency founded in 2000. Having started out as four people in a small Porto Alegre office, it has since opened branches in London and São Paulo and recruited personnel from all walks of life. The agency is currently concerned with creation, planning and general media.
**<www.w3haus.com>**

# Einleitung

## Leo Prestes

Bob Garfield, Kolumnist bei „Advertising Age", besuchte eine Veranstaltung über digitale Kommunikation in Brasilien. Dort erwähnte er das erste Musikvideo überhaupt, das bei dem nordamerikanischen Sender MTV gezeigt wurde („*Video Killed the Radio Star*" von der Band Buggles), und er sprach von der Ironie, die auch dreißig Jahre später noch darin steckt. Heute hat MTV den größten Teil der Musikvideos aus dem Sendeplan genommen und konzentriert sich auf Reality-Shows und Unterhaltungssendungen. Garfield bringt die Gründe für diese Entwicklung auf den Punkt: „*Online video killed the MTV Star*". Die Leichtigkeit, mit der wir heute Musikvideos auf YouTube schauen können – angefangen bei solchen Dinosauriern wie den Buggles, digitalisiert von einem alten VHS-Video, bis hin zu der Band *OK Go*, die sich mit einem einzigen YouTube-Video auf dem Markt durchgesetzt hat –, hat dem berühmten Musiksender keine andere Wahl gelassen.

Programmumstellungen dieser Art lösen allerdings die Probleme von MTV und anderen massentauglichen Sendern nicht. Denn der Tag ist nicht mehr weit, an dem Reality-Shows, Nachrichtensendungen und sogar Live-Events wie Fußballspiele und Konzerte genauso selbstverständlich auf dem Computer geschaut werden wie über den Fernseher.

Bis dahin müssen sich diese Formate mit den zahllosen Arbeiten der Unterhaltungsindustrie abfinden, die die Macht der Online-Videos immer noch unterschätzt. Trotzdem gibt es mittlerweile einige Medienformate, bei denen die Möglichkeiten, die sich „online" und „offline" bieten, intelligent und ergänzend genutzt werden. Die TV-Serie *Heroes* ist ein gutes Beispiel dafür. Hier werden nicht nur Episoden online präsentiert oder lediglich im Abspann der Tipp gegeben, die Website zu besuchen. *Heroes* ist vielmehr von Grund auf interaktiv angelegt. Im Internet werden Episoden ergänzt, Informationen und neue Inhalte vermittelt und nicht zuletzt Werbekunden angesprochen.

*Heroes* liefert uns wichtige Erkenntnisse, lässt Trends erkennen und versorgt uns mit den wichtigsten Informationen, um in unseren PowerPoint-Präsentationen und Grundsatzreden die aktuellsten Tendenzen analysieren zu können. Die alten Schlagwörter wie „Die Macht dem Verbraucher", „Nur der Inhalt zählt" und „Massentauglicher Inhalt" zählen nicht mehr. Was also können wir in einer Agentur tun, um diese Veränderungen positiv zu nutzen und im Abspann des nächsten Web-Videos unseren Namen zu sehen?

Mir drängt sich dabei unmittelbar die Frage auf: Soll das Online-Video wirklich auf eine amateurhaftere Weise produziert werden als das traditionelle? Wächst das Interesse des Publikums, wenn es merkt, dass kein professionelles Team am Werk war? Oder hat die Nachfrage nach solchen Videos nur diese Ausmaße angenommen, weil in den digitalen Bereich weniger investiert wurde und innovative Drehbücher daher nur auf diese Art geschrieben werden konnten?

Je höher die Übertragungsraten, desto schneller werden die Computer und Tools. Das hat zur Folge, dass Websites mittlerweile komplett aus Videoanimationen bestehen können (zum Beispiel bei quitdoingit.com von AgencyNet) und Video-Mashups mit mehreren APIs zusammengebracht werden können (auf takethisdance.com sieht man sehr gut, was ich meine). Möglicherweise ist die Mode der Amateurvideos auch bald wieder vorbei. Tatsächlich haben zahlreiche Marken bereits schmerzlich erfahren müssen dass für jedes „Coca Cola"- und „Mentos"-Video 1000 neue ins Web gestellt werden, die allesamt so anonym sind wie das der Abschlussfeier irgendeines Cousins zweiten Grades.

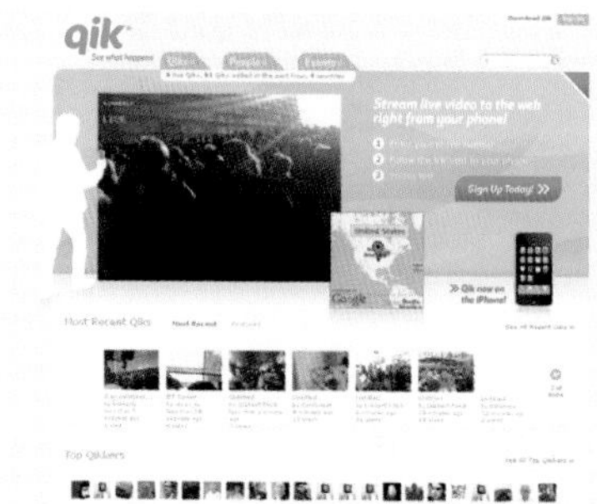

www.qik.com

Kampagnen wie „Kreiere deinen eigenen Werbespot", die derselben Logik folgen wie die Doritos-Kampagne „Crash the Superbowl", werden in der ganzen Welt verbreitet, auch wenn sie nie den Erfolg des Originals erreichen. In ihrem Bestreben, auf den Zug der „Viral Videos" aufzuspringen, haben viele Kunden vergessen, dass man sich vor der Produktion eines Videos intensiv damit auseinandersetzen muss, wie der Konsument am besten erreicht werden kann. Die schier unermessliche Zahl an „Viral Videos", die keinen wirklichen Inhalt vermitteln, könnte dazu führen, dass dieses Format irgendwann verpönt ist und die Unternehmen wieder zu professionellen Werbungsformaten übergehen.

Diese Möglichkeit lässt eine weitere Frage bei den Agenturen aufkommen: Sollten Agenturen Produzenten beauftragen, um Videos zu drehen, oder sollten sie in ihre eigene Infrastruktur investieren? Die wichtigsten Digitalagenturen – so zum Beispiel R/GA und AgencyNet – verfügen über eigene Studios, und auch meine Agentur W3Haus ist jetzt gerade dabei, ihr eigenes Studio aufzubauen. Auf den ersten Blick scheint dies ein Widerspruch zu sein, denn einige Werbeagenturen sind gerade deshalb erfolgreich, weil ihre Arbeitsweise sich von den überholten Methoden der traditionellen Werbung unterscheidet. In einem Bereich, in dem das finanzielle Budget noch immer beschränkt ist, wo die Rückmeldung vom Publikum unmittelbar erfolgt und wo die Reaktionen auf die Veröffentlichungen einen entscheidenden Einfluss auf das Geschehen des nächsten Tages haben, ist es trotzdem eine unbestreitbare Tatsache, dass man auf die Bedürfnisse des Kunden am besten mit einem professionellen Produzenten reagiert.

Das alles sind Fragen und Antworten, die nur genau jetzt, in diesem Moment zählen. Sie haben vielleicht nicht einmal mehr Gültigkeit, wenn dieser Text veröffentlicht wird. Jeden Tag werden wir bei unserer Arbeit mit neuen Bewertungskriterien konfrontiert – sogar bei *YouTube* kann man sich seit einiger Zeit darüber informieren, wie häufig Videos an bestimmten Orten geschaut werden. Jeden Tag entsteht ein neuer Videokanal. Vor einigen Wochen bekam ich einen Link zu qik.com, einer Seite, die es ermöglicht, Videos direkt vom Handy aus ins Internet zu stellen und mit den anderen Usern zu interagieren. Haben Sie einmal daran gedacht, welche Möglichkeiten eine solche Technologie bietet – für ein Fußballspiel, eine Show oder auf der Damentoilette?

Neue und noch präzisere Methoden zur Bestimmung von Zielgruppen und zur Personalisierung von Nachrichten schießen wie Pilze aus dem Boden. Mit jedem neuen Tag werden solche Prophezeiungen wie die im *Buggles*-Song kurzlebiger. Die Formate ändern sich ständig, verdrängen andere und schaffen beim Publikum neue Begehrlichkeiten. Man hat inmitten all dieser Veränderungen nur noch die Möglichkeit, sich ständig über Neuerungen zu informieren, sie zu interpretieren und dabei immer wieder neue, innovative Ideen zu entwickeln. Genau deshalb besteht nicht das geringste Risiko, dass Bücher wie dieses vom letzten Trend überrollt werden.

Der vor 30 Jahren im brasilianischen Porto Alegre geborene **Leo Prestes** arbeitet seit seinem 19. Lebensjahr in der Kommunikationsbranche. Heute ist er bei **W3Haus** für Konzeption und Planung verantwortlich. Seit Gründung im Jahr 2000 eröffnete diese erfolgreiche Digitalagentur Filialen in London und São Paulo und beschäftigt Mitarbeiter jeglicher Couleur. Ihre Schwerpunkte liegen in den Bereichen Konzeption, Planung und allgemeine Medien. <www.w3haus.com>

# Introduction

Leo Prestes

Bob Garfield, chroniqueur pour *Advertising Age*, a récemment participé à un événement sur la communication numérique au Brésil. Lors de la conférence qu'il y a donnée, il a mentionné le premier clip vidéo diffusé sur la chaîne américaine MTV, « Video Killed the Radio Star » des Buggles (la vidéo a tué la star de la radio), et a relevé son ironie plus de trente ans plus tard. Aujourd'hui, MTV a en fait éliminé les clips de sa programmation, et a décidé de diffuser des émissions de télé-réalité et de divertissement. Garfield a révélé la raison de ce choix : *« Online video killed the MTV Star »* (la vidéo sur le web a tué la star de MTV). La facilité avec laquelle nous pouvons aujourd'hui regarder des clips vidéo sur YouTube – de véritables dinosaures, comme les Buggles, en versions numérisées à partir de vieilles cassettes VHS, à OK Go, un groupe qui a investi le marché grâce à l'un de ses clips diffusé directement sur YouTube – n'a pas laissé d'autre choix à la célèbre chaîne de télévision.

Pourtant, cela ne suffira peut-être pas à résoudre les problèmes que MTV et toutes les autres chaînes à grande audience rencontrent actuellement. Après tout, avant longtemps la télé-réalité, les informations et même les événements en direct comme les matchs de football et les concerts seront tout aussi couramment vus sur les écrans d'ordinateur qu'ils le sont actuellement sur les écrans de télévision.

En attendant, elles devront faire avec les sorties en cascade de l'industrie du divertissement, qui persiste à ignorer l'importance des vidéos en ligne. Il existe cependant certains supports de communication qui utilisent intelligemment les modes « online » et « offline », dans un esprit de complémentarité. La série télévisée *Heroes* en est un bon exemple. Il ne s'agit pas seulement de mettre des épisodes en ligne, ni de se contenter de la mention « consultez notre site Internet pour en savoir plus » à la fin des épisodes diffusés à la télévision. *Heroes* est une série interactive, et ce, depuis la création des scripts, pour améliorer les épisodes, apprendre à connaître le public, créer des contenus supplémentaires et, avant tout, pour attirer les annonceurs publicitaires.

Toutes ces informations forcent les producteurs à rester vigilants, font apparaître des tendances et établissent des références qui nous permettent de faire des présentations et des programmes plus solides. La série se repose également moins sur de vieilles rengaines comme « le pouvoir est aux consommateurs », « le contenu est roi » et « contenu collaboratif ». Mais que peut faire une agence pour que tous ces changements lui soient favorables, et que le prochain site vidéo à succès porte son nom ?

La question qui vient immédiatement à l'esprit est « est-ce que la vidéo sur Internet devrait vraiment être produite avec plus d'amateurisme que la vidéo traditionnelle ? » L'intérêt du public augmente-t-il lorsqu'il n'y a pas d'équipe professionnelle derrière la caméra ? Ou bien la demande pour ce type de vidéo n'a-t-elle atteint ses proportions actuelles que parce que les investissements dans le secteur numérique étaient plus faibles, et que c'était le seul moyen de produire des scripts innovants ?

La bande passante ne cesse de s'élargir, les ordinateurs sont de plus en plus puissants et des outils apparaissent qui permettent d'intégrer la vidéo aux graphismes des sites (avez-vous vu quitdoingit.com, d'AgencyNet ?) et de réaliser des vidéos composites à partir de plusieurs interfaces API (allez visiter takethisdance.com, et vous verrez de quoi je parle). La mode des vidéos amateurs disparaîtra peut-être.

www.quitdoingit.com

En fait, de nombreuses marques ont déjà réalisé, à leur grande déception, que pour chaque vidéo « Coke + Mentos » qui fait irruption sur le web, il y a 1 000 autres vidéos tout aussi anonymes que la cérémonie de remise de diplôme du petit cousin de quelqu'un.

Les campagnes du genre « créez votre propre publicité », qui suivaient la même logique que la campagne « Invitez-vous au Superbowl » de Doritos en 2006, ont bourgeonné aux quatre coins du globe de la même manière, même s'ils n'ont pas toujours eu le même succès que l'originale. Beaucoup de clients et d'agences veulent tellement faire des campagnes virales qu'ils ont oublié que, avant de réaliser une vidéo, il faut créer un univers conceptuel qui donne au consommateur une bonne raison de dégainer sa caméra. L'explosion des campagnes virales sans véritable contenu à diffuser a fini par condamner le format et a conduit les marques à s'adresser une fois de plus aux professionnels.

Cette possibilité sème un autre doute dans les couloirs des agences : devraient-elles engager des producteurs pour réaliser les vidéos, ou devraient-elles plutôt investir dans leurs propres infrastructures ? Les grandes agences numériques, comme R/GA et AgencyNet, ont leurs propres studios et, à l'heure où j'écris, mon agence, W3Haus, est en train de monter le sien. À première vue, cela pourrait sembler un peu contradictoire pour les sociétés de communication dont l'expansion est due, précisément, à un mode de fonctionnement qui diffère des formules pesantes et obsolètes de la publicité traditionnelle. Il n'en reste pas moins que, dans un secteur où le soutien financier est toujours insuffisant, où la réponse du public est immédiate, et où les réactions à tout ce qui se produit ont un effet décisif sur ce qui se fera le lendemain, la présence d'un producteur dans la pièce d'à côté est la meilleure façon de satisfaire les besoins du client.

Ces questions et réponses ne sont cependant valides que jusqu'au moment présent. Le temps que ce texte soit rédigé et publié dans un livre, elles seront peut-être déjà obsolètes. Chaque jour, de nouveaux paramètres d'évaluation apparaissent pour notre travail, et même YouTube à commencé il y a quelque temps à révéler l'origine de ses accès. Un nouveau canal de diffusion de vidéos apparaît chaque jour. Il y a quelques semaines, on m'a envoyé un lien vers qik.com, où l'on peut transmettre en direct à partir d'un téléphone mobile et interagir avec les visiteurs du site. Pouvez-vous envisager les possibilités que cette technologie peut offrir pour un match de football, un spectacle, ou dans des toilettes pour femmes ?

De nouvelles façons de segmenter le public, plus précises, et de personnaliser les messages envoyés apparaissent sans cesse. Les formats changent, se remplacent les uns les autres et créent de nouvelles attentes chez le public. La seule façon de naviguer entre tous ces changements, c'est de les suivre de très près et de les interpréter constamment, pour identifier et évaluer les idées innovantes. C'est pour cela que les livres comme celui que vous tenez entre les mains ne risquent pas d'être balayés par les dernières tendances.

**Leo Prestes** est né à Porto Alegre, au Brésil. Il a 30 ans, et a commencé à travailler dans la communication à 19 ans. Aujourd'hui, Leo est responsable de la création et de la planification chez **W3Haus**, une agence numérique bourdonnante d'activité créée en 2000. Composée au départ de quatre personnes dans un petit bureau à Porto Alegre, elle a depuis ouvert des succursales à Londres et à São Paulo, et son personnel vient des horizons les plus divers. Elle se consacre actuellement à la création, à la planification et aux médias. **<www.w3haus.com>**

CASE:01

## HBO Voyeur

Michael Lebowitz

Discover what people do when they think no one is watching. Peer into every window. You'll soon learn that the sinister behaviour of dark alleys and bawdy nights is not as strange as what's happening right next door... even in broad daylight.

What if you were to tear down the outer walls of a New York City apartment building, exposing the grit and the underbelly for anyone to see? This is the question HBO posed when developing its multimedia marketing campaign, HBO Voyeur. The centrepiece was a short film that set out to capture what lurks behind closed doors. With director Jake Scott and a skeleton key in hand, twelve such doors were unlocked, divulging brash fantasies and mysteries.

HBO, working with BBDO, approached digital creative agency Big Spaceship to look for a place for the film to live online. Big Spaceship responded by creating a virtual Manhattan where the footage would not just live, but thrive and expand in a digital environment.

The end result, which launched in June 2007, was <www.hbovoyeur.com>, a seductive experiment and an invitation to continue the perverse pleasure of voyeurism in an online setting. Voyeurs witness mere snippets of life, sordid tales of romance, temptation, lust and betrayal. A glimpse into the apartments of ordinary New Yorkers proves only that nothing is ordinary. And it takes place without a single spoken word.

The objective from inside Big Spaceship's DUMBO office was to substitute a window and binoculars for a monitor and a mouse. In this digital landscape, the voyeur is shrouded in the courage that the shadows provide. But he is always kept at arm's length, lest he divulge his presence. Within a living, breathing urban setting, where detailed architectural facades house HBO's poignant video vignettes, Big Spaceship created a vicarious world as rich as it was secretive.

One of the toughest technical challenges was streaming the high-quality video and audio for the stories in perfect harmony. Big Spaceship had to accomplish this in a way that would register with users no matter what their processor or connection speed. The outcome: a finely tuned but alluring look at life with the surface peeled back. It is stark, messy and raw — at times eerie or amusing, but always moving.

It was absolutely essential that the voyeuristic point of view not be violated anywhere within the site experience. The user — or voyeur, in this case — can peer just deep enough into New York's concrete building blocks to see the blood that flows within them. Through intuitive and seamless navigation, a sense of slyness and intimacy is always maintained. Sliders and buttons disappear while one watches a vignette, but they furtively reappear to act as a guide through the city as needed.

Another credit to the campaign's effectiveness is the voyeur's commanding role. From his window, the black sky glimmers with city lights as he selects a window to his liking. The main action unfolds in a tenement on the Lower East Side at Ludlow and Broome. But there are also four other apartment buildings throughout the city, all of which he can peek into and zoom in and out of. A game of strip poker is greeted with a twist. Across town a proposal goes awry. A temptress toys with a businessman. Secrets climb up and down the staircase. All the while the murderess grins.

The voyeur sits frozen and trapped, watching every move from a covert vantage point. Perhaps he's so enthralled that he downloads the entire wall of stories, choosing from one of seven soundtracks — some

www.hbovoyeur.com

melodic, others haunting. Or maybe it is only the commotion in apartments 2A and 3A that intrigues him. He uses the slider to review a specific scene. He can download the stories (in addition to the trailer and screensaver) in a variety of formats.

HBO Voyeur was a tremendous success, in part because it placed the film in a larger, richer context, one that created an online conversation with the HBO audience. Following its launch, which involved projecting the film on to an actual New York City building, the site garnered significant press coverage. TV ads and an On Demand feature helped drive web traffic, while generating an active fan following — HBO among them. The website received a Site of the Day and Site of the Month Favorite Website Award, a Pixel Award in the TV category, and a Runner-up Pixel for Best in Show. It was also a winner of the Design Week Awards in the UK and HOW Magazine's International Design Awards.

From the combined efforts of Big Spaceship and BBDO, the project raised the standard of what to expect from the entertainment industry. HBO Voyeur is life unfolding and tangling up again in front of you. It is a complex story and a clear reminder of why HBO is known as the sophisticated source of storytelling.

Go ahead, pick up the binoculars. No one is watching you... promise.

**Michael Lebowitz** founded Big Spaceship in early 2000 and serves as its CEO. He has lectured and led seminars internationally on creativity, emerging trends, entertainment and its role in digital engagement. He is a member of the AIGA's Visionary Design Council and the International Academy of Digital Arts & Sciences and a founding board member of SoDA — the Society of Digital Agencies. He is also a regular juror for the world's top creative awards.
**Big Spaceship** is an innovation-led digital creative agency that partners with brands to create and evolve deeply engaging experiences, products and relationships. Telling stories and starting conversations across the digital landscape, the company has garnered countless accolades for its work, including the highly coveted One Show, Clio, Webby Awards and the Cannes Lion. Holding more FWAs than any other firm, it was the first American agency inducted into its Hall of Fame. **<www.bigspaceship.com>**

CASE:01

# HBO Voyeur

Michael Lebowitz

Entdecken Sie, was andere Menschen tun, wenn sie sich unbeobachtet fühlen. Spähen Sie in jedes Fenster, und Sie werden bald herausfinden, dass das Geschehen in dunklen Gassen und schwülen Nächten längst nicht so absonderlich ist wie das, was in der Nachbarwohnung geschieht ... am helllichten Tag.

Was wäre, wenn man die Außenwände eines Wohnblocks in New York City einfach wegreißen würde und jeder bis in alle Einzelheiten beobachten könnte, was sich darin zuträgt? Genau diese Frage hat sich der Fernsehsender HBO gestellt, als er seine Multimedia-Marketingkampagne „HBO Voyeur" entwickelte. Im Mittelpunkt standen dabei kurze Filme, die das festhielten, was sonst hinter verschlossenen Türen geschieht. Regisseur Jake Scott öffnete mit seinem Generalschlüssel zwölf solcher Türen und enthüllte aufregende Fantasien und Geheimnisse.

HBO arbeitete für dieses Projekt mit der Werbeagentur BBDO zusammen und beauftragte die Kreativagentur Big Spaceship damit, diesen Film im Internet zu präsentieren. Big Spaceship schuf daraufhin ein virtuelles Manhattan, wo das Filmmaterial nicht nur präsentiert werden sollte, sondern sich in einem digitalen Umfeld weiterentwickeln und wachsen konnte.

Das Ergebnis, das im Juni 2007 veröffentlicht wurde, heißt <www.hbovoyeur.com> – ein verführerisches Experiment und eine Einladung für jeden, sein perverses voyeuristisches Begehren innerhalb einer Online-Kulisse zu befriedigen. Voyeure erleben kleine Ausschnitte aus fremden Leben mit – schmutzige kleine Romanzen, Lust, Verführung und Betrug. Ein flüchtiger Blick in das Apartment ganz gewöhnlicher New Yorker beweist uns, dass einfach *nichts* normal ist. Und all dies findet statt, ohne dass der Beobachter auch nur ein Wort hört.

Ziel der zu Big Spaceship gehörenden Agentur DUMBO war es, Fenster und Fernglas durch Monitor und Maus zu ersetzen. In dieser digitalen Landschaft hat der Voyeur die Gewissheit, stets im Verborgenen zu bleiben. Gleichzeitig befindet er sich immer in einer gewissen Distanz zum Geschehen. Big Spaceship schuf mitten in einer lebendigen und pulsierenden urbanen Kulisse eine eigene kleine Welt, die genauso aufschlussreich wie verschwiegen ist. Hinter ganz realistisch wirkenden Fassaden spielen sich die ergreifenden Vignetten-Filme von HBO ab.

Eine der härtesten technischen Herausforderungen für Big Spaceship war es, eine hohe Video- und Audioqualität zur Verfügung zu stellen und diese exakt aufeinander abzustimmen. Eine der Bedingungen war dabei, dass es keine Rolle spielt, über welchen Prozessor oder welche Internetverbindung der Internet-User verfügt. Das Resultat: ein fein abgestimmter und verführerischer Blick auf das wahre Leben unter der Oberfläche. Intensiv, chaotisch und rau, manchmal unheimlich, manchmal amüsant – aber immer bewegend.

Sehr wichtig war dabei, dass der voyeuristische Standpunkt stets realistisch dargestellt wurde. Das heißt, der User – also der Voyeur – kann wie ein wirklicher Voyeur nur gerade so weit in die Betonblöcke New Yorks hineinspähen, dass er das Leben darin pulsieren sieht. Bei der intuitiven und fließenden Navigation durch die Wohnungen bleibt jedoch immer ein Gefühl von Heimlichkeit und Intimität erhalten. Symbole und Schaltflächen verschwinden während des Betrachtens eines der Filme, aber danach erscheinen sie sofort wieder und bieten sich dem User als kleine digitale „Stadtführer" an.

Ein weiterer Punkt trug zu dem enormen Erfolg der Kampagne bei: die Rolle des Voyeurs als lenkende

www.hbovoyeur.com

Instanz. Von seinem Fenster aus sieht er die blinkenden Lichter des nächtlichen Stadtpanoramas und kann sich eines der Fenster nach Belieben aussuchen. Die Haupthandlung findet in einem Wohnblock in der Lower East Side an der Ecke Ludlow Street und Broome Street statt. Es gibt aber noch vier weitere, in der Stadt verteilte Wohnblöcke, in die der Voyeur hineinspähen bzw. hinein- und hinauszoomen kann. Ein Strip-Poker-Spiel erfährt eine überraschende Wendung. Am anderen Ende der Stadt misslingt ein Heiratsantrag. Eine Verführerin spielt mit einem Geschäftsmann. Die Geheimnisse steigen treppauf und treppab. Und all das, während eine Mörderin ihr Werk vollbringt.

Der Voyeur ist von der Neugierde gepackt und kann nicht anders, als von seinem verborgenen Plätzchen aus jede Bewegung zu verfolgen. Vielleicht ist er so fasziniert, dass er alle Geschichten auf einmal auf seinen Computer herunterlädt und sich den passenden von sieben Soundtracks – von melodisch bis gespenstisch – dazu heraussucht. Oder vielleicht interessiert ihn nur die aufregende Handlung in den Apartments 2A und 3A. Er benützt das Menü, um eine bestimmte Szene noch einmal anzusehen. Er kann die einzelnen Geschichten in verschiedenen Formaten herunterladen (zusätzlich zum Trailer und Bildschirmschoner).

HBO Voyeur verzeichnete einen enormen Erfolg. Ein Grund dafür ist, dass das HBO-Publikum online dabei mitwirkte, den Gesamtfilm in einen größeren Kontext einzubetten. Die Veröffentlichung der Website, die unter anderem die Projektion des Films auf ein New Yorker Gebäude umfasste, wurde von der Presse mit Begeisterung aufgenommen. Fernsehwerbung und On-Demand-Angebote trugen zu einer enormen Steigerung der Besucherzahl auf der Website bei. Bald entstand eine rege Fangemeinde – darunter auch HBO. Die Website erhielt die Preise Site of the Day und Site of the Month, den Pixel Award in der Kategorie TV und auf dem zweiten Platz einen Pixel Award in der Kategorie Beste Show. Außerdem gewann sie den Design Week Award in Großbritannien und den International Design Award des *HOW-Magazins*.

Big Spaceship und BBDO schafften es, ihrem Gemeinschaftsprojekt einen hohen qualitativen Standard zu verleihen, der die Erwartungen der Unterhaltungsindustrie mit Bravour erfüllt hat. HBO Voyeur enthüllt das wahre Leben, dessen Irrungen und Wirrungen sich direkt vor unseren Augen abspielen. Diese vielschichtige Geschichte ist eines von vielen Beispielen, die zu dem Ruf von HBO beigetragen haben, ein anspruchsvoller Geschichtenerzähler zu sein.

Los geht's: Nehmen Sie Ihr Fernglas in die Hand. Niemand sieht Ihnen zu ... versprochen!

**Michael Lebowitz**, CEO von Big Spaceship, gründete die Agentur Anfang 2000. Er hielt weltweit Vorlesungen und Seminare über Kreativität, Trends, Unterhaltung und ihre Rolle in der digitalen Arbeit. Lebowitz ist Mitglied des AIGA Visionary Design Council und der International Academy of Digital Arts & Sciences und Mitbegründer sowie Vorstandsmitglied von SoDA – (Society of Digital Agencies). Außerdem fungiert er regelmäßig als Juror bei den international renommierten Kreativ-Awards.

**Big Spaceship** ist eine innovative, auf digitale Arbeiten spezialisierte Kreativagentur. Sie arbeitet für verschiedene Firmen, für die sie Produkte und erfahrbare Konzepte entwickelt, die das Zielpublikum fesseln und faszinieren sollen. In der digitalen Welt Geschichten erzählen und Gespräche führen – mit diesen beiden Konzepten hat es die Agentur zu zahlreichen Auszeichnungen gebracht, einschließlich der begehrten Preise One Show, Clio, Webby und eines Löwen in Cannes. Big Spaceship hat mehr FWAs als jedes andere Unternehmen bekommen und wurde als erste amerikanische Agentur mit der Aufnahme in die FWA Hall of Fame ausgezeichnet. **<www.bigspaceship.com>**

CASE·01

# HBO Voyeur

Michael Lebowitz

Découvrez ce que les gens font lorsqu'ils pensent que personne ne les voit. Regardez à travers toutes les fenêtres. Vous comprendrez sans tarder que les comportements sinistres des ruelles obscures et des nuits de débauche ne sont pas aussi étranges que ce qui se passe juste à côté de chez vous… même en plein jour.

Que se passerait-il si l'on démolissait les murs extérieurs d'un immeuble d'appartements new-yorkais, et que l'on en exposait l'ossature et les entrailles à la vue de tous ? C'est la question que la chaîne HBO a posée lors du développement de sa campagne de marketing multimédia, HBO Voyeur. La pièce centrale était un court-métrage qui se proposait de révéler ce qui se cache derrière les portes closes. Avec l'aide du réalisateur Jake Scott et d'un passe-partout, douze de ces portes ont été ouvertes, et ont laissé échapper les fantasmes et les mystères les plus provocants.

HBO, en collaboration avec BBDO, a demandé à l'agence créative Big Spaceship de trouver le moyen de faire perdurer le film sur Internet. Big Spaceship a répondu en créant un Manhattan virtuel où les séquences peuvent non seulement perdurer, mais également prospérer et grandir dans un environnement numérique.

Le résultat final, lancé en juin 2007, est < www.hbovoyeur.com >, une expérience fascinante et une invitation à continuer d'explorer sur le web le plaisir pervers du voyeurisme. Les voyeurs assistent à des bribes de vie, des histoires sordides d'amour, de tentation, de luxure et de trahison. Il suffit d'un coup d'œil dans les appartements de New-Yorkais ordinaires pour se rendre compte que rien n'est ordinaire. Et tout cela sans qu'un seul mot soit prononcé.

Pour le bureau DUMBO de Big Spaceship, l'objectif était de remplacer la fenêtre et les jumelles par le moniteur et la souris. Dans ce paysage numérique, le voyeur est armé du courage que lui donne l'obscurité. Mais il est toujours maintenu à une certaine distance, de peur de révéler sa présence. Dans un décor citadin vivant, où des façades très détaillées abritent les fascinants portraits vidéo d'HBO, Big Spaceship a créé un monde par procuration aussi riche que secret.

L'un des plus grands défis techniques était de permettre un visionnage sans anicroche des flux vidéo et audio haute qualité. Big Spaceship devait faire en sorte d'atteindre tous les utilisateurs, quels que soient leur processeur ou leur vitesse de connexion. Le résultat : un regard sur mesure et fascinant sur la face cachée de la vie. C'est brut, désordonné et cru, parfois sinistre ou amusant, mais toujours en mouvement.

Il fallait absolument que le point de vue du voyeur soit toujours respecté tout au long du site. Le regard de l'utilisateur (ou du voyeur, dans ce cas précis), peut plonger juste assez profondément dans le ciment des immeubles de New York pour voir le sang qui y circule. La navigation intuitive et harmonieuse entretient l'impression de clandestinité et d'intimité. Les curseurs et les boutons disparaissent lorsque l'on regarde une vignette, mais ils réapparaissent furtivement pour guider le voyeur à travers la ville.

L'une des raisons de l'efficacité de cette campagne est également que tout se passe depuis le point de vue du voyeur. Depuis sa fenêtre, le ciel nocturne brille des feux de la ville pendant qu'il sélectionne la fenêtre qui l'intéresse. L'action principale se déroule dans un immeuble du quartier du Lower East Side, au coin de Ludlow et de Broome. Mais il y a aussi quatre autres immeubles disséminés dans toute la ville, sur lesquels le voyeur peut zoomer à loisir. Une partie de strip-poker est assaisonnée d'un rebondissement inattendu.

www.hbovoyeur.com

À l'autre bout de la ville, une proposition en mariage tourne mal. Une tentatrice s'amuse avec un homme d'affaires. Les secrets montent et descendent dans l'escalier. Pendant ce temps, la tueuse vaque à ses occupations.

Sur sa chaise, le voyeur est pétrifié, piégé, et peut voir les moindres mouvements depuis son poste d'observation clandestin. Il est peut-être tellement captivé qu'il télécharge tout le mur d'histoires, avec un choix de sept bandes sonores, douces et mélodieuses, ou envoûtantes. Ou peut-être n'est-il intéressé que par l'agitation des appartements 2A et 3A. Il utilise le curseur pour revoir une certaine scène. Il peut télécharger les histoires (en plus de la bande-annonce et de l'économiseur d'écran) sous plusieurs formats différents.

HBO Voyeur a été un succès énorme, en partie parce que le projet plaçait le film dans un contexte plus général et plus riche, qui créait une conversation en ligne avec le public d'HBO. Après le lancement du projet, avec la projection du film sur un immeuble new-yorkais, le site a bénéficié d'une couverture importante dans la presse. Les spots télévisés et la fonction On Demand ont participé à stimuler le trafic, tout en créant une base de fans actifs – HBO parmi eux. Le site a reçu plusieurs récompenses, notamment Site of the Day et Site of the Month des Favorite Website Awards, un Pixel Award dans la catégorie TV, et un Runner-up Pixel pour la catégorie Best in Show. Il a également gagné les Design Week Awards au Royaume-Uni, et les International Design Awards de *HOW Magazine's*.

Grâce aux efforts combinés de Big Spaceship et de BBDO, le projet a relevé les critères de ce que l'on peut attendre de l'industrie du divertissement. HBO Voyeur, c'est la vie elle-même qui se déroule et s'emmêle devant vos yeux. C'est une intrigue complexe, et elle nous rappelle clairement pourquoi HBO a la réputation de savoir conter des histoires raffinées.

Allez-y, prenez les jumelles. Personne ne vous voit… promis.

**Michael Lebowitz** a créé Big Spaceship en 2000. Il en est le directeur général. Il a donné des conférences et des séminaires dans le monde entier sur la créativité, les tendances émergentes, le divertissement et son rôle dans la sphère numérique. Il est membre du Visionary Design Council de l'AIGA et de l'International Academy of Digital Arts & Sciences, et membre fondateur de la SoDA – Society of Digital Agencies. Il fait souvent partie des jurés des récompenses décernées à la créativité les plus prestigieuses au monde.

**Big Spaceship** est une agence créative axée sur l'innovation, qui travaille en partenariat avec les marques pour créer et faire évoluer des projets, des produits et des relations à l'impact profond. La société raconte des histoires et engage des conversations dans le paysage numérique, et a récolté de nombreuses récompenses pour son travail, notamment les prix très convoités One Show, Clio, Webby Awards et le Lion de Cannes. Elle détient plus de distinctions FWA que n'importe quelle autre société, et a été la première agence américaine à entrer dans son Hall of Fame.
**<www.bigspaceship.com>**

CASE 01

CLINT MANSELL

LEARN MORE HBO FORUMS HBO TERMS OF USE THESTORYGETSDEEPER.COM

CLINT MANSELL

LEARN MORE HBO FORUMS HBO TERMS OF USE THESTORYGETSDEEPER.COM

www.hbovoyeur.com

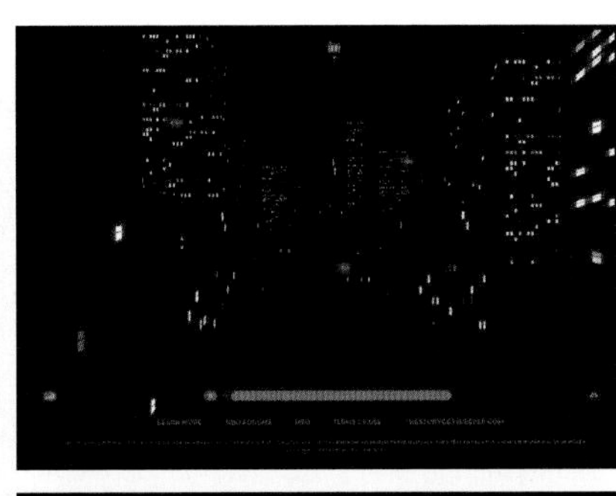

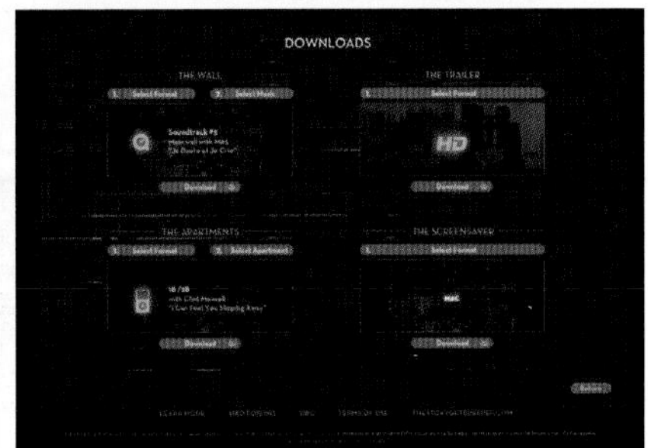

CASE·02

# Evolve

Junichi Saito

From a global perspective, the infrastructure for internet use in Japan has advanced significantly in the past few years. The diffusion rate of PCs to population is at 70%, and over 50 million people now have regular access to broadband. Such improvements in infrastructure, matched with many new communication technologies and advanced PC specifications, give Japan a unique environment for expression on the web. In recent years, Japan has seen an increase in new forms of websites with much 3D and high-capacity video content. As the delivery of such websites becomes easier, they increase their value as realistic and practical business solutions. Here at ARCHETYP, we are receiving more and more requests for broadband web content production. Video expression on the web has now become an indispensable method of communication, and effective strategies for efficient dispatch are a growing requirement by Japanese businesses.

Although the main focus may be in video production, video for web use requires a much different planning approach from that in other mediums such as television. The website does not conclude by simply broadcasting the video; rather, it must incorporate it as a part of the user experience online. So, as with any website planning, one must keep in mind the overall objective to decide whether the application of video content provides a suitable solution. When directing and editing the video content, the director must be aware of this objective. He or she must take into account a number of factors, such as what the video content needs to express, and also how the content is to be used on a website with clear technical limitations. For example, how dynamic can a small, compressed video be? Will reduced size and higher resolution provide more effect? Such questions always arise in the planning stage.

Even if the planning is executed properly, one cannot control the environment of the user viewing the website. As every end-user environment varies, we must be aware of the communication infrastructure immediately surrounding us and plan accordingly to balance carefully the number of videos, their resolution, size and bit rate. Such user environments advance and change constantly at recognisable speeds, and therefore we must always be prepared for the possibility that current plans may become obsolete and impractical in the near future. Through this awareness, we aim to further web expression with our experience in video application, as the technology and infrastructure of this country advances. We will continue to explore new possibilities of video in web expression and offer fresh and novel websites which impress people and get them talking.

### 100 Cheergirls

A campaign website dedicated to users through 100 video messages where cheer girls face 100 separate challenges. The videos, also posted on YouTube, are expressed in an original way on the website, encouraging users to repeat viewing whilst promoting the e-career brand to their core target of 20-35-year-old males. The large volume of video content allows for a longer durational experience for users on the website, whilst offering multiple opportunities for encounters with the brand and branding message.

### The Choice of Hiraya

A promotional site for Sumitomo Forestry's housing project called "Grand Life Hiraya". Targeted at a senior

www.sony.co.jp/united/momoko

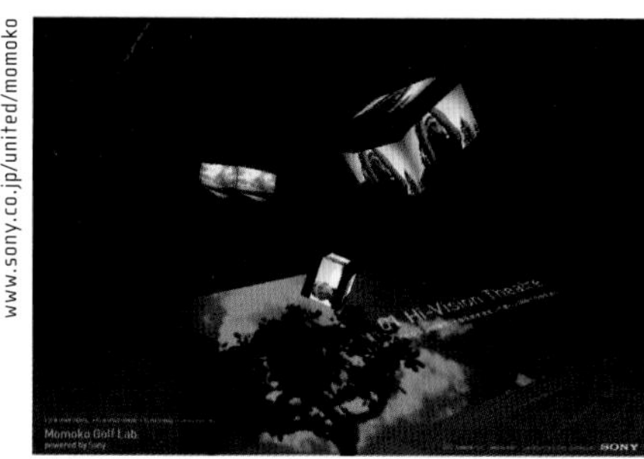

age group, the website suggests a new, comfortable and alternative lifestyle of a "Hiraya". It offers a stress-free experience by adjusting to the user's environment with calm music and atmosphere. With a simple layout that is centred on photographs and the message of the users' "choice", the site also synchronises with various forms of advertisements whilst guiding users to click on documentation requests, thus enabling the user to select the ideal product through a choice of his or her desired lifestyle.

**Junichi Saito** is the head of ARCHETYP Inc., a young interactive agency based in Tokyo. Founded in 2007, **ARCHETYP** has been providing the creative industry with interactive solutions for any internet-related client, ranging from execution of websites to strategic plans for product launches. In this short period they have been highly regarded as a leading agency for working with video on the web, and have received a number of awards in the field.
<www.archetyp.jp>

CASE:02

## Fortschritt

Junichi Saito

Global gesehen ist die Infrastruktur des Internets in Japan in den letzten Jahren enorm gewachsen. Mehr als 70 % der Bevölkerung besitzt einen PC, über 50 Millionen Menschen haben Zugang zu Breitband-Internet. Diese Entwicklung sowie zahlreiche neue Kommunikationstechnologien und fortschrittliche Computeranwendungen schaffen einzigartige Voraussetzungen für verschiedene Ausdrucksformen im Internet. Seit einigen Jahren gibt es immer mehr japanische Websites, die neuartige Darstellungsmethoden anwenden – so zum Beispiel 3D-Effekte und hochentwickelte Videoinhalte. Die Konzeption komplexer Internetseiten lässt sich mittlerweile immer einfacher realisieren und bietet daher eine realistische und profitable Möglichkeit, einen solchen Service anzubieten. Hier bei ARCHETYP erhalten wir eine steigende Anzahl von Nachfragen nach der Konzeption von komplexen und anspruchsvollen Webinhalten. Videos im Internet sind heute ein unentbehrliches Kommunikationsmittel geworden, und mehr und mehr suchen japanische Unternehmen effektive Strategien, um Botschaften zu vermitteln.

Obwohl bei uns der Schwerpunkt auf der Videoproduktion liegt, gilt es, einen wichtigen Aspekt zu berücksichtigen: Videos für das Internet erfordern eine ganz andere Herangehensweise als andere Medien wie etwa das Fernsehen. Bei einer Website reicht es nicht aus, das Video einfach nur auszustrahlen, sondern es muss zum Bestandteil der gesamten Interneterfahrung des Users werden. Daher muss man bei der Planung einer Website ihr Gesamtbild berücksichtigen, um sicherzugehen, dass sich das Video optimal einfügt. Der Regisseur muss sich dessen während der Dreharbeiten und bei der Nachbearbeitung des Videos stets bewusst sein. Er muss eine ganze Reihe von Faktoren berücksichtigen, zum Beispiel, was das Video dem Betrachter vermitteln soll, oder wie der Inhalt auf einer Website dargestellt werden kann, die nicht über ausreichende technische Standards verfügt. Oder auch, ob ein kleines, komprimiertes Video trotz seiner Größe dynamisch wirken kann. Kann ein kleineres, aber dafür höher aufgelöstes Video effektiv sein? Solche Fragen kommen in der Planungsphase auf.

Auch wenn die Planung so sorgfältig wie möglich ausgeführt wird, kann niemand wissen, unter welchen Bedingungen der User die Website besucht. Dass diese Bedingungen und Möglichkeiten bei jedem User variieren, müssen wir berücksichtigen und genau überlegen, wie viele Videos eine Website haben soll, wie hoch deren Auflösung und Übertragungsrate sein dürfen und wie groß sie sind. Die Möglichkeiten der Internet-User entwickeln sich stetig und in hoher Geschwindigkeit weiter; daher müssen wir stets darauf vorbereitet sein, dass aktuelle Konzepte in nächster Zukunft bereits veraltet sein können. Mit diesem Bewusstsein und unseren Erfahrungen im Bereich der Videoanwendungen tragen wir dazu bei, die Ausdrucksmöglichkeiten im Internet weiterzuentwickeln – einhergehend mit dem wachsenden technologischen Fortschritt in Japan. Wir werden immer neue Möglichkeiten der Videodarstellung im Internet entdecken und überraschende Websites kreieren, die die Menschen beeindrucken und miteinander ins Gespräch bringen.

### 100 Cheergirls

Diese Website wurde für eine Werbekampagne entwickelt. Den Usern werden 100 Videobotschaften präsentiert, in denen 100 Cheergirls 100 verschiedene Aufgaben bewältigen müssen. Die auf der Website auf originelle Weise präsentierten Videos, die auch bei

www.sony.co.jp/united/momoko

YouTube zu sehen sind, regen dazu an, sie wiederholt anzuschauen. Zielgruppe dieser Werbekampagne eines E-Career-Unternehmens sind männliche User im Alter zwischen 20 und 35. Die zahlreichen Videos laden dazu ein, länger auf der Website zu verweilen – so kann das Unternehmen seine Werbebotschaft ideal vermitteln.

### The Choice of Hiraya

Diese Werbesite wurde für Sumitomo Forestrys Wohnprojekt „Grand Life Hiraya" gestaltet. Die Website, die sich an eine vorwiegend ältere Zielgruppe richtet, stellt den neuen und komfortablen, alternativen Lebensstil eines „Hiraya" vor. Dabei wird eine stressfreie Atmosphäre geschaffen, die mittels ruhiger Musik und anderer Elemente an die Umgebung des Users angepasst werden kann. Die schlichte, auf Fotografien basierende Oberfläche, die sich in erster Linie auf ihre Werbebotschaft konzentriert, motiviert den User mithilfe verschiedener Werbeformen dazu, Formulare anzufordern, mit denen er das für ihn perfekte Produkt und somit seinen gewünschten Lebensstil auswählen kann.

**Junichi Saito** ist Chef von ARCHETYP Inc., einer im Jahr 2007 gegründeten Internetagentur aus Tokio. **ARCHETYP** hat sich mit Internetauftritten für zahlreiche Kunden aus der Kreativbranche einen Namen gemacht. Ihr Angebot reicht von der Erstellung von Internetseiten bis hin zur umfassenden Planung von Product Launches. Die junge Agentur erwarb sich als Wegbereiter für Webvideos einen internationalen Ruf und erhielt bereits zahlreiche Auszeichnungen. **<www.archetyp.jp>**

CASE 02

# Evolve

Junichi Saito

Globalement, au Japon l'infrastructure Internet a beaucoup avancé ces dernières années. Le taux de diffusion des PC dans la population est de 70 %, et plus de 50 millions de personnes ont régulièrement accès au haut débit. Ces progrès infrastructurels, alliés aux nombreuses nouvelles technologies de la communication et aux configurations avancées des PC, donnent au Japon un environnement unique pour l'expression sur Internet. Ces dernières années, le Japon a connu une augmentation des nouvelles formes de sites web, avec beaucoup de contenus en 3D et en vidéo haute capacité. Le public a accès à ces sites web de plus en plus facilement, ce qui augmente leur valeur en tant que solutions réalistes et pratiques pour les entreprises. Chez ARCHETYP, nos clients nous demandent de plus en plus de produire des contenus spécifiquement pour le haut débit. Sur Internet, la vidéo est maintenant une méthode de communication indispensable, et les entreprises japonaises demandent des stratégies efficaces pour la transmettre au public dans les meilleures conditions.

Bien que le plus gros de l'activité soit centré sur la production, la vidéo pour Internet requiert une approche très différente de celle utilisée pour les autres supports, la télévision par exemple. Le site web ne se contente pas de diffuser la vidéo, il doit aussi l'intégrer à l'expérience du visiteur. Comme pour toute planification de site web, il faut donc penser à l'objectif général pour décider si la vidéo est une solution convenable. Lorsqu'il réalise ou monte la vidéo, le réalisateur doit être bien conscient de cet objectif. Il ou elle doit tenir compte de plusieurs facteurs, notamment ce que la vidéo doit exprimer, et comment le contenu sera utilisé sur un site web limité par des contraintes techniques bien précises. Par exemple, une vidéo compressée visionnée dans une petite fenêtre sera-t-elle assez dynamique ? L'effet sera-t-il meilleur avec une taille plus réduite et une plus grande résolution ? Ce type de question se pose toujours au moment de la planification.

Même si l'on planifie correctement, on n'a aucune prise sur l'environnement des internautes qui visitent le site web. Puisque chaque utilisateur final évolue dans un environnement différent, nous devons connaître l'infrastructure de communication qui nous est proche et équilibrer en conséquence le nombre de vidéos, leur résolution, leur taille et leur débit binaire. Les environnements des utilisateurs évoluent constamment et à grande vitesse, nous devons donc toujours être préparés au cas où les plans actuels deviendraient obsolètes et inapplicables dans un futur proche. C'est grâce à cette vigilance que nous voulons faire avancer l'expression sur Internet, avec notre expérience dans les applications vidéo, au fur et à mesure des progrès technologiques et infrastructurels de ce pays. Nous continuerons d'explorer les nouvelles possibilités de la vidéo sur Internet et de proposer des sites web inattendus qui font sensation.

### 100 Cheergirls

Un site web publicitaire tourné vers les visiteurs grâce à 100 messages vidéo où des supportrices sont confrontées à 100 défis différents. Les vidéos, également publiées sur YouTube, sont présentées avec originalité sur le site web et encouragent les utilisateurs à des visionnages multiples tout en faisant la publicité de la marque d'e-carrière auprès de son public cible de jeunes hommes de 20-35 ans. La quantité de vidéos permet aux utilisateurs d'allonger leur visite sur le site web tout en créant

www.sony.co.jp/united/momoko

de nombreuses opportunités de contact avec la marque et son message.

**The Choice of Hiraya**

Un site promotionnel pour le projet résidentiel de Sumitomo Forestry, « Grand Life Hiraya ». Il cible un public de séniors, et propose un nouveau style de vie « Hiraya », confortable et différent. Il évite tout stress en s'adaptant à l'environnement de l'utilisateur avec une atmosphère détendue et de la musique relaxante. La mise en page simple est axée sur les photographies et sur le message de leur « choix ». Le site est également synchronisé avec plusieurs formes de publicité et encourage les utilisateurs à cliquer pour demander de la documentation en les aidant à choisir le produit qui leur convient le mieux en fonction de leur choix de style de vie.

**Junichi Saito** est le directeur d'ARCHETYP Inc., une jeune agence interactive basée à Tokyo. Créée en 2007, **ARCHETYP** a fourni à l'industrie de la création des solutions interactives pour n'importe quel client sur Internet, depuis la réalisation de sites web jusqu'à la mise au point de plans stratégiques pour des lancements de produit. En très peu de temps, elle s'est positionnée en première ligne des agences travaillant dans le secteur de la vidéo sur Internet, et a reçu de nombreuses récompenses. **<www.archetyp.jp>**

CASE:02

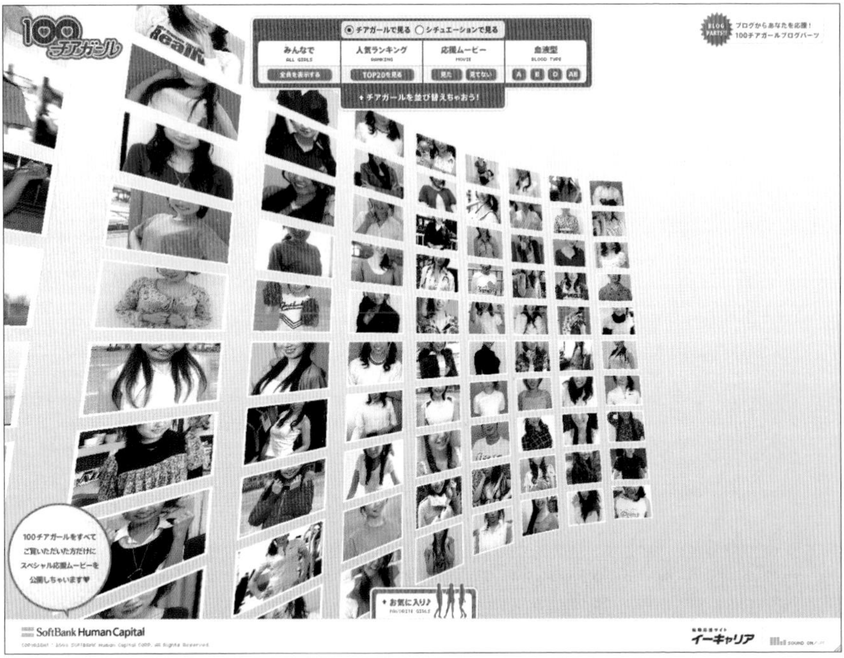

http://100cheergirl.jp

http://sfc.jp/ie/lineup/grandlife

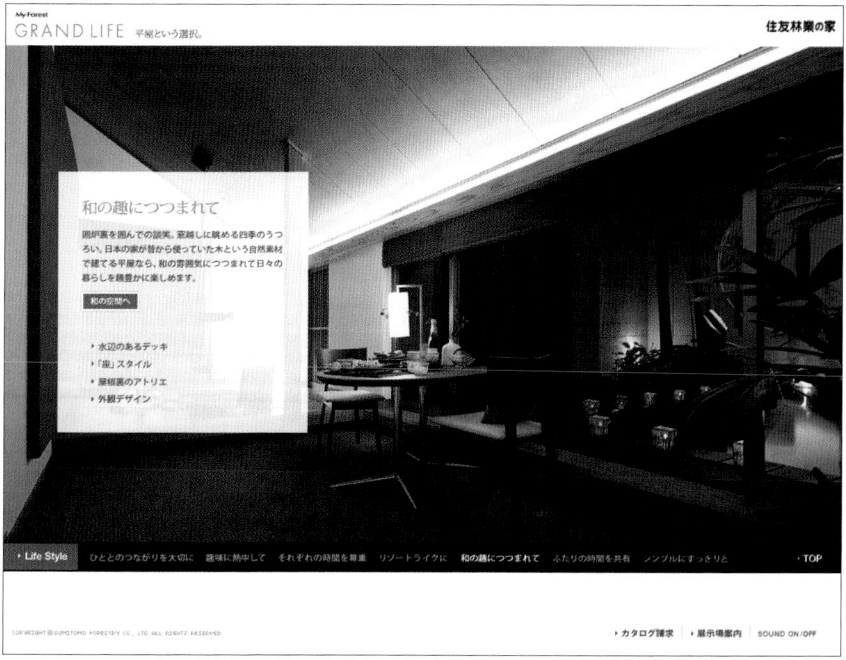

My Forest
GRAND LIFE 平屋という選択。

住友林業の家

和の趣につつまれて

囲炉裏を囲んでの談笑。窓越しに眺める四季のうつろい。日本の家が昔から使っていた木という自然素材で建てる平屋なら、和の雰囲気につつまれて日々の暮らしを趣豊かに楽しめます。

和の空間へ

- 水辺のあるデッキ
- 「座」スタイル
- 屋根裏のアトリエ
- 外観デザイン

Life Style | ひととのつながりを大切に | 趣味に熱中して | それぞれの時間を尊重 | リゾートライクに | 和の趣につつまれて | ふたりの時間を共有 | シンプルにすっきりと | TOP



カタログ請求 | 展示場案内 | SOUND ON/OFF

# AAA TOWN

USA

www.aaatown.com

2008

Concept

**The campaign relies on an innovative navigation approach in which the viewer moves back and forth in time via synchronous live-action clips.** /// Diese Kampagne arbeitet mit einer innovativen Navigation, bei der sich der Betrachter auf einer Zeitleiste anhand von synchronen Live-Action-Clips vor und zurück bewegen kann. /// **La campagne s'appuie sur une navigation innovante : l'utilisateur se déplace dans le temps grâce à des clips synchronisés d'action en direct.**

Info

**DESIGN:** Publicis & Hal Riney <www.hrp.com>; Perfect Fools <www.perfectfools.com>: Roger Camp, Dominic Goldman, Rikesh Lal, Rich North, Tony Högqvist, Christian Mezöfi. /// **PROGRAMMING:** David Genelid. /// **VIDEO:** Andrew Douglas (Director); Digital Domain (Visual Effects); Gino Nave (Sound Design). /// **OTHERS:** Sam Moore, Justin Kramm, Adam Koppel (Copy); David Verhoef (Director of Integrated Production); Dora Lee (Agency Producer); Fredrik Heghammar (Producer); Björn Kummeneje (Sound). /// **CLIENT:** AAA. /// **TOOLS:** Flash.

Change ZIP ▸ Send to a friend ▸ Members, register at AAA.com ▸ Sound off ▸
COVERAGE IN ANY CAR
LARGE NETWORK OF SERVICE VEHICLES
STAY ON THE ROAD (AND OUT OF THE SHOP)
TECHNOLOGY FOR SMOOTH TRAVEL
The most experience getting drivers out of jams.
Join AAA, and help is as close as the phone. Your Membership may pay for itself with just one Road Service call to 800-AAA-HELP or a request for assistance through Road Service online at AAA.com.
JOIN AAA TODAY
Insurance Road Service Shopping Dining AAA Branch Office
CLICK | COME IN | Terms & Conditions | Privacy Policy | © 2008 CSAA

Change ZIP ▸ Send to a friend ▸ Members, register at AAA.com ▸ Sound off ▸
Some things are easier in person.
In addition to AAA Maps and TourBook® guides available at AAA offices, many branches feature a full-service Travel Agency that offers international driving permits, passport photos, travel money products and more. Explore AAA Travel Services or find out what's offered at your local branch.
JOIN AAA TODAY
Insurance Road Service Shopping Dining AAA Branch Office
CLICK | COME IN | Terms & Conditions | Privacy Policy | © 2008 CSAA

# ABSOLUT DISCO

WORLDWIDE

http://www2.absolut.com/disco

2007

Concept

Special packaging turns the Absolut bottle into a disco ball. It's all part of a new integrated campaign with microsite produced by Perfect Fools for Great Works. Create your own disco films, either with your keyboard or a webcam. /// Durch eine spezielle Verpackung wird die Absolut-Flasche in eine Discokugel verwandelt. Das ist Bestandteil einer neuen, integrierten Kampagne mit einer Microsite, die von Perfect Fools für Great Works produziert wurde. Hier können Sie entweder mit Tastatur oder Webcam eigene Discofilme erstellen. /// Grâce à son emballage, la bouteille Absolut se transforme en boule de discothèque. Ce projet fait partie d'une nouvelle campagne intégrée avec un microsite produit par Perfect Fools, pour Great Works. Créez vos propres films disco, avec votre clavier ou une webcam.

Info

**Design:** Great Works <www.greatworks.com>: Mathias Päres (Art Director); Perfect Fools <www.perfectfools.com>: Vinh Kha (Creative Director), Christian Mezöfi, Fredrik Stutterheim (Art Directors). /// **Programming:** Perfect Fools: Björn Kummeneje (Tech Director); Jonathan Pettersson (Tech); Great Works: Jocke Wissing (Lead Tech). /// **Others:** Perfect Fools: Kathrin Spaak (Producer); Great Works: Charlotta Rydholm (Account Lead), Linn Tornéhielm, Sofie Vestergren (PL). /// **Client:** Absolut Vodka. /// **Tools:** Flash, Photoshop, After Effects, Eclipse.

◂ BACK TO ABSOLUT.COM
ABSOLUTDRINKS.COM
ABSOLUT
DISCO
PUT YOUR HAND IN THE AIR AND WAVE IT LIKE YOU JUST DON'T CARE!
SHOW US YOUR HAND MOVES! (WITH WEBCAM)
SHOW US YOUR LIGHTNING SKILLS! (WITHOUT WEBCAM)
USE YOUR KEYBOARD TO CREATE DISCO MAGIC
PRESS HERE TO RECORD YOUR MOVES
ABSOLUT DISCO GIFT PACK
ABSOLUT DISCO DRINKS
DOWNLOADS
SOUND OFF
TERMS & CONDITIONS
PRIVACY POLICY
SEND TO A FRIEND

# ADIDAS ORIGINALS HANDBAGS

GERMANY

www.neue-digitale.de/projects/originals_hff

2008

Concept

The main character is a photographer, who visits the subway. Every time the train stops, people leave and enter the scenario. Through the windows the user can see different subway stations named after the different lines in the collection. /// Die Hauptperson ist eine Fotografin, die mit der U-Bahn fährt. Immer wenn die Bahn anhält, betreten Menschen die Szenerie oder verlassen sie. Durchs Fenster sieht der User U-Bahn-Stationen, die nach den verschiedenen Produktlinien der Kollektion benannt sind. /// Le personnage principal est un photographe qui visite le métro. Chaque fois que le métro s'arrête, les gens sortent et entrent dans le scénario. À travers les fenêtres, l'utilisateur peut voir différentes stations de métro qui portent les noms des lignes de la collection.

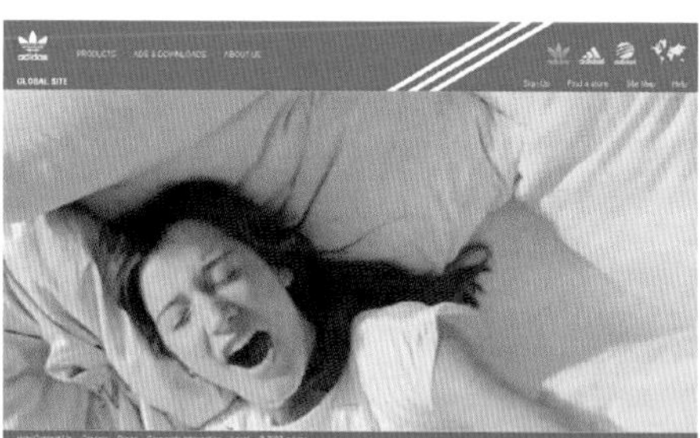

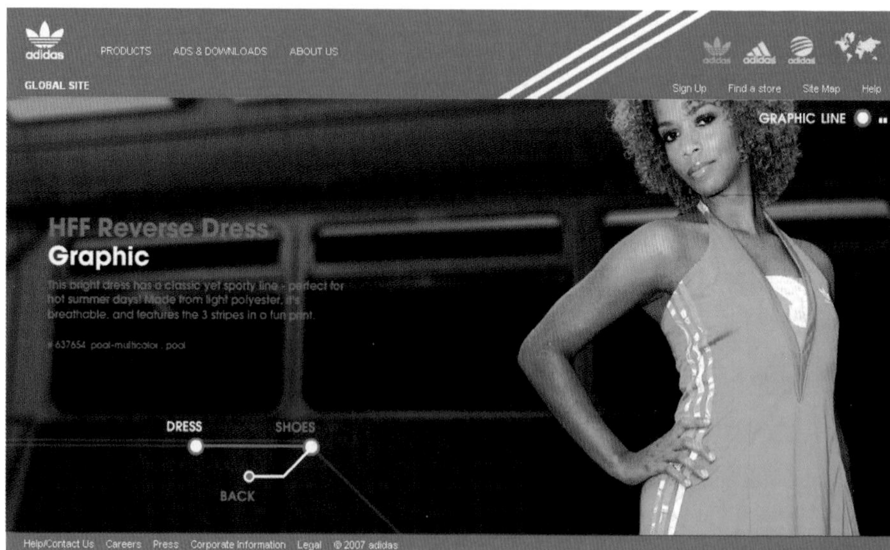


Info

**Design:** Neue Digitale GmbH <www.neue-digitale.de>: Elke Klinkhammer, Carsten Jamrow, Nico Schwenke. /// **Programming:** Oliver Greschke, Mathis Moder. /// **Others:** Katrin Bergfeld (Account Manager). /// **Client:** adidas AG. /// **Tools:** Cinema 4D, Flash, Premiere Pro, After Effects, Photoshop, Illustrator. /// **Awards:** FWA (Site of the Day), Mobius Award (Outstanding Creativity), ADC Germany (Distinction), New York Festivals (Bronze).

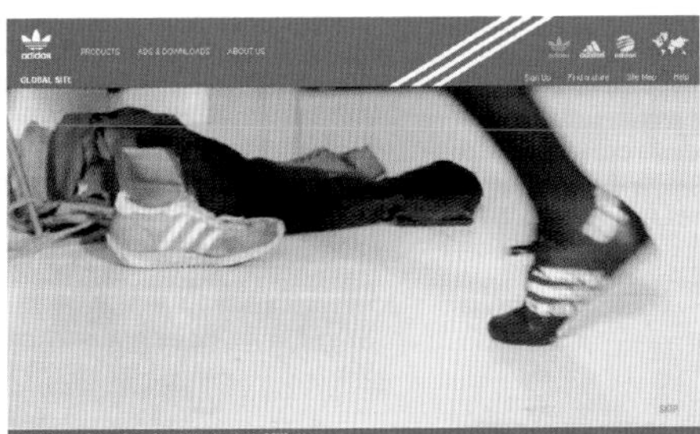

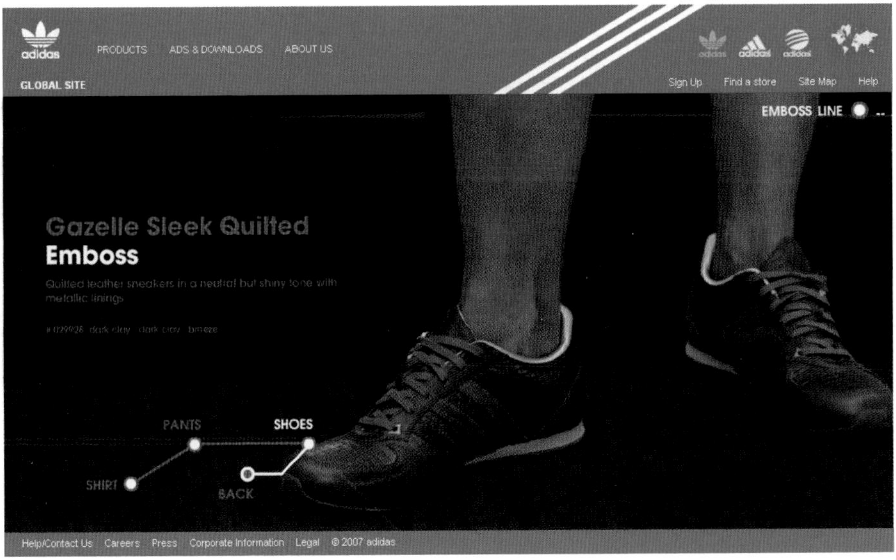

adidas
PRODUCTS
ADS & DOWNLOADS
ABOUT US
GLOBAL SITE
Sign Up
Find a store
Site Map
Help
EMBOSS LINE
Gazelle Sleek Quilted
Emboss
Quilted leather sneakers in a neutral but shiny tone with metallic linings
PANTS
SHOES
SHIRT
BACK
Help/Contact Us
Careers
Press
Corporate Information
Legal
© 2007 adidas

# ADIDAS Y-3 TIME SHIFTED

GERMANY

www.neue-digitale.de/projects/y-3_fw2007/2008

2007

Concept

**Space and time play an essential role in the Y-3 campaign in which models walk through a futuristic environment on time delay. Users themselves become the director and can decide what path the models take.** /// Raum und Zeit spielen bei der Kampagne Y-3 eine zentrale Rolle. Hier spazieren die Models zeitverzögert durch eine futuristische Umgebung. Die User können als Regisseur selbst festlegen, welche Pfade die Models nehmen sollen. /// **L'espace et le temps jouent un rôle essentiel dans la campagne Y-3, où des mannequins évoluent dans un décor futuriste avec un décalage temporel. Les utilisateurs deviennent réalisateurs, et peuvent décider du chemin que prendront les mannequins.**

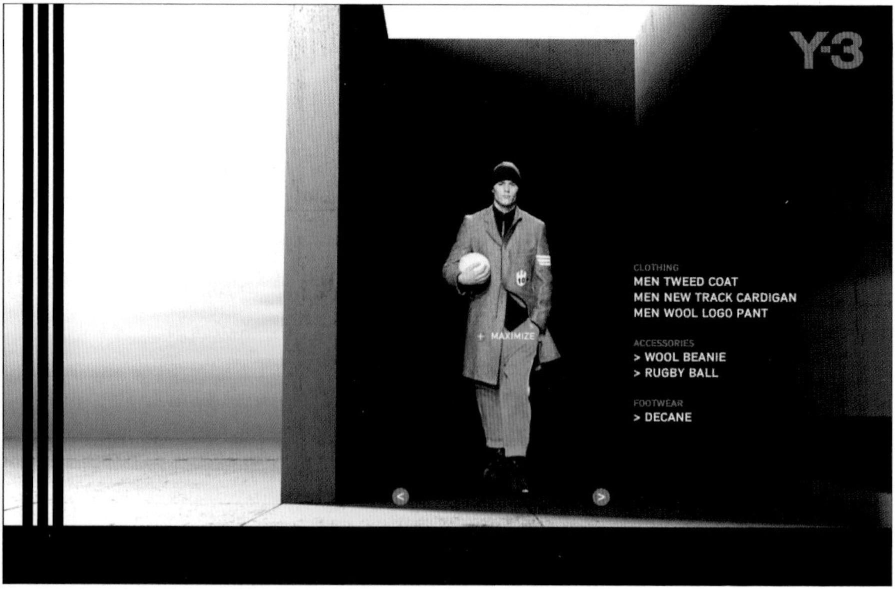

Info

**DESIGN:** Neue Digitale GmbH <www.neue-digitale.de>: Elke Klinkhammer, Steffen Bärenfänger, Oliver Hinrichs, Carsten Jamrow. /// **PROGRAMMING:** Andreas Diwisch, Jens Steffen, Marius Bulla. /// **VIDEO:** Dropout Films. /// **OTHERS:** Katrin Bergfeld (Account Manager); Christoph Riebling (Sound Design). /// **CLIENT:** adidas AG. /// **TOOLS:** Photoshop, Cinema 4D, After Effects, Flash, Eclipse. /// **AWARDS:** FWA (Site of the Day), Mobius Award (Outstanding Creativity), ADC Germany (Distinction), New York Festivals (Bronze).

Y-3

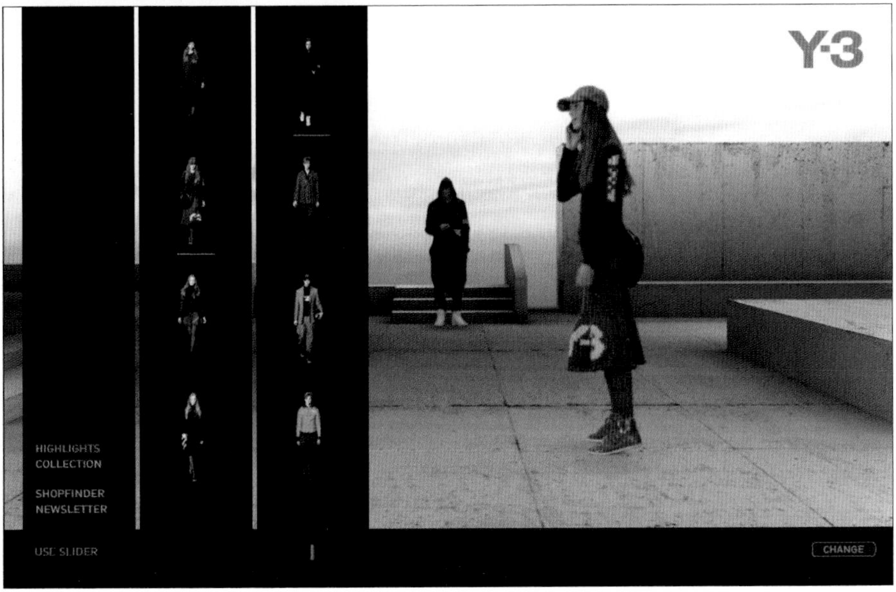

HIGHLIGHTS
COLLECTION

SHOPFINDER
NEWSLETTER

USE SLIDER

CHANGE

# ADULT SWIM

USA

www.adultswim.com

2008

Concept

Redesign of show pages for Adult Swim, featuring animated shows, including original programming, syndicated shows, and Japanese anime, generally with minimal or no editing for content. /// Ein Redesign der Show-Seiten für Adult Swim mit Animationsshows, zu der die Originalprogrammierung, Syndication-Shows und japanische Animes gehören (hier generell wenige oder keine Bearbeitungsmöglichkeit des Inhalts). /// Remodelage des pages consacrées aux émissions d'Adult Swim, avec des dessins animés, notamment des séries originales, des émissions indépendantes, de l'anime japonais, en général avec peu ou pas d'édition des contenus.

Info

**DESIGN:** HUGE <www.hugeinc.com>: David Skokna (Creative Director); Joe Stewart (Associate Creative Director); Kirsten Lawton, Aron Wahl (Interaction Designers). /// **PROGRAMMING:** Martin Olson, Josef Pfleger. /// **VIDEO:** Adult Swim. /// **CLIENT:** Turner Entertainment. /// **TOOLS:** Photoshop, Flash, Final Cut Pro. /// **COST:** 6 months.

[adult swim] SHOWS VIDEO DOWNLOADS GAMES MOBILE BOARDS MUSIC SHOP LOG IN SEARCH
10 Worst Dads on Adult Swim
Happy Father's Day. Suck it.
GAMES DON'T GET CAUGHT

Adult Swim
Meet the all-new Tiguan.
A big idea wrapped in a smaller frame.
It's what the people want. Learn more
Das Auto.

VIDEO
[adultswim.com] VIDEO
Noble Micronauts on [adult swim]
SHARE
CLIP OF THE DAY

FULL EPISODES WORDS FAIL
The Venture Bros.
The Invisible Hand of Fate
Metalocalypse
Dethrace
Fat Guy Stuck in Internet
Threshold
Assy McGee
The Ballad of Blind Anthony
Death Note
Vigilance

CLIPS LITTLE ANGEL BABIES
Venture Bros.
Slotted for #2
Family Guy
Tons of Clips
Assy McGee
Long Time
Robot Chicken
Tons of Clips
Metalocalypse
The Soup of My Beloved Husband

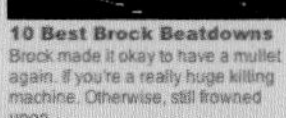
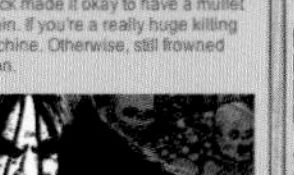

HEY GUESS WHAT STUFFED WITH TACOS
10 Great Tim and Eric Guest Stars
No star too big, no skit too ridiculous.
Ode to the Nerd
For anyone out there who's ever been thrown into a locker or raped by a unicorn.
10 Worst Dads on Adult Swim
Stop crying and read your list, or I'll give you something to cry about.
Ode to Evil Monkey
When buying a new home, always check the closets for monkeys.
Free Music: World Wide Renewal
Discover good new music without having to trudge through crappy new music.
10 Best Brock Beatdowns
Brock made it okay to have a mullet again. If you're a really huge killing machine. Otherwise, still frowned upon.
Meg's Most Humiliating Moments
Meg just does not deserve this abuse. Which is why it's hilarious.
Best Mayor West Clips
Will Adam West ever stop enriching our lives?
Dethklok Tour in June
Every time you buy a ticket, a demon gets his horns. Subject yourself to Ticketmaster Terms and Conditions now!
10 Best Family Guy Fights
With all the overblown fight scenes out there, it's refreshing to see something that overblows the rest out of the water.
10 Sexiest Moments from Adult Swim
Yes, it's another sex list. 10 Gruelingest Social Responsibility Seminars just keeps getting rejected.

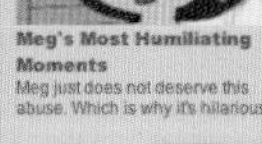

MISE EN SCÉNE PRET A PORTER
Dethklok Poster
The perfect counterbalance to that kitty on a branch poster you insist on displaying.
Tim & Eric: Awesome Record, Great Songs!
Uneasy listening.
Venture Bros. Season 3 Trailer
This season, it's personal.
Wanna put your junk on a shirt?
Brought to you by the 2008 Honda Fit. (external link)
Radiohead Video Contest
See if the semi-finalists are worthy of their semi-title at aniboom.com. (external link)
MySpace for Williams St
Our cyber friendship would mean so much to you. (external link)
Boondocks Comic
Read today's Boondocks comic.
Web Cam
Closed for Naked Week. Sorry.
Aqua Teen Movie Central: KingColon.com

# ALFA ROMEO EXPERIENCE 159 FRANCE

www.experience159.com 2008

Concept

**Experience the colorful universe of the Alfa 159 from Alfa Romeo in this full-screen walkthrough.** /// Erleben Sie in diesem Walkthrough das farbenprächtige Universum des Alfa 159 von Alfa Romeo auf dem ganzen Bildschirm. /// **Explorez l'univers coloré de l'Alfa 159 d'Alfa Romeo avec cette visite en plein écran.**

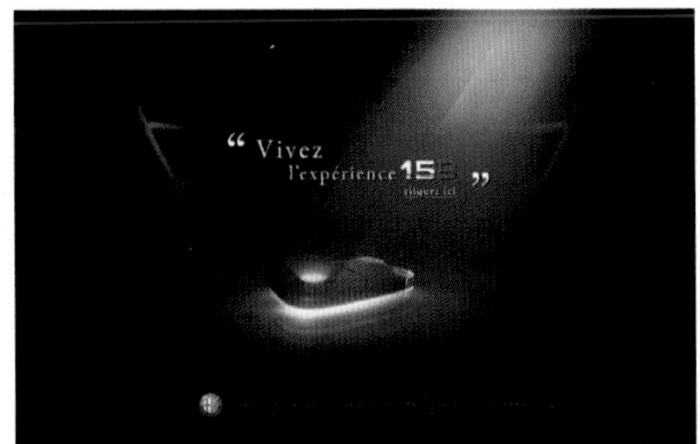


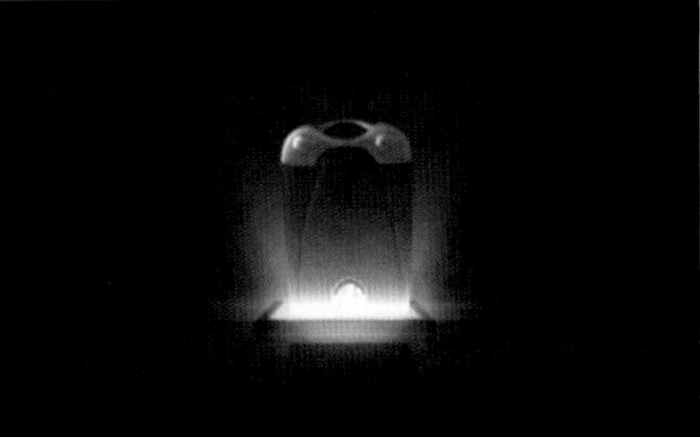

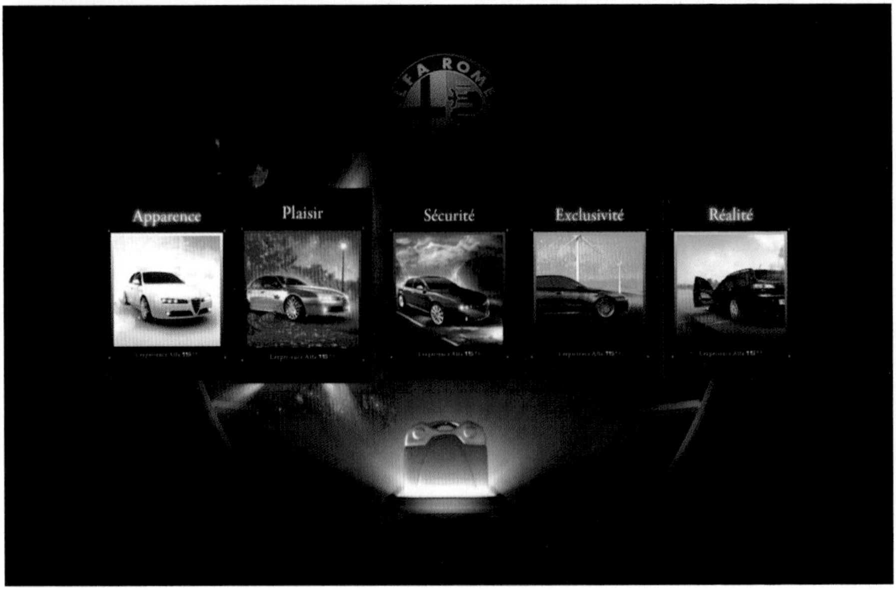

Info

**DESIGN:** Soleil Noir <www.soleilnoir.net>. /// **CLIENT:** Alfa Romeo. /// **TOOLS:** Photoshop, Flash, Flash Media Server, After Effects, Maya. /// **AWARDS:** FWA (Site of the Month). /// **COST:** 3 months.

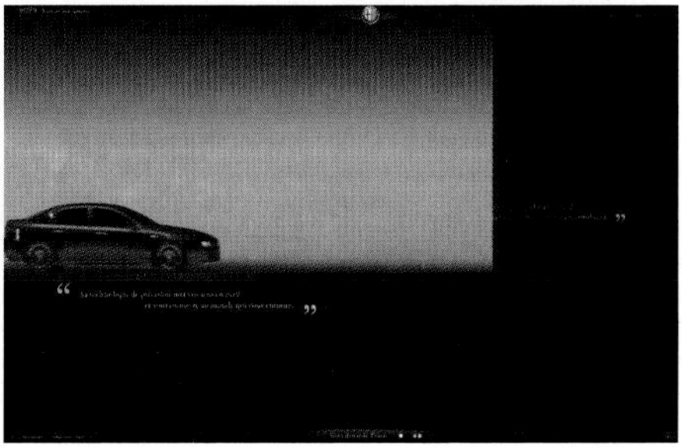

Elle vous fascinera par ses lignes pures
regard.
beauté intérieure

Prolongez

# ALL-BRAN 10 DAY CHALLENGE

USA

2008

Concept

With work by Leo Burnett, this project features a series of interactive banners and an online game that includes a healthy serving of John McEnroe in its video content. /// Mit der Arbeit von Leo Burnett stellt dieses Projekt eine Serie von interaktiven Bannern und ein Online-Spiel vor, zu dessen Videoinhalten viel Material mit John McEnroe gehört. /// Avec la collaboration de Leo Burnett, ce projet propose une série de bandeaux interactifs et de jeux en ligne qui comprend dans ses contenus vidéo une bonne portion de John McEnroe.

Info

**Design:** Domani Studios <http://domanistudios.com>. /// **Client:** Leo Burnett; Kellog's. /// **Tools:** Flash.

Yahoo! - Groups Home - Help

Join this Group **The All-Bran Day 10 Club** Already a member? Sign in to access this group!

home messages

Welcome to the All-Bran® Day 10 Club
I'm John McEnroe. I'm not only the spokesman for the All-Bran 10 Day Challenge™, I've done it myself. After 10 days, you too could be amazed at the results.
Become part of a regular movement in the All-Bran® 10 Day Club. See what Club members from coast-to-coast are saying about the benefits of All-Bran® products.


**Success Stories**

Hi, I'm Sue J.
"I can tell I have lost a lot of the bloating in my stomach and I am much more regular. That is a good thing for me."

Hi, I'm Yvette F.
"At first I thought, BRAN cereal!?? But this stuff really tastes great!"

Hi, I'm Julie N.
"Since I am getting more fiber in my diet, I feel like I have more energy when I exercise in the evening and I wake up feeling very good."

Hi, I'm Kendra N.
"I am sticking to the plan very easily. I love the challenge."

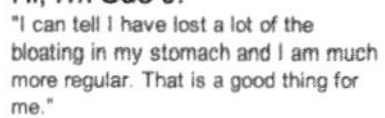

**Hot Topics & New Tools**

- Introduce yourself!
- Get motivated by reading how people are feeling on Day 10 of the Challenge.
- Just starting the All-Bran 10 Day Challenge™? Let us know what you're expecting.
- You're halfway through the All-Bran 10 Day Challenge TM, are you feeling any different?
- You did it! Tell us how the All-Bran 10 Day Challenge™ went for you.
- Send a personalized message from John McEnroe to a friend.
- Check out All-Bran® recipe ideas – or share one of your own.
- Have John McEnroe tell you about 10 ways to eat All-Bran®.
- How much fiber have you been eating? Try the Fiber Tabulator.

**Messages**

| | |
|---|---|
| Re: new members to the Bran 10 Day Club | linsuara@... posted june 11, 2008, 4:12 am |
| Re: My All-Bran 10 Day Success!!!! | debra corrica posted june 5, 2008, 9:27 pm |
| Re: Of all the good/best things you listed, | c_m_eden54@... posted june 4, 2008, 1:05 pm |
| Made It Through the 10 Day Challenge ! | c_m_eden54@... posted june 4, 2008, 1:05 pm |

**About This Group**

Kellogg started this group by recruiting more than 100 people to take the **All-Bran 10 Day Challenge™**. These "founding members" were asked questions about the challenge each day and asked to post their thoughts. The group has now been opened to the public for anyone who is interested in the benefits of fiber.

**Challenge Overview**

Take the All-Bran® cereal 10-Day Challenge
Here's your step-by-step plan to becoming a more regular you:

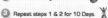

1. Get All-Bran® cereal 
2. Eat one serving of All-Bran®
3. Repeat steps 1 & 2 for 10 Days. 

New to this fiber thing? Increase your fiber intake gradually and drink plenty of water everyday.

**Group Information**

To ensure that **All-Bran®** cereal Day 10 Club Yahoo Group is a place where everyone can feel comfortable posting messages, sharing what is on their mind, and providing support to one another, we require that everyone adhere to the Yahoo Groups guidelines. All photos uploaded to the group must be of the user themselves. All-Bran® does not test or endorse any recipe submitted by users.

**Group info**

**Web:**
http://groups.yahoo.com/allbrangroup
**Post to:**
allbrangroup@yahoogroups.com

# AMERICAN IDOL DREYERS

USA

http://idol.dreyers.slowchurned.com/idol/index.html

2008

Concept

**This site Domani Studios created for Goodby, Silverstein & Partners uses former American Idol contestants to introduce and sing about five new ice cream flavors.** /// Diese Site, die Domani Studios für Goodby, Silverstein & Partners geschaffen hat, stellt fünf neue Sorten Eiscreme vor, die von Kandidaten aus *American Idol* besungen werden. /// **Sur ce site que Domani Studios a créé pour Goodby, Silverstein & Partners, cinq anciens concurrents d'American Idol présentent et mettent en chanson cinq nouveaux parfums de glace.**

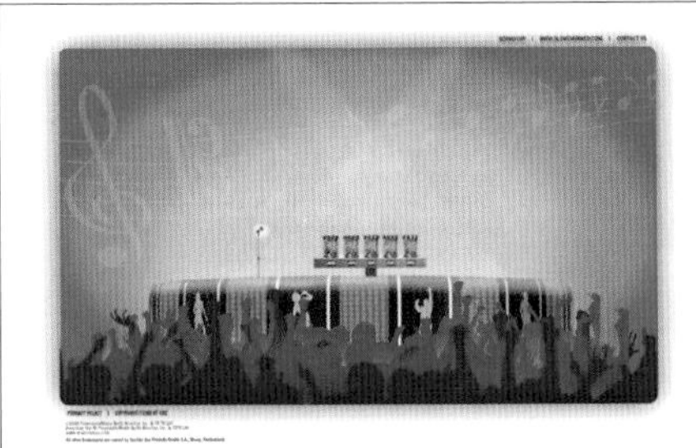

Info

**DESIGN:** Domani Studios <http://domanistudios.com>. /// **CLIENT:** Goodby, Silverstein & Partners; Dreyers. /// **TOOLS:** Flash, FCP, After Effects, Photoshop.

Dreyer's
Slow Churned
DREYER'S IDOL ICE CREAM TOUR
Get an all-access pass to Chris Richardson and Melinda Doolittle's tour!

Dreyer's
Slow Churned
DREYER'S IDOL ICE CREAM TOUR
Get an all-access pass to Chris Richardson and Melinda Doolittle's tour!

Dreyer's
Slow Churned
DREYER'S IDOL ICE CREAM TOUR
Get an all-access pass to Chris Richardson and Melinda Doolittle's tour!

Dreyer's
Slow Churned
DREYER'S IDOL ICE CREAM TOUR
Get an all-access pass to Chris Richardson and Melinda Doolittle's tour!

SOUND OFF | WWW.SLOWCHURNED.COM | CONTACT US
Dreyer's
Slow Churned
RICH & CREAMY
FLAVOR PERFORMANCES
DREYER'S IDOL ICE CREAM TOUR
SPECIAL PERFORMANCES
FAQ
PERFORMANCES
EXCLUSIVE INTERVIEWS
SEND TO A FRIEND
PRIVACY POLICY | COPYRIGHT/TERM OF USE

# AS THE WORLD TURNS

USA

http://atwt.freedominteractivedesign.com

2007

Concept

"As The World Turns" is the 2nd-longest running program in daytime television history. Its first official site takes visitors behind the scenes at the television studio, where content is cleverly delivered. /// „As The World Turns" ist das am zweitlängsten laufende Programm der Fernsehgeschichte. Auf der ersten offiziellen Website können die Besucher hinter die Kulissen des Aufnahmestudios schauen, wo die Inhalte auf pfiffige Weise vermittelt werden. /// « As The World Turns » est la deuxième émission la plus ancienne toujours diffusée actuellement dans l'histoire des programmes télévisés de la journée. Son premier site officiel fait entrer les visiteurs dans les coulisses du studio de télévision, où les contenus sont présentés avec beaucoup d'intelligence.

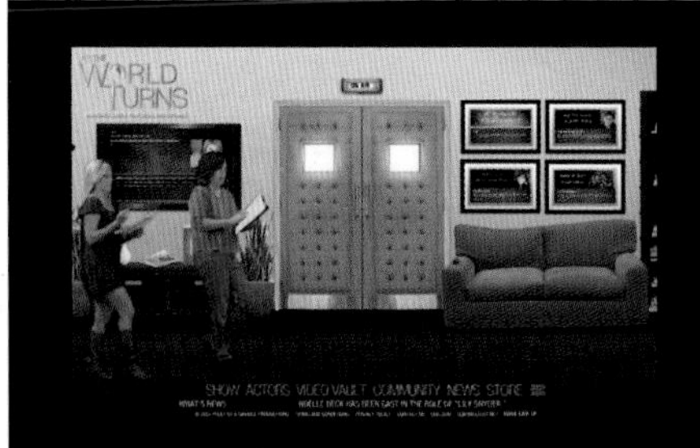

Info

**Design:** Freedom Interactive Design <www.freedominteractivedesign.com>: Mark Ferdman (Creative Director); Matt Sundstrom (Senior Art Director). /// **Programming:** Shea Gonyo (Tech Director); Gicheol Lee (Senior Action Script Developer); Brian Kadar (Senior Action Script Developer). /// **Video:** Mark Ferdman (Executive Producer); Shea Gonyo (Director); Nick Kircos (Post-production). /// **Others:** Danny Chang (Production Artist/ Post-production). /// **Client:** Procter & Gamble Productions. /// **Tools:** Flash, Microsoft ASP.net.

AS THE
WORLD
TURNS
WEEKDAYS: CHECK YOUR LOCAL CBS LISTINGS.
HOME SHOW ACTORS VIDEO VAULT COMMUNITY NEWS STORE
FEATURES BEHIND THE SCENES ARCHIVES
© 2007 PROCTER & GAMBLE PRODUCTIONS TERMS AND CONDITIONS PRIVACY POLICY CONTACT US CBS.COM EMAIL SIGN-UP

AS THE
WORLD
TURNS
WEEKDAYS: CHECK YOUR LOCAL CBS LISTINGS
ATWT BLOOPERS AND OUTTAKES
FULL SCREEN
HOME SHOW ACTORS VIDEO VAULT COMMUNITY NEWS STORE
FEATURES BEHIND THE SCENES ARCHIVES
© 2007 PROCTER & GAMBLE PRODUCTIONS TERMS AND CONDITIONS PRIVACY POLICY CONTACT US CBS.COM EMAIL SIGN-UP

# B2S

THE NETHERLANDS

www.b2s.nl

2007

Concept

From b2s, dutch leader in dance events, the request came in to develop an umbrella site which covered all of their event brands whilst maintaing a unified look. /// b2s, der niederländische Marktführer bei Dance-Events, vergab den Auftrag, eine Umbrella-Site zu entwickeln, die alle ihre Event-Marken unter einem einheitlichen Aussehen vereinen sollte. /// Le leader néerlandais des spectacles de danse, b2s, voulait développer un site qui regrouperait toutes ses marques d'événement tout en conservant un style homogène.

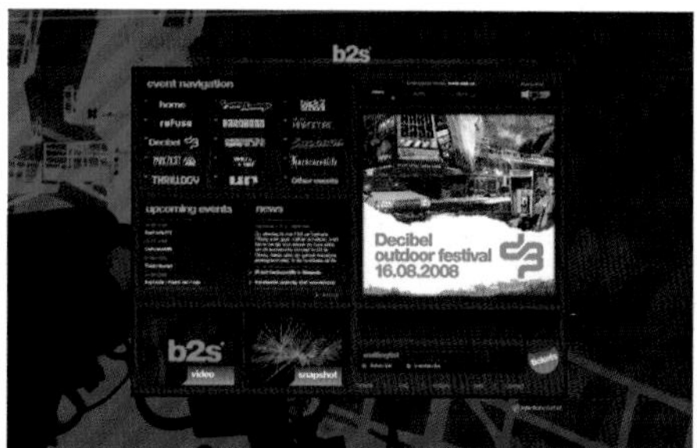

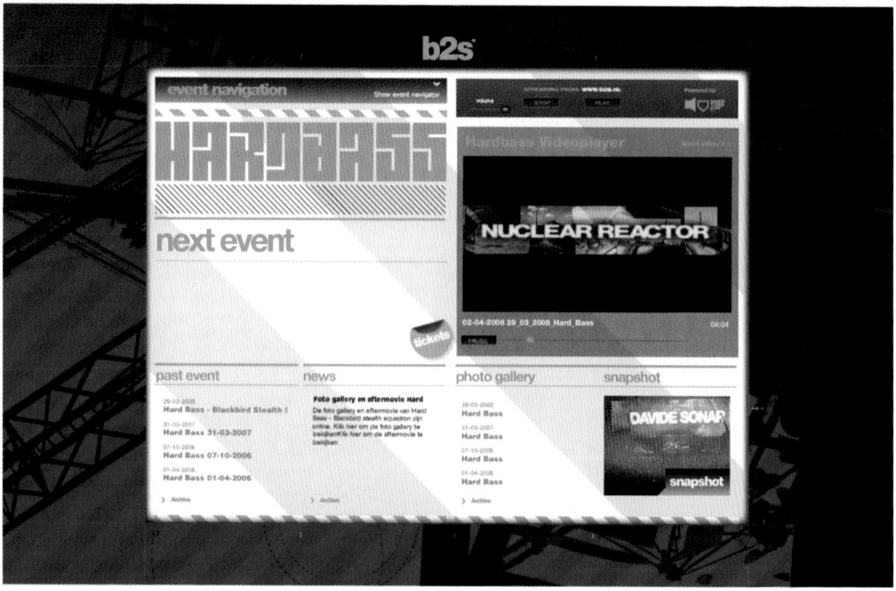

Info

**Design:** THEPHARMACY <www.thepharmacymedia.com>: Joeri Tan, Jackson Chang, Krijn Elders. /// **Programming:** Jan-Willem Reuling, Dirk van Hout. /// **Video:** Edwin Schutjes (b2s). /// **Tools:** Flash, Photoshop, Illustrator, PHP, MySQL. /// **Cost:** 200 hours.

b2s
next event

b2s
Darkness4life Videoplayer
31-05-2008
snapshot

b2s
next event
THRILLOGY

b2s
07-06-2008
Pussy lounge
Pussy Lounge Videoplayer
snapshot

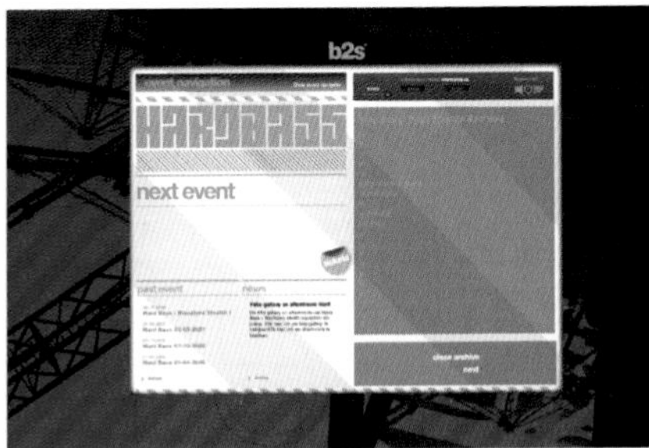

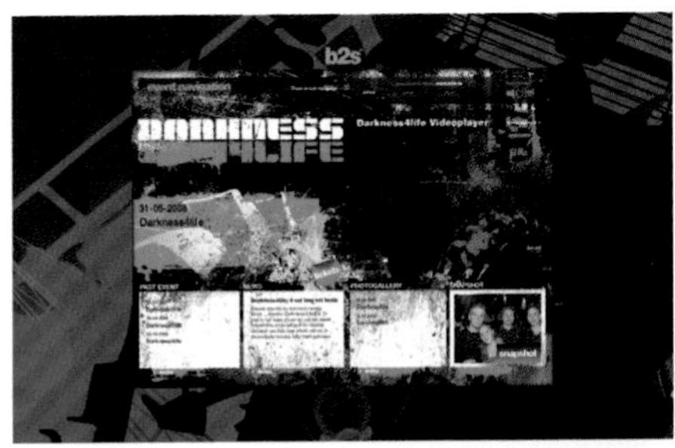

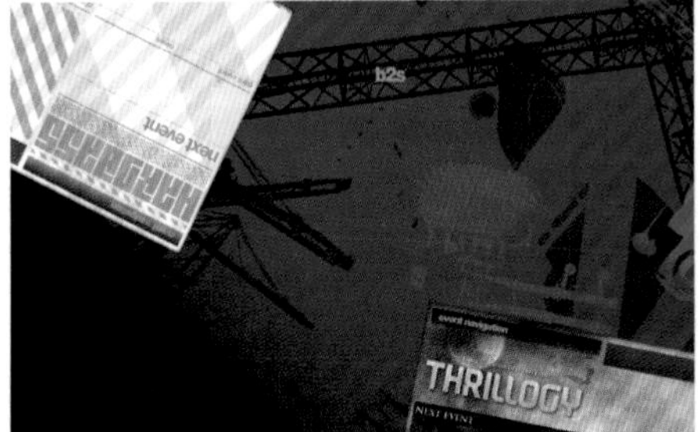

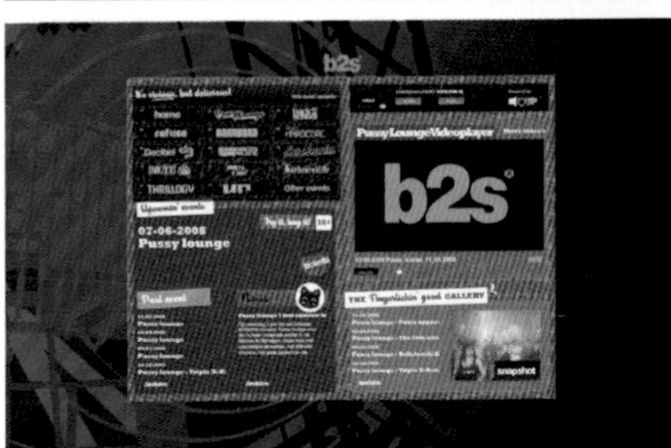

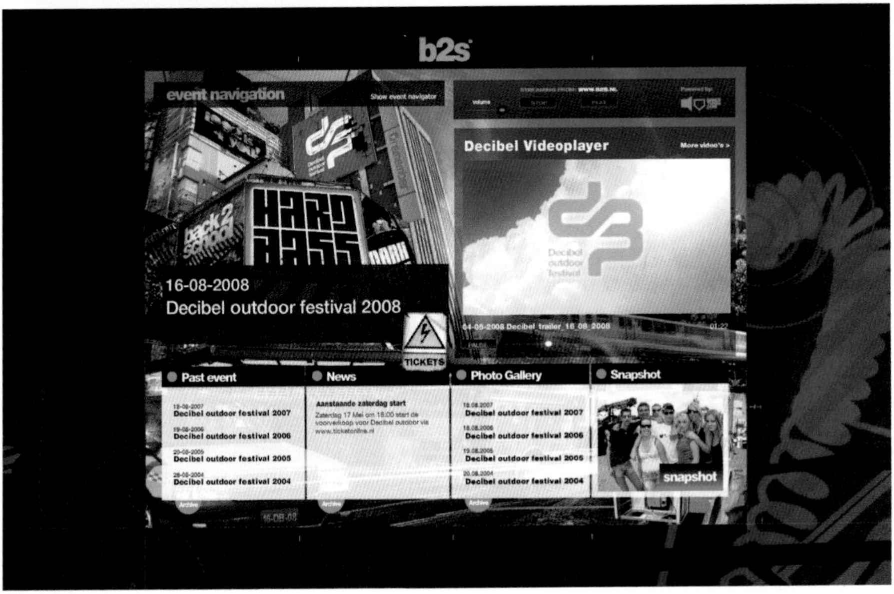

b2s
event navigation
Show event navigator
Decibel Videoplayer
More video's >
16-08-2008
Decibel outdoor festival 2008
TICKETS
04-05-2008 Decibel trailer 16 08 2008
01:22
Past event
18-08-2007
Decibel outdoor festival 2007
19-08-2006
Decibel outdoor festival 2006
20-08-2005
Decibel outdoor festival 2005
28-08-2004
Decibel outdoor festival 2004
News
Aanstaande zaterdag start
Zaterdag 17 Mei om 18.00 start de voorverkoop voor Decibel outdoor via www.ticketonline.nl
Photo Gallery
18.08.2007
Decibel outdoor festival 2007
18.08.2006
Decibel outdoor festival 2006
19.08.2005
Decibel outdoor festival 2005
20.08.2004
Decibel outdoor festival 2004
Snapshot
snapshot
Archive

# BALDINI NI

www.baldinini.it

ITALY

2007

Concept

The website makes good use of videos taken from the fashion show for each collection released. /// Die Website arbeitet für jede vorgestellte Kollektion mit umfangreichen, bei der Fashion-Show aufgenommenen Videos. /// Ce site web utilise habilement les vidéos extraites du défilé de chaque collection présentée.

Info

**Design:** Extera <www.extera.com>. /// **Programming:** Extera. /// **Client:** Baldinini. /// **Tools:** Flash, Javascript, PHP, CSS.

Baldinini

BALDININI footwear factory
COLLECTION
SPECIAL ITEMS
SALES POINTS
PRESS/NEWS
CONTACTS

The footwear factory in San Mauro Pascoli, Rimini, which over the years has retained the complex structure of an enormous workshop with a factory attached, recently underwent a full restyling. New structures have been designed and integrated with the original buildings to enhance the flexibility of the spaces in each division.

At the premises, which occupy about 15.000 sq m (161,458 sq ft.), all design and manufacturing activities are performed around the hub of the central management offices, including the work of the design division, modeling workshops, raw materials warehouse, display and sales areas, and quality control areas. The premises also include a large factory outlet that, among its many customers, attracts numerous buyers from outside Italy.

Baldinini S.r.l.
via Rio Salto, 1°
47030 San Mauro Pascoli (FC) - Italia

Tel. + 39 0541 932898
Fax + 39 0541 932960

03

Sound on/off 2008 © Baldinini Privacy policy Credits

# BBC THREE LIVE ARENA

UK

http://www.bbc.co.uk/bbcthree/livearena

2008

Concept

**Live Arena is an immersive, playful space in the new BBC Three web presence. The space is dominated by a big screen where users watch premieres, simulcasts and live content.** /// Live Arena ist ein beeindruckender, verspielter Ort der neuen Webpräsenz von BBC Three. Auf einem großen, dominanten Bildschirm können die User Premieren, Simulcasts und Live-Sendungen anschauen. /// **Live Arena est un espace ludique et fascinant qui fait partie du nouvel arsenal web de BBC Three. Il est dominé par un grand écran où les utilisateurs peuvent regarder des premières, des simulcasts et des émissions en direct.**

Info

**DESIGN:** Nexus Productions <www.nexusproductions.com>: Tim Dillon (Art Direction); Gareth Bourne (Producer); Red Bee Media <www.redbeemedia.com>: Ken Lum. /// **PROGRAMMING:** Red Bee Media. /// **VIDEO:** Fletch Moules, Mark Davies, Florian Mounie, Simon Goodchild, Matt Howard, Jonathan Gallagher, Eoin Coughlan (3D Design, Modelling, Animation, Rendering). /// **CLIENT:** Red Bee Media for BBC Three. /// **TOOLS:** 3D Studio Max, After Effects, Flash, HTML, Photoshop, BBC iPlayer. /// **COST:** 8 weeks.

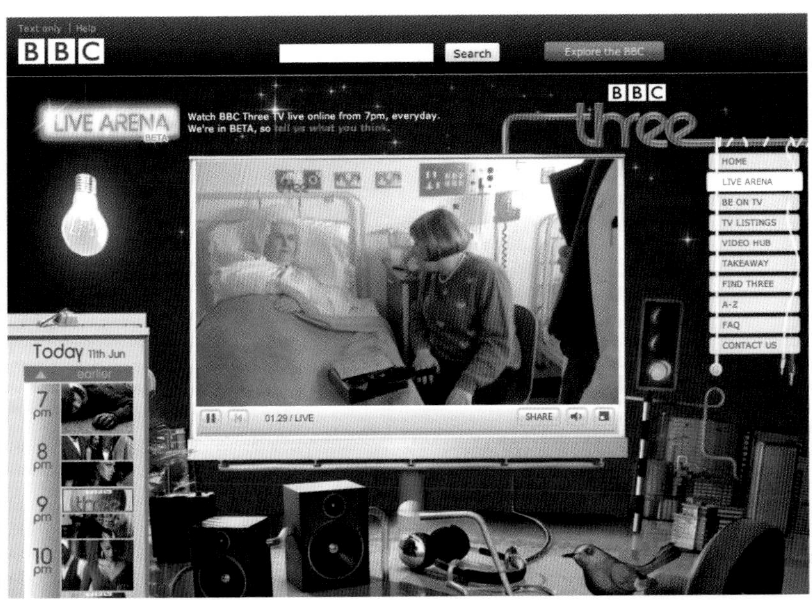
Text only | Help
BBC
Search
Explore the BBC
LIVE ARENA
BETA
Watch BBC Three TV live online from 7pm, everyday.
We're in BETA, so tell us what you think.
BBC three
HOME
LIVE ARENA
BE ON TV
TV LISTINGS
VIDEO HUB
TAKEAWAY
FIND THREE
A-Z
FAQ
CONTACT US
Today 11th Jun
earlier
7 pm
8 pm
9 pm
10 pm
01.29 / LIVE
SHARE

Text only | Help
BBC
Search
Explore the BBC
VIDEO HUB
A selection of clips and your videos
BBC three
HOME
LIVE ARENA
BE ON TV
TV LISTINGS
VIDEO HUB
TAKEAWAY
FIND THREE
A-Z
FAQ
CONTACT US
00:05|00:05
Gideon & Stacey 2
Gideon loves Gavin & Stacey
Created by: Be_on_TV - 9th Jun 2008
Link to this: http://www.bbc.co.uk/bbcthree/videohub/show/1371/
IDEAL: NEW SERIES
MOST RECENT
TAGGED AS

# BIBI

BRAZIL

www.bibi.com.br/clubBoy/bibiTv

2007

Concept

On Bibi's website users can watch videos produced for TV Bibi, a TV program made by the brand, with content designed for children. /// Auf der Website von Bibi betrachtet man für *TV Bibi* produzierte Videos. Dieses Fernsehprogramm wurde von der Marke Bibi produziert und richtet sich vom Inhalt her an Kinder. /// Sur le site web de Bibi, les visiteurs peuvent regarder des vidéos produites pour TV Bibi, une émission réalisée par la marque, avec des contenus conçus pour les enfants.

Info

**Design:** W3Haus <www.w3haus.com.br>. Diego Chiarelli, Chico Baldini. /// **Programming:** Luiz Ricardo Sordi, Marcelo Arocha, Julio Silva, Filipe Silvestrim, Eduardo Costa. /// **Video:** TGD Filmes. /// **Others:** Leo Prestes (Creative); Joseane Janner (Account Executive); Diego Grandi (Project Manager). /// **Client:** Bibi Calçados. /// **Tools:** HTML, PHP, Flash, Photoshop, Action Script. /// **Cost:** 1300 hours.

Bibi
PORT ENG ESP
BUSCA
HOME
INSTITUCIONAL
COLEÇÃO
CLUBIBINHO
CLUBE DA MAMÃE
ONDE ENCONTRAR
CONTATO
CLUBIBINHO
MENINO
TV BIBI
Menuzinho
LOGIN
E-MAIL:
SENHA:
ESQUECI MINHA SENHA
ENVIAR
CADASTRO
06
NICKOLASAMANDA
Estilo para se vestir
▶PLAY ‖PAUSE ■STOP
OUTROS PROGRAMETES
01 02 03 04 05 06 07
TV Bibi
TODAS AS QUARTAS ENTRE
19:00>19:30H
NO CARTOON NETWORK
BLOG
CLIQUE AQUI
Calçados Bibi Ltda. | RS 239 Km 28,4 no 3600 | Tel.: 55 51 3512 3344 | Parobé RS Brasil | Todos os Direitos Reservados | Copyright 2008 |

CLUBIBINHO
MENINO
TV BIBI
AMANDINHA
Estilo para se vestir
▶PLAY ‖PAUSE ■STOP

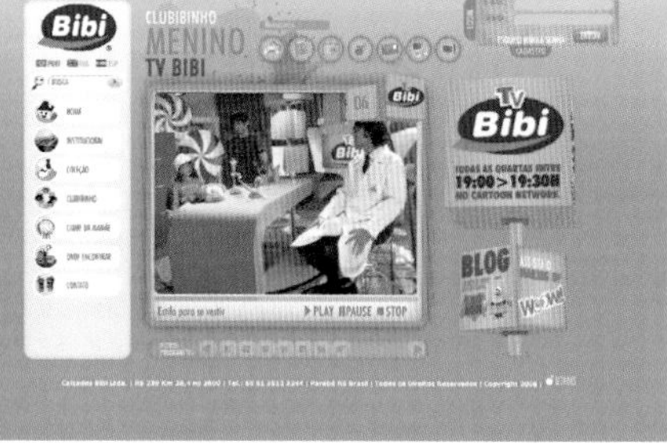
CLUBIBINHO
MENINO
TV BIBI
▶PLAY ‖PAUSE ■STOP

CLUBIBINHO
MENINO
TV BIBI
LAÇO
TEIA
DE
ARANHA
▶PLAY ‖PAUSE ■STOP

CLUBIBINHO
MENINO
TV BIBI
www.bibi.com.br
▶PLAY ‖PAUSE ■STOP

# BLACKBELTMONKEY

GERMANY

www.blackbeltmonkey.com

2008

Concept

Agency website using interactive video sequences integrated into the Flash framework used to display their philosophy, culture and previous cases. /// Die Website der Agentur arbeitet mit interaktiven Videosequenzen, die in das Flash-Framework integriert sind, um die eigene Philosophie, Kultur und Referenzarbeiten darzustellen. /// Site web d'agence qui utilise des séquences vidéo interactives intégrées à un environnement Flash qui présente sa philosophie, sa culture et les projets qu'elle a réalisés.

Info

**DESIGN:** blackbeltmonkey, digital advertising agency <www.blackbeltmonkey.com>: Mike John Otto, Oliver Bentz (Creative Directors); Mike John Otto (Art Director); Marcellus Gau (Project Manager); Oliver Bentz (Copy). /// **PROGRAMMING:** Nikolai Bockholt, mploj. /// **VIDEO:** Verena Knemeyer (Photo), Jasper Jones (Model). /// **OTHERS:** V8 Studio (Sound), Paul picts (Photo). /// **TOOLS:** Flash, Photoshop, Freehand, After Effects. /// **AWARDS:** Cannes Cyber Lions (Shortlist), FWA, Screenfluent, Qbn (News Today), Website Design Awards. /// **COST:** 3 months.

blackbeltmonkey
hello@blackbeltmonkey.com

blackbeltmonkey, digital communication and design studio
++49 (0) 40/ 431 792 10 / 18:43:54

BLACKBELTMONKEY, HEAD OF CREATION

/ awards /

mail:

We brought this little fella back with us from one of our jungle expeditions.
It was June 1st when we found him. He was sitting under a big banana tree leaf shielding himself from the monsoon rain, shivering. Obviously his tribe had abandoned him.
We wrapped him in a blanket and carried him with us back to our basecamp.

We quickly discovered that he was different from all the other monkeys that we had met over the years. He was special. He could do the most amazing things and he suprised every member of our expedition on a daily basis with his ideas. He was a quick and eager learner, always curious.

That must have been the reason why his tribe had left him all alone in the jungle – his wild creativity probably had disturbed the social dynamics of stability and continuity that are typical for many monkey tribes. His specialness was not only obvious from his extraordinary skills and behaviour. You could see it, too.

NEWS
RULES
CASES

PROFILES

HEY, HEY, WE'RE THE MONKEYS ...

MIKE JOHN OTTO
OLIVER BENTZ MARCELLUS GAU NIKOLAI BOCKHOLT
CARSTEN GUETH FREELANCERS + PRODUCTION COMPANIES

JOBS
CONTACT

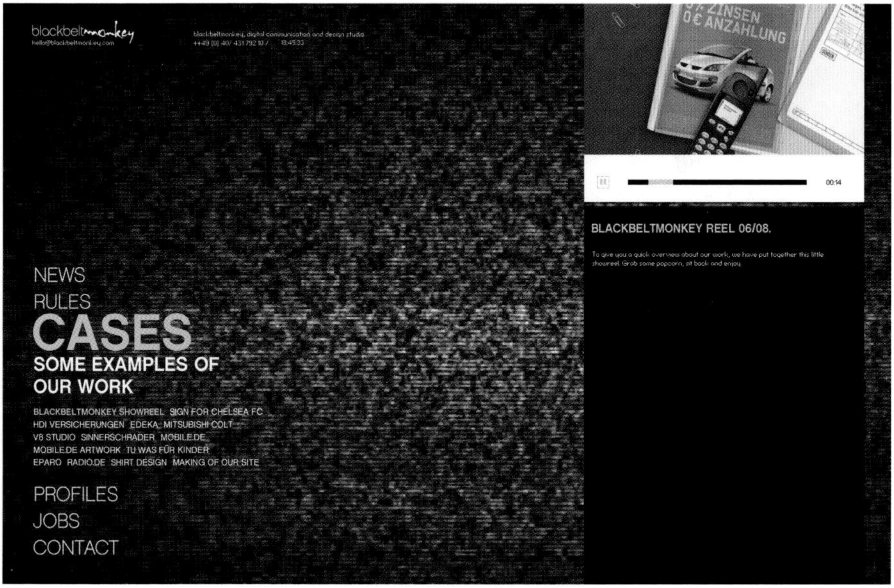

blackbeltmonkey
hello@blackbeltmonkey.com

blackbeltmonkey, digital communication and design studio
++49 (0) 40/ 431 792 10 / 18:45:33

0% ZINSEN
0 € ANZAHLUNG

00:14

BLACKBELTMONKEY REEL 06/08.

To give you a quick overview about our work, we have put together this little showreel. Grab some popcorn, sit back and enjoy.

NEWS
RULES

CASES

SOME EXAMPLES OF OUR WORK

BLACKBELTMONKEY SHOWREEL SIGN FOR CHELSEA FC
HDI VERSICHERUNGEN EDEKA MITSUBISHI COLT
V8 STUDIO SINNERSCHRADER MOBILE.DE
MOBILE.DE ARTWORK TU WAS FÜR KINDER
EPARO RADIO.DE SHIRT DESIGN MAKING OF OUR SITE

PROFILES
JOBS
CONTACT

# BLASON BY LOUIS VUITTON

FRANCE

www.louisvuitton.com

2008

Concept

**Presentation of a jewelry line from Louis Vuitton.** /// Präsentation einer Schmuckkollektion von Louis Vuitton. /// **Présentation d'une ligne de bijoux de la maison Louis Vuitton.**

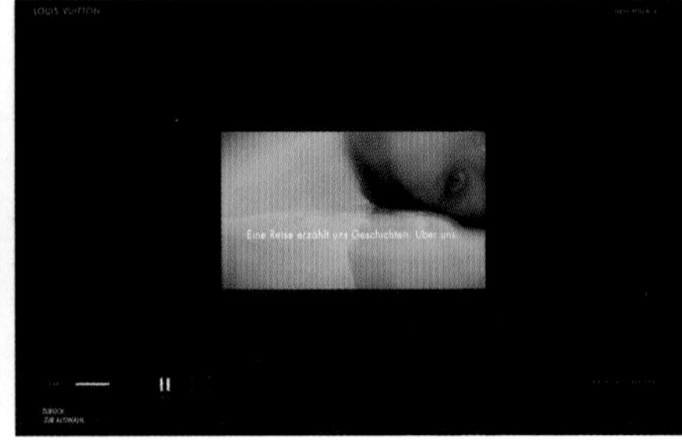

Info

**DESIGN:** Spill <www.spill.net>: Liz Stirling, Nicholas Mir Chaikin, Virginie Nguyen Tan Hon, Guilhem Moreau, Malte Ludwig, François Chay. /// **PROGRAMMING:** Christophe Le Bars, Guilhem Moreau, Malte Ludwig, François Chay. /// **VIDEO:** Guilhem Moreau. /// **OTHERS:** Design Coordination/Producer: Pierre-Alexis Corson for Spill with Audrey Montacel and Claire Foulain for Louis Vuitton, and the film "Blason" by S2A Paris/Jeremy Rozan. /// **CLIENT:** Louis Vuitton. /// **TOOLS:** Adobe CS, Flash, After Effects. /// **COST:** 200 hours.

LOUIS VUITTON
www.louisvuitton.com

MOSCOW
BY MIKHAIL GORBACHEV

LOUIS VUITTON
MEHR REISEN
KAPITEL 4.
EINE STADT IM SMOG
KLICKEN SIE, UM DAS KAPITEL ANZUSEHEN
MOSKAU
BY MICHAIL GORBATSCHOW
HAUPTMENÜ

# CALLIOPE

ITALY

www.calliope.info

2008

Concept

The contents of each issue of this fashion magazine are displayed in large-sized spreads. /// Die Contents jeder Ausgabe dieses Modemagazins werden in großformatigen Spreads dargestellt. /// Les contenus de chaque numéro de ce magazine de mode sont affichés sur de grandes doubles pages.

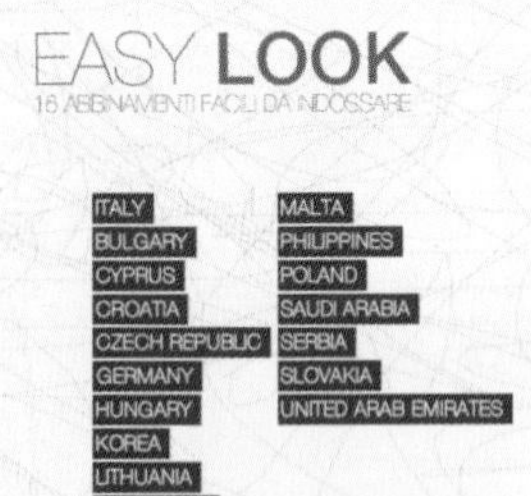

Info

**Design:** Extera <www.extera.com>. /// **Programming:** Extera. /// **Video:** Lavinia <www.laviniastyle.com>. /// **Client:** Teddy. /// **Tools:** Flash, ASP, CSS, Javascript.

calliop

CALLIOPE
SPRINGSUMMER08
MAGAZINE
trend
style
08
JEANS
SPECIAL
BON TON &
BACK TO 60
MODERN
MIX
A CRUISE BACK
INTO THE 20'S
A TRIP
SICILY
IN THE SIDE
BACKSTAGE
DOWNLOAD
STORES
CONTACT
BUSINESS
Credits
Versione Italiana
© 2008 Teddy spa

# COKE ZERO – BLITZ VERÃO

BRAZIL

www.cokezeroveraors.w3haus.co.uk

2007

Concept

Created to support the Coke Zero live-marketing action, the website is based on the brand's communication campaign. With the concept "the same flavor, zero sugar", the project is led by its characters: two tongues and an eye. /// Diese Website basiert auf der Kommunikationskampagne der Marke Coke Zero und wurde als Unterstützung für das Live-Marketing geschaffen. Das Konzept „Echter Geschmack, zero Zucker" wird von den Hauptpersonen dieses Projekts vermittelt: zwei Zungen und einem Auge. /// Créé pour soutenir les actions de marketing direct de Coke Zero, ce site web se base sur la campagne de communication de la marque. Avec le concept « le goût de Coca-Cola avec zéro sucre », le projet est mené par ses personnages : deux langues et un œil.

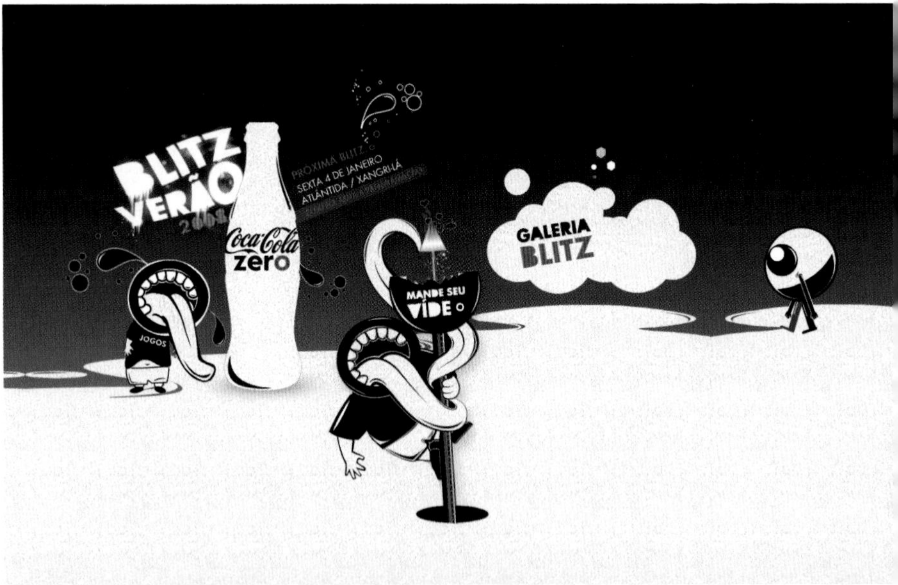

Info

**DESIGN:** W3Haus <www.w3haus.com.br>: Chico Baldini, Diego Chiarelli. /// **PROGRAMMING:** Matias Causa, Carolina Sebben, Filipe Silvestrin, Marcelo Arocha. /// **OTHERS:** Tiago Ritter (Account Manager), Kátia Rosa (Account Executive), Leo Prestes (Creative), Rodrigo Meurer (Project Manager), Ricardo Gimenes (Designer Assistant). /// **CLIENT:** Coca-Cola. /// **TOOLS:** Photoshop, Flash, PHP, HTML, XML. /// **COST:** 212 hours.

BLITZ
VERÃO
HOME
GALERIA
VÍDEOS
MANDE SEU
VÍDEO
MANDE SEU VÍDEO

BLITZ
VERÃO
HOME
GALERIA
VÍDEOS
MANDE SEU
VÍDEO
MANDE SEU VÍDEO

BLITZ
VERÃO
HOME
GALERIA
VÍDEOS
MANDE SEU
VÍDEO
MANDE SEU VÍDEO

BLITZ
VERÃO
HOME
GALERIA
MANDE SEU
VÍDEO
VEJA OS VÍDEOS

BLITZ
VERÃO
HOME
AGENDA
GALERIA
BLITZ
JOGOS
VÍDEOS
MANDE UM VÍDEO MOSTRANDO
QUE A LÍNGUA JAMAIS SE ENGANA
ASSISTA AO COMERCIAL
DA CAMPANHA
CLIQUE AQUI
MANDE SEU
VÍDEO
MANDE SEU VÍDEO
Coca-Cola
zero

# CONCEPT 10

UK

www.concept10.co.uk

2007

Concept

Online clothing store and lifestyle magazine. Guest artists contribute video animations that introduce the site. /// Online-Modegeschäft und Lifestyle-Magazin. Gastkünstler stellen die Site über Videoanimationen vor. /// Boutique de vêtements et magazine d'art de vivre. L'introduction du site est composée d'animations vidéo réalisées par des artistes invités.

Info

**Design:** Onscreen Creative <www.onscreencreative.com>: Tim Dillon; Gavin Renz (Frizbee). /// **Programming:** Rob Thomson, Marotori. /// **Video:** Tim Dillon (Animation). /// **Client:** Concept 10. /// **Tools:** After Effects, Flash, HTML, Photoshop, Illustrator. /// **Cost:** 8 weeks.

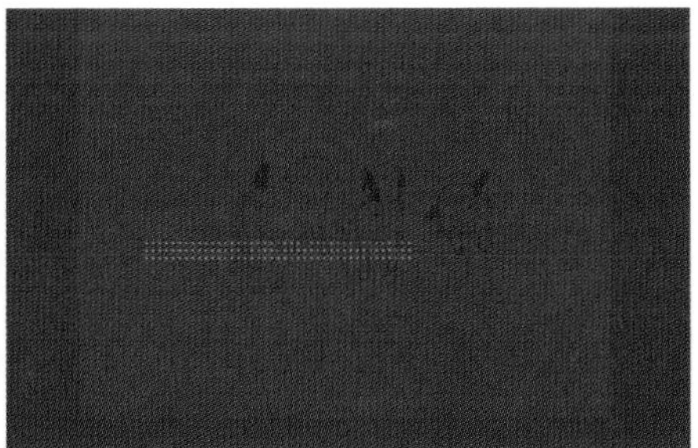

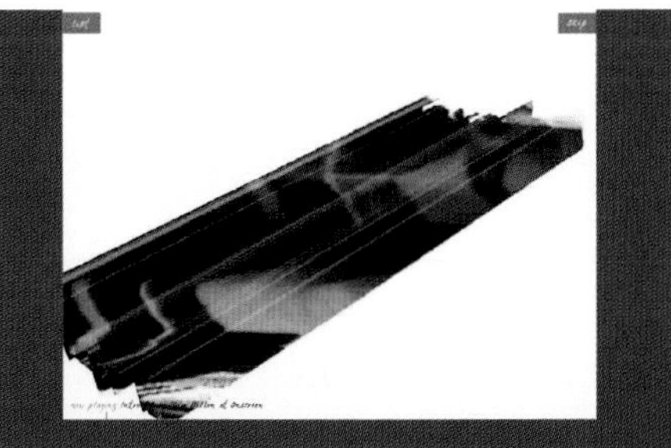
list
skip

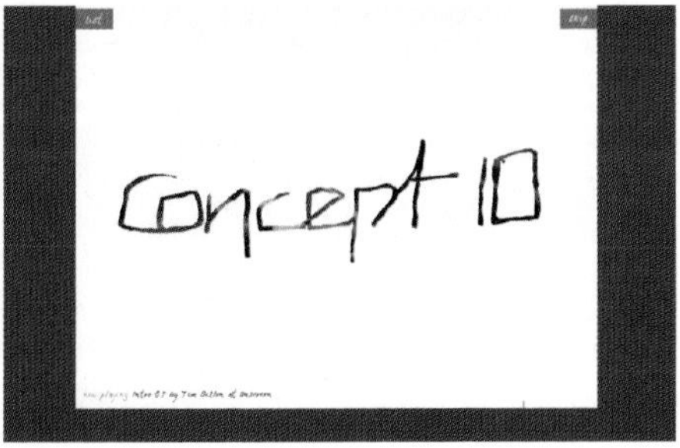

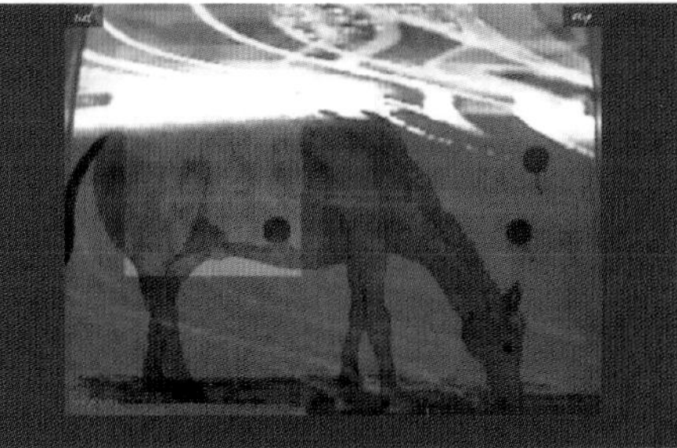
list
skip

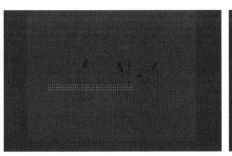

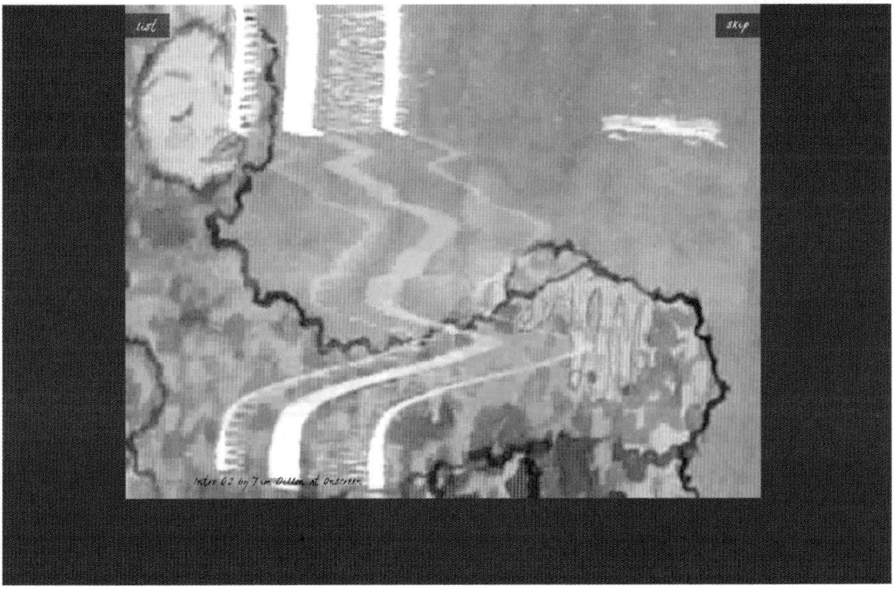

# CUENTA SUELDO BCP

PERU

www.viacompras.com/cuentasueldo/juegos/bailedeldiadepago/index.asp

2008

Concept

**A viral marketing campaign inviting people to celebrate their pay day interactively, with a lot of dancing (three types of music: disco, mambo and reggae). The campaign got more than 10,000 people dancing on the site.** /// Eine virale Marketing-Kampagne, bei der die Besucher eingeladen werden, mit viel Tanz den eigenen Zahltag interaktiv zu feiern (es gibt die Musikarten Disco, Mambo und Reggae). Bei dieser Kampagne tanzten mehr als 10.000 Menschen auf dieser Site. /// **Une campagne de marketing viral invite les gens à fêter leur jour de paie interactivement, par le biais de la danse (trois types de musique : disco, mambo et reggae). La campagne a réussi à rassembler plus de 10 000 personnes dansant simultanément sur le site.**

Info

**DESIGN:** Asix S.A. <www.asixonline.com>. Carlos Vidal. /// **PROGRAMMING:** Martin Bailetti. /// **VIDEO:** Quien Producciones. /// **OTHERS:** Leo Burnett (TV, Radio, BTL Advertising campaign). /// **CLIENT:** Banco de Credito del Peru. /// **TOOLS:** Photoshop, Final Cut Pro, Flash. /// **COST:** 1600 hours.

Cuenta Sueldo BCP
BCP
preguntas frecuentes
Cuenta sueldo BCP
Compras en línea
Juegos y videos
Contáctanos

Viernes
30
El baile del día de pago
3 Recorta tu cara
Tamaño
Rotación
Regresar
Continuar

Cuenta Sueldo BCP
BCP
preguntas frecuentes
Cuenta sueldo BCP
Compras en línea
Juegos y videos
Contáctanos

Viernes
30
El baile del día de pago
Bailar otra vez
Enviar a un amigo
Crear Nuevo Baile

# CUERVO SEASON

USA

http://cuervoseason.domanidev.com:8080/index5_1.html

2008

Concept

"Cuervo Season" is celebrated in this mock news site featuring commentators who coach users through the site. In addition Domani Studios created "The Shot Poured Around the World", which strung together uploaded video footage of people taking Cuervo shots. /// Diese Pseudo-Newssite feiert „Cuervo Season", und Kommentatoren leiten die User durch die Site. Dazu schufen Domani Studios „The Shot Poured Around The World": Man konnte dort Video-Clips hochladen, in denen Leute Cuervo trinken. /// « Cuervo Season » se fête sur ce faux site d'information où des commentateurs guident les visiteurs. Domani Studios a en outre créé « The Shot Poured Around the World », qui met bout à bout des clips vidéo de gens buvant des shots de Cuervo.

Info

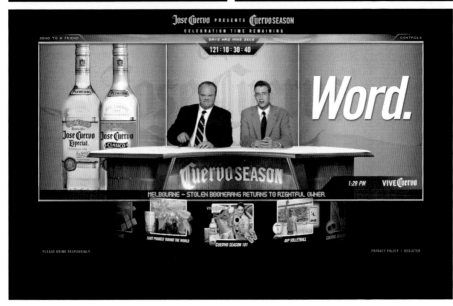

**Design:** Domani Studios <http://domanistudios.com>; Tribal DDB. /// **Programming:** Domani Studios. /// **Video:** Domani Studios. /// **Client:** Tribal DDB; Jose Cuervo. /// **Tools:** Flash, HTML, ASP.net, FCP.

Jose Cuervo PRESENTS Cuervo SEASON
CELEBRATION TIME REMAINING
SEND TO A FRIEND
DAYS HRS MINS SECS
CONTROLS
121 : 10 : 28 : 56
IN STUDIO
TODAY
92º
BACK TO STUDIO
87º
90º
90º
90º
92º
CUERVO SEASON 5-DAY FORECAST / HEIDI
1:30 PM
VIVE Cuervo
AVP VOLLEYBALL
CUERVO SEASON 5-DAY FORECAST (WITH HEIDI)
CUERVONATION
CUERVO.COM
PLEASE DRINK RESPONSIBLY
PRIVACY POLICY | REGISTER

121 : 10 : 29 : 02
IN STUDIO
TODAY
92º

121 : 10 : 23 : 40

121 : 10 : 28 : 50

IN STUDIO
TODAY
90º
121 : 10 : 27 : 55

# CURRENT TV - AWAITING INPUT USA

www.evergrowing.net/archives/awaiting_input 2006

Concept

Awaiting Input's campaign website for Current TV. The site features a series of web-episodes created and directed by Mekanism. /// Die Website von Awaiting Input für die Kampagne von Current TV. Diese Site stellt verschiedene, von Mekanism entworfene und produzierte Webepisoden vor. /// Le site web de la campagne d'Awaiting Input pour Current TV. Il présente une série d'épisodes web créés et réalisés par Mekanism.

Info

**Design:** Ever Growing Studio <www.evergrowing.net>: Arron Bleasdale. /// **Programming:** Arron Bleasdale. /// **Video:** Tommy Means, Ian Kovalik (Mekanism). /// **Others:** Arron Bleasdale (Photo). /// **Client:** Current TV. /// **Tools:** PhotoShop, Illustrator, Flash, Final Cut Pro, After Effects, JavaScript, PHP, HTML ActionScript. /// **Cost:** 300 hours.

current_
EPISODES:
SAN FRANCISCO
LOS ANGELES
NEW YORK
PHILADELPHIA
CHICAGO
ATLANTA
MIAMI
DO IT YOURSELF
_awaiting input
CLOSE
STAY CURRENT
SEND TO A FRIEND
ABOUT CURRENT
MEET VIC
CONTRIBUTORS

current_
awaitinginput.com

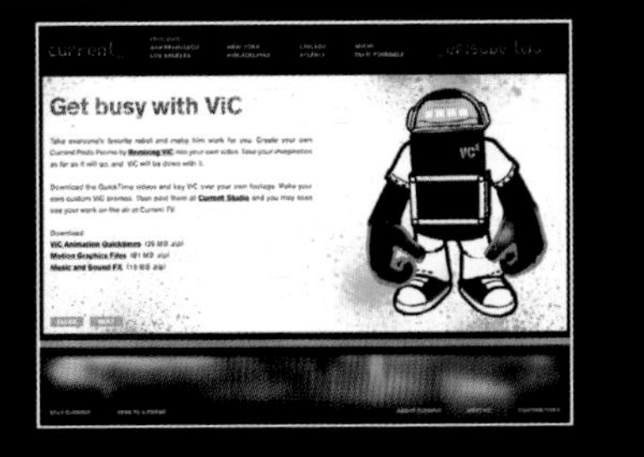
Get busy with ViC

# DIESEL STYLE LOUNGE

GERMANY

www.neue-digitale.de/projects/diesel_stylelounge

2007

Concept

**The Diesel Style Lounge offers an unusual product-presentation that also serves as an emotional introduction to the online shop. The user is sent on a journey through a surreal 3-D underwater world into the current Diesel collection.** /// Die ungewöhnliche Produktpräsentation der Diesel Style Lounge ermöglicht eine gefühlsbetonte Vorstellung des Online-Shops. Der User wird in einer surrealen 3-D-Unterwassserwelt auf die Reise zur aktuellen Diesel-Kollektion geschickt. /// **Le Diesel Style Lounge propose une présentation de produits inhabituelle qui fait également office d'introduction pleine d'émotion pour la boutique en ligne. Le visiteur est catapulté dans un monde sous-marin et surréel en 3D qui le plonge dans la collection actuelle de Diesel.**

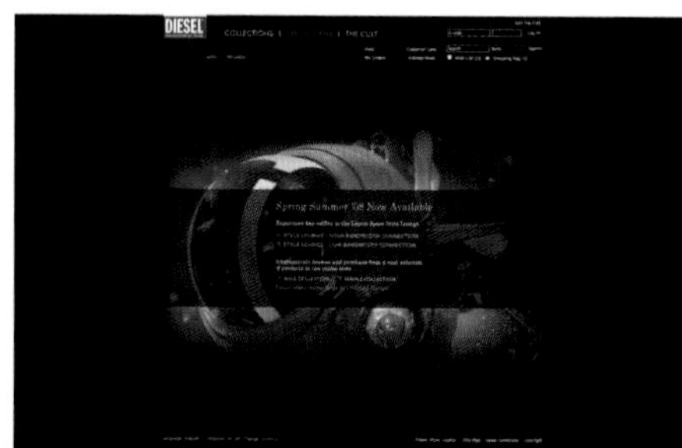

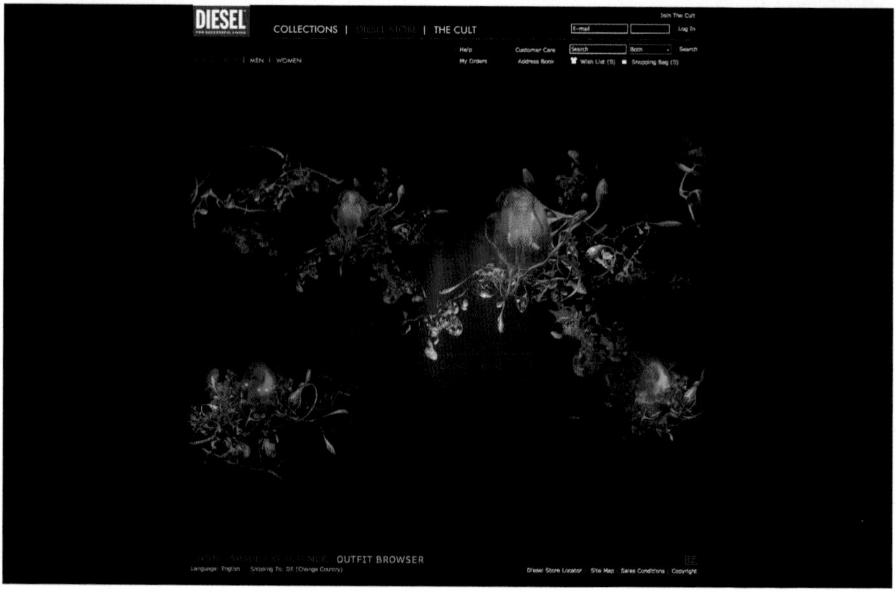

Info

**DESIGN:** Neue Digitale GmbH <www.neue-digitale.de>: Sven Küster, Stefanie Knoren, Alfredo Picardi, Oliver Hinrichs, Robert Woloschanowski. /// **PROGRAMMING:** Mathis Moder, Dorian Roy. /// **VIDEO:** Kay Kienzler (Film-styler). /// **OTHERS:** Mathias Sinn (Account Management); Jana Wardag (Project Management); Christiane Haid (Photo). /// **CLIENT:** Diesel S.p.A. /// **TOOLS:** Flash, After Effects, Photoshop. /// **AWARDS:** FWA (Site of the Day), ADC Germany (Bronze), New York Festivals (Bronze).

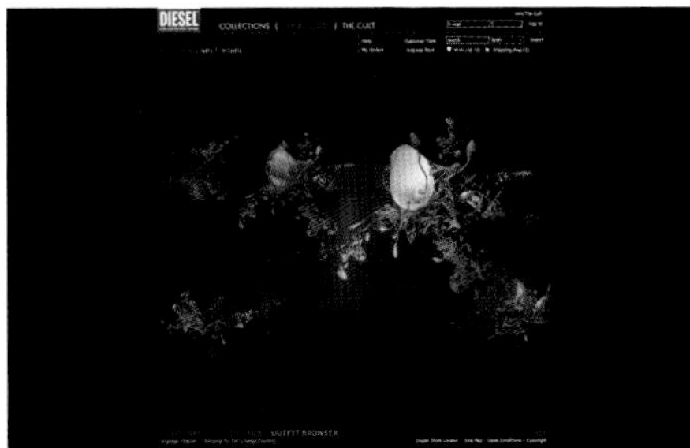

DIESEL
Join The Cult
COLLECTIONS | DIESEL STORE | THE CULT
E-mail
Log In
Help
Customer Care
My Orders
Address Book
Search
Both
Search
Wish List (0)
Shopping Bag (0)
MEN | WOMEN
01/12
BACK
OUTFIT BROWSER
Language: English Shipping To: DE (Change Country)
Diesel Store Locator | Site Map | Sales Conditions | Copyright


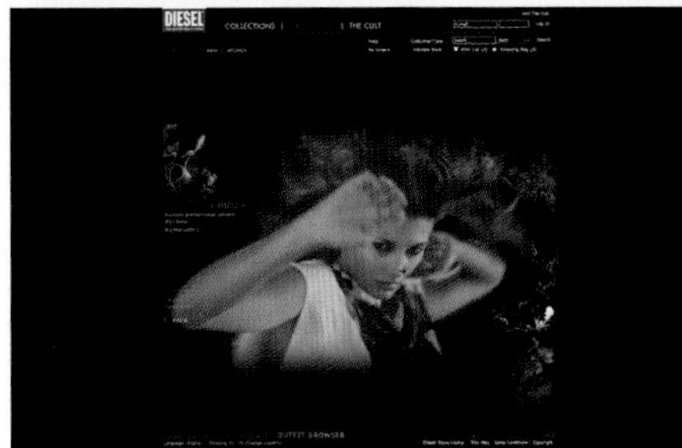

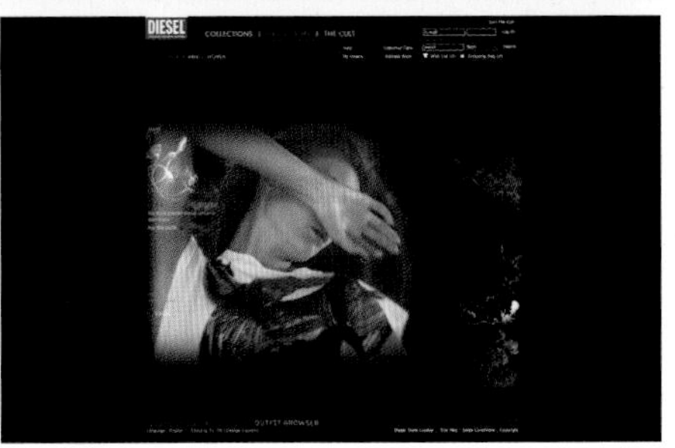

# DIPNA HORRA

CANADA

www.dipnahorra.com

2006

Concept

Dipna Horra's practice is based in both mixed-media and interdisciplinary explorations. The video segments cycle through on the screen and are layered with handwritten content created by the artist. /// Dipna Horras Arbeit basiert auf Mixed Media und interdisziplinären Erforschungen. Die Videosegmente kreisen auf dem Bildschirm und werden von handgeschriebenen Inhalten der Künstlerin überlagert. /// Le travail de Dipna Horra se base sur le mélange des supports et sur les explorations interdisciplinaires. Des fragments de vidéo sont diffusés en séquence à l'écran et servent de toile de fond aux contenus écrits à la main par l'artiste.

Info

**Design:** Analogue <www.analogue.ca>: Jory Kruspe, Craig Hooper. /// **Programming:** Jory Kruspe, Craig Hooper. /// **Video:** Dipna Horra. /// **Client:** Dipna Horra. /// **Tools:** Flash, Photoshop, Dreamweaver, Quicktime, HTML. /// **Awards:** FWA (Site of the Day). /// **Cost:** 2 months.

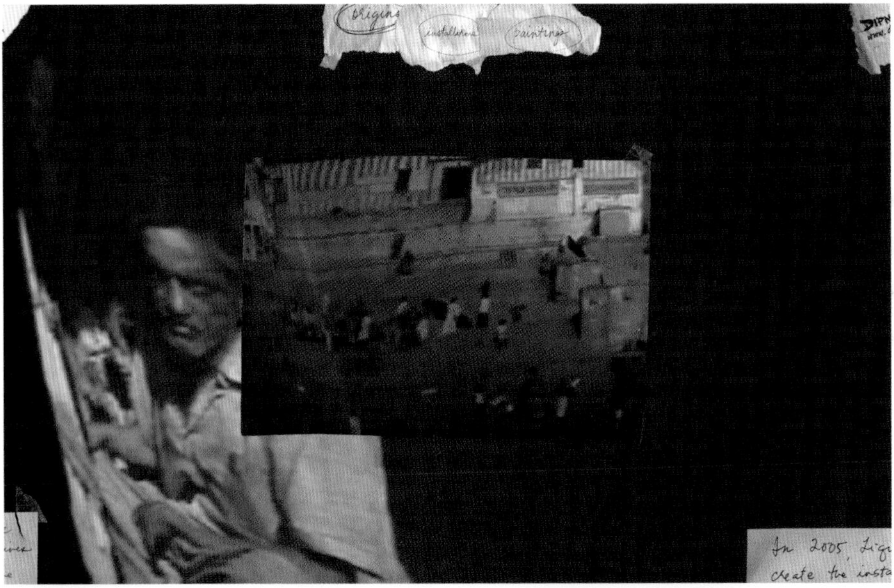
origins
installations
paintings

origins
installations
paintings
Dreaming
36" X 84"
91 cm X 213 cm
2000
BROOKLYN
70" X 54"

# DISCOVER SATURN AURA

CANADA

http://gm.ca/ss/gm/feature.do?param=aura&lang=en_CA&brand=saturn

2007

Concept

This video-driven interactive site and brand development includes a red glow, or aura, around the car. Using the Northern Lights as a style cue, Velocity developed a fluid, organic glow that follows the silhouette of the vehicle. /// Zu dieser videogesteuerten interaktiven Site für die Entwicklung der Marke gehört eine Art rotes Glühen oder Aura um den Wagen. Velocity hat als Style-Motto das Polarlicht genommen und ein flüssiges, organisches Leuchten entwickelt, das der Silhouette des Fahrzeugs folgt. /// Sur ce site vidéo interactif de développement de marque, la voiture est entourée d'une lueur rouge, comme une sorte d'aura. Velocity s'est inspiré des aurores boréales pour créer une lueur fluide et organique qui épouse la silhouette du véhicule.

Info

**Design:** Velocity Studio & Associates <www.velocitystudios.com>: Marco Di Carlo, Shane Stuart. /// **Programming:** Jonathan Coe. /// **Video:** Marco Di Carlo. /// **Client:** Cossette Communications. /// **Tools:** Flash, After Effects.

GM Canada | Vehicles | Finance | Parts & Services | About Us | Dealers/Retailers | My GM Canada | Help

Rethink. SATURN | SHOWROOM | THE SATURN DIFFERENCE | SATURN SERVICE | NEWS & EVENTS |

menu

AURA new york launch video | color selector | 360 | press room mute audio

Home > Saturn > Saturn Offers

Privacy Policy | Legal | Français

Search Enter Keyword(s) GO

gm.ca Saturn

Dealers/Retailers | Contact Us | Site Map | Help

# ELAN NEW RACE

SLOVENIA

www.newrace.elanskis.com

2008

Concept

**Meet the idea! Meet the spirit! Elan presents New Race. The idea was to incorporate the branding of the company in a video-driven website.** /// Meet the idea! Meet the spirit! Elan präsentiert New Race. Das Branding des Unternehmens wird in einer von Videos dominierten Website eingebunden. /// **Rencontrez l'idée ! Rencontrez l'esprit ! Elan présente New Race. L'idée était d'intégrer la stratégie de marque de l'entreprise à un site vidéo.**

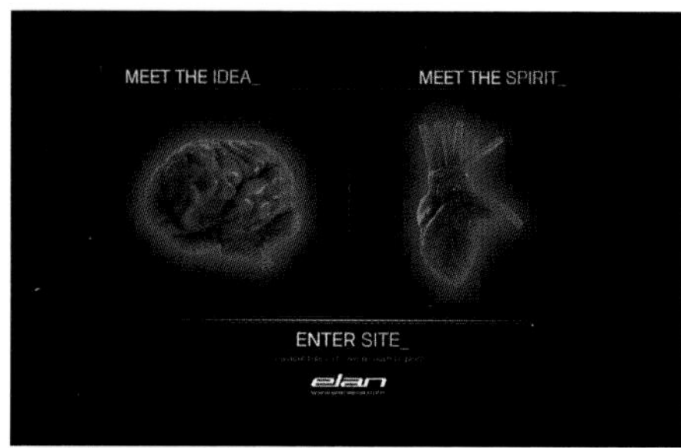

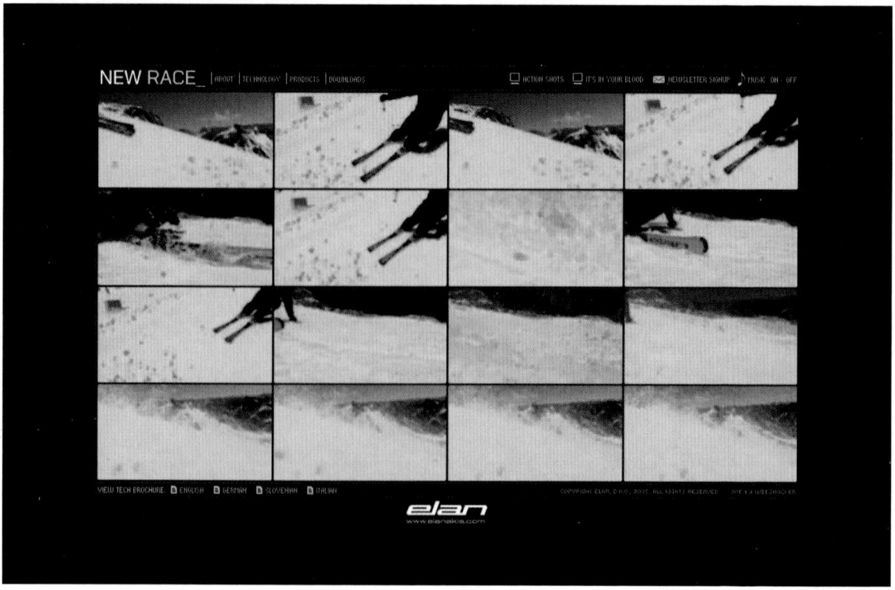

Info

**DESIGN:** Webshocker <www.webshocker.net>: Matjaz Valentar. /// **PROGRAMMING:** Matjaz Valentar, Grega Carni. /// **VIDEO:** Elan Skis, Webshocker. /// **CLIENT:** Elan Skis. /// **TOOLS:** Flash, ASP. /// **AWARDS:** DOPE, Creative Website Awards. /// **COST:** 180 hours.

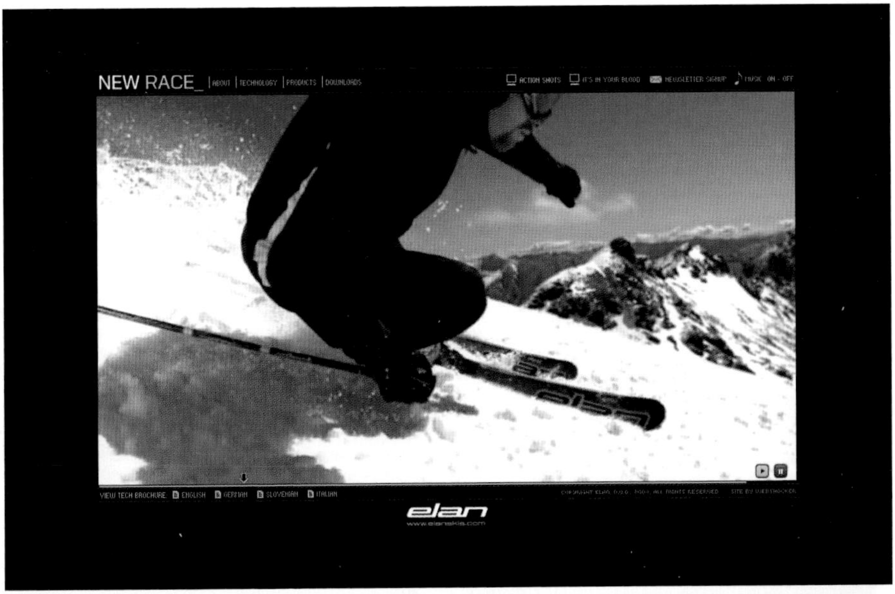

NEW RACE_
ABOUT
TECHNOLOGY
PRODUCTS
DOWNLOADS
ACTION SHOTS
IT'S IN YOUR BLOOD
NEWSLETTER SIGNUP
MUSIC ON - OFF
VIEW TECH BROCHURE
ENGLISH
GERMAN
SLOVENIAN
ITALIAN
elan
www.elanskis.com

NEW RACE_
elan

NEW RACE_
elan

NEW RACE_
elan

NEW RACE_
elan

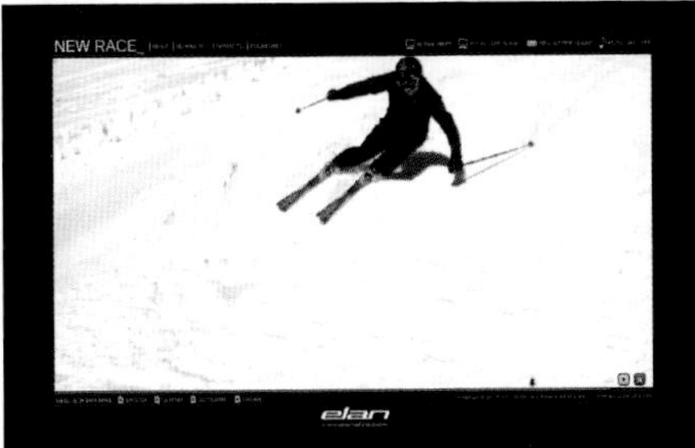

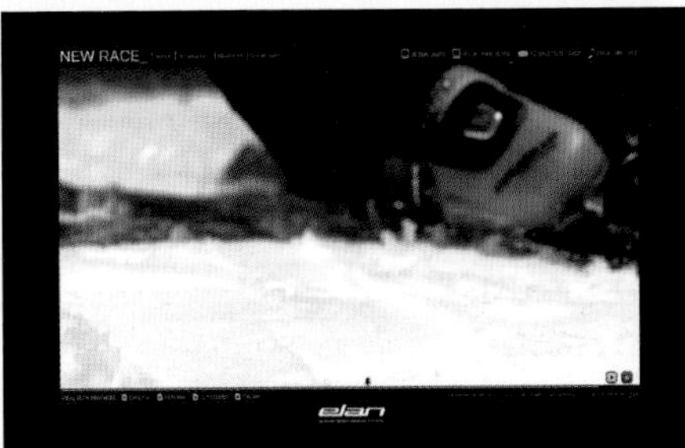

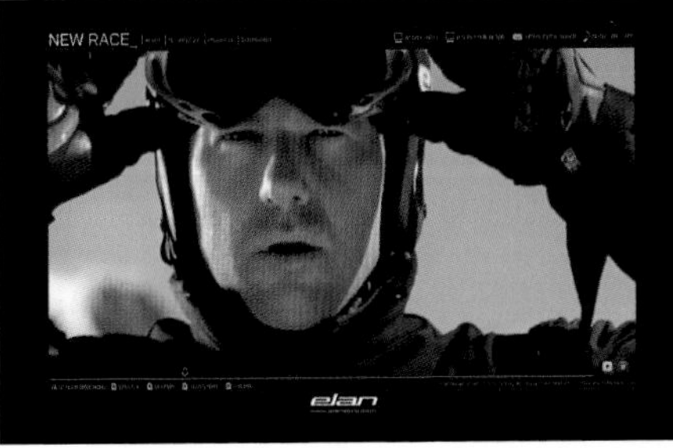

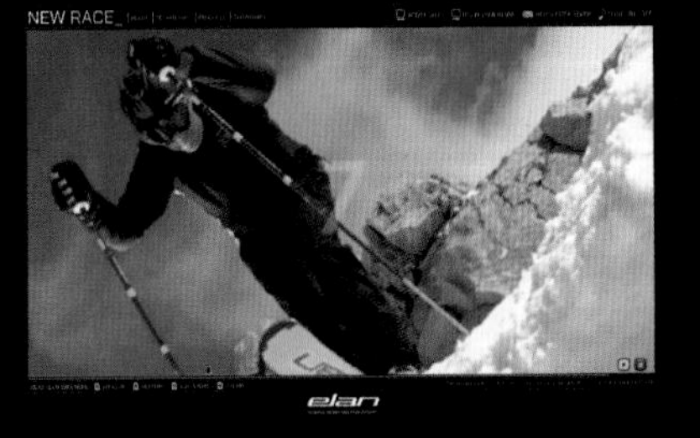

# ELAN SKI SELECTOR

SLOVENIA

http://skiselector.elanskis.com

2006

Concept

In this project the user can choose their perfect Elan skis through an interactive ski selector. /// In diesem Projekt wählt der User anhand eines interaktiven Ski-Selectors die perfekten Elan-Skier aus. /// Avec ce projet, le visiteur peut choisir les skis Elan qui lui conviennent le mieux grâce à un sélecteur interactif.

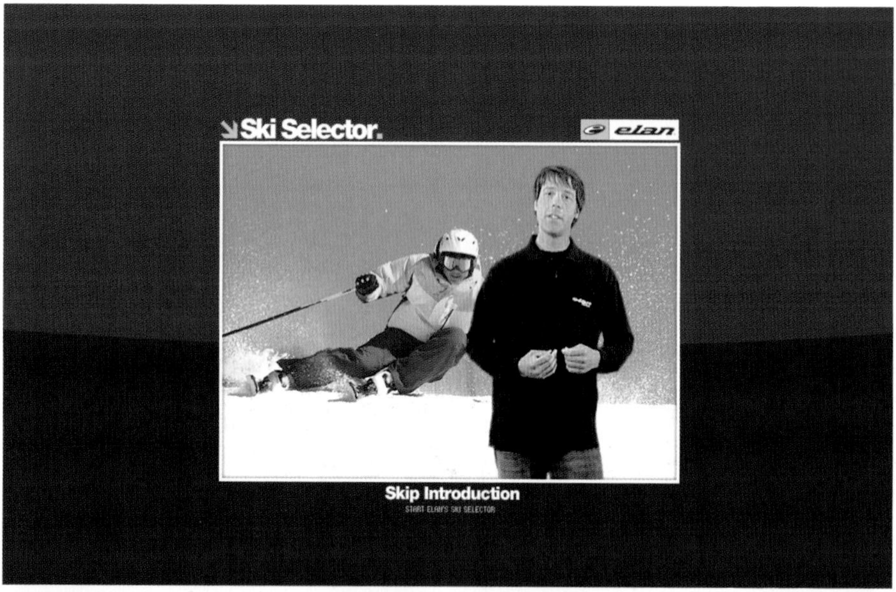

Info

**Design:** Webshocker <www.webshocker.net>: Matjaz Valentar. /// **Programming:** Matjaz Valentar, Grega Carni. /// **Video:** Elan Skis, Webshocker. /// **Client:** Elan Skis. /// **Tools:** Flash, ASP, Webshocker Flash CMS. /// **Awards:** FWA, DOPE, Creative Website Awards, WDA, Fcukstar. /// **Cost:** 220 hours.

Ski Selector.

Ski Selector.

Ski Selector.

Ski Selector.

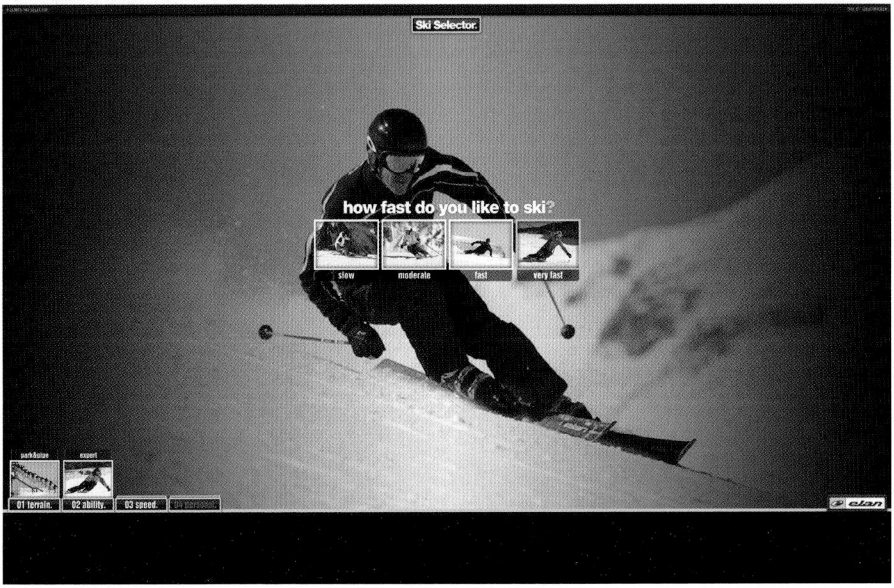

Ski Selector.
how fast do you like to ski?
slow
moderate
fast
very fast
park&pipe
expert
01 terrain.
02 ability.
03 speed.
04 personal.
elan

# ELAN TEAM GREEN

SLOVENIA

www.teamgreen.elanskis.com

2006

Concept

This website presents Elan's international freeride and freestyle riders, the Team Green, and the newest Elan freeride and freestyle skis. /// Diese Website präsentiert die internationalen Freeride und Freestyle Rider von Elan, das Team Green und die neuesten Freeride- und Freestyle-Skier von Elan. /// Ce site web présente les skieurs freeride et freestyle d'Elan, la Team Green, et les derniers skis freeride et freestyle de la marque.

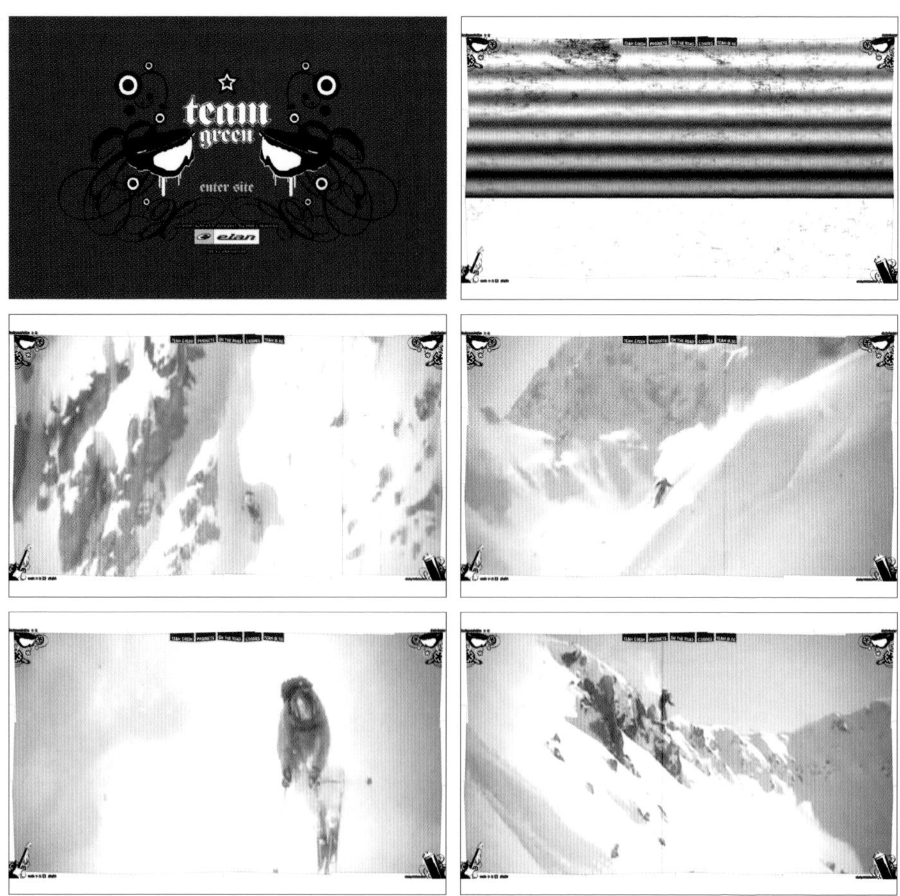


Info

**DESIGN:** Webshocker <www.webshocker.net>: Matjaz Valentar. /// **PROGRAMMING:** Matjaz Valentar, Grega Carni. /// **VIDEO:** Elan Skis, Webshocker. /// **CLIENT:** Elan Skis. /// **TOOLS:** Flash, ASP, Webshocker Flash CMS. /// **AWARDS:** DOPE, ITA, Creative website awards, Coolwebsites.dk. /// **COST:** 280 hours.

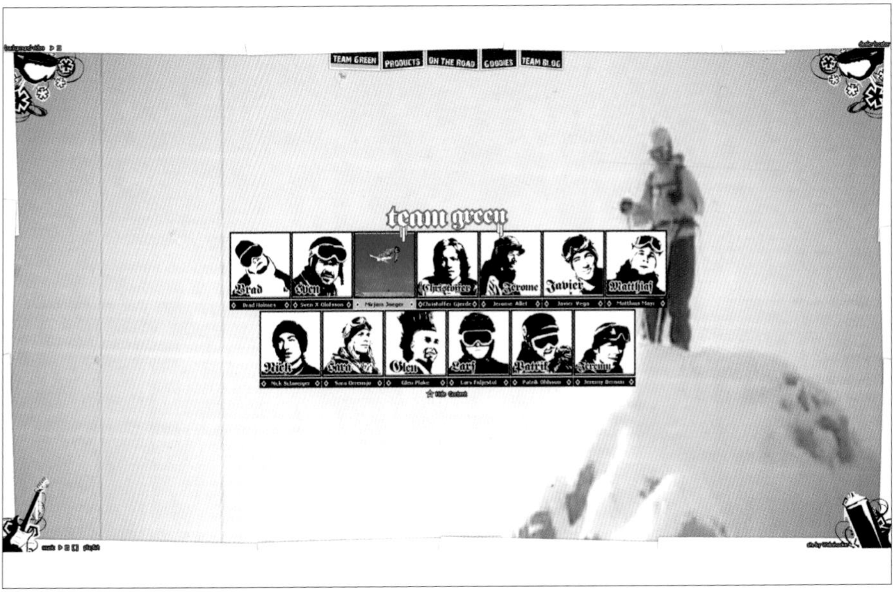
TEAM GREEN
PRODUCTS
ON THE ROAD
GOODIES
TEAM BLOG
team green

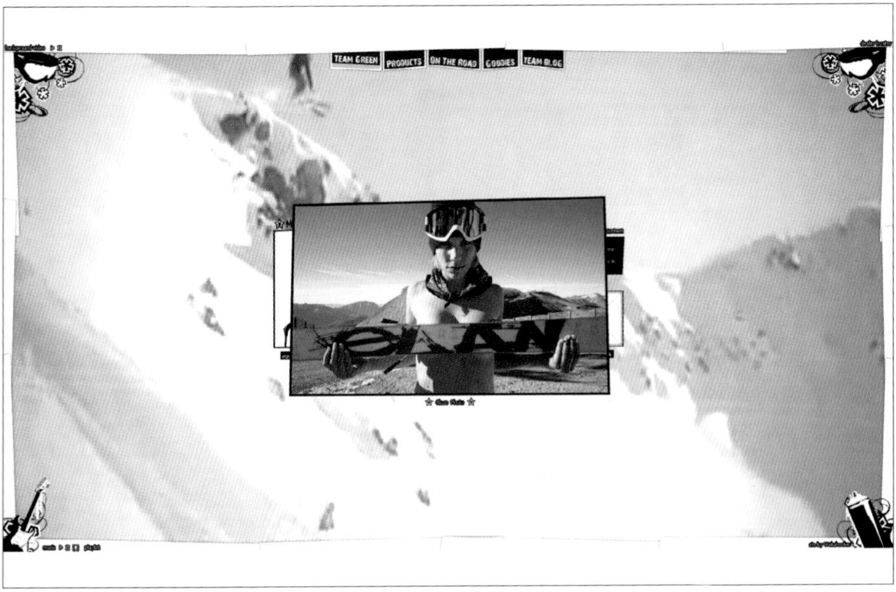
TEAM GREEN
PRODUCTS
ON THE ROAD
GOODIES
TEAM BLOG

# ENTERTAINMENT AFRICA

SOUTH AFRICA

www.sterkinekor.com/video_demo.html

2008

Concept

This banner showcases how EntertainmentAfrica.com has the latest music videos and enables users to watch snippets of them in the banner itself. /// Dieses Banner präsentiert die neuesten Musikvideos von EntertainmentAfrica.com. Die User können im Banner Ausschnitte daraus betrachten. /// Ce bandeau montre qu'EntertainmentAfrica.com a les toutes dernières vidéos musicales, et permet aux visiteurs d'en voir des extraits directement dans le bandeau.

Info

**DESIGN:** Prezence <www.prezence.co.za>: Jonathan Beech, Wesley Reyneke. /// **PROGRAMMING:** Jonathan Beech, Neil Aves. /// **CLIENT:** EntertainmentAfrica.com. /// **TOOLS:** Flash. /// **COST:** 5 hours.

click the artists below to watch right now!
30 SECONDS TO MARS
HARRIS TWEED
JACK JOHNSON
MUSE
PANIC AT THE DISCO
HI
MED
LO
TICKETLINE
082 16789
vas rates apply
HOME
MOVIEMAIL
CINEMA NOUVEAU
SCREENED BY JAMESON
I'M IN THE MOOD FOR
MOVIES SHOWING
SELECT A DAY

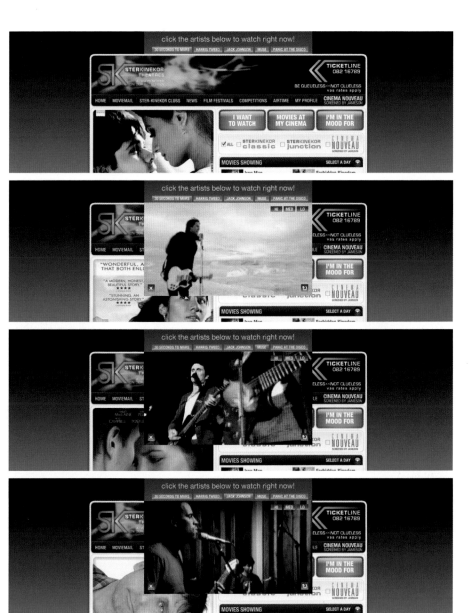

# FANSHAWE COLLEGE

CANADA

http://www.fanshawec.ca

2008

Concept

Complete redesign of existing website that includes Adobe Flash and TV Spot. The home page features a custom fluid and dynamic Flash Dynamic transition, driving users to view the 30-second "We Do That!" TV Commercial and various other elements. /// Das vollständige Redesign einer vorhandenen Website mit Adobe Flash und TV Spot. Auf der Homepage wird eine eigene flüssige und dynamische Dynamic Transition in Flash gezeigt, die den Besucher zum Betrachten des 30 Sekunden langen Fernsehspots „We do that!" und verschiedenen anderen Elementen animieren soll. /// Remodelage complet du site web existant, avec Adobe Flash et TV Spot. Sur la page d'accueil, une transition fluide et dynamique en Flash Dynamic conduit les visiteurs au spot télévisé « We Do That! » et à plusieurs autres éléments.

Info

**Design:** Velocity Studio & Associates <www.velocitystudios.com>: Marco Di Carlo, Shane Stuart. /// **Programming:** Jonathan Coe. /// **Video:** Marco Di Carlo. /// **Client:** Fanshawe College. /// **Tools:** Flash, After Effects.

ACCESS FANSHAWE ONLINE
Search Our Website
Fanshawe College
Visit • Contact • Newsroom • Jobs • Employers • Alumni • Research
Community Driven
Student Focused
Notices
Admissions
Event - Girls Rock I.T.
Registration Conditions
Summer Term Start-Up
Quick Links
About Fanshawe
Accessibility
AskFanshawe
Athletics
Donate Now!
Campus Locations
Fanshawe Facts
Financial Aid (OSAP)
Graduation
Photo Gallery
President's Blog
Programs
T2202A Tax Forms
Video Gallery
Virtual Library
WebAdvisor Services
Full Time Programs...
Over 100 programs leading to certificates, diplomas and degrees. The choice is yours.
Get A Head Start and Apply Now...
Build your future today, at one of Ontario's best post-secondary institutions.
Graduate Studies
Graduate to a job with programs in Business & Management, Health & Human Services, Art & Design or Media & Communication Arts!
Book Your Tour Today!
See for yourself. Ontario's best College experience.
Student Success
We're all about student success. Check out services we offer to help you succeed.
Let us kick start YOUR FUTURE.
What's On Your Mind?
Want to help improve our new site?
CLICK HERE - WE'RE LISTENING!

ACCESS FANSHAWE ONLINE
Search Our Website
Fanshawe College
Visit • Contact • Newsroom • Jobs • Employers • Alumni • Research
Notices
Admissions
Event - Girls Rock I.T.
Registration Conditions
Summer Term Start-Up
Quick Links
About Fanshawe
Accessibility
AskFanshawe
Athletics
Donate Now!
Campus Locations
Fanshawe Facts
Financial Aid (OSAP)
Graduation
Photo Gallery
President's Blog
Programs
T2202A Tax Forms
Video Gallery
Virtual Library
WebAdvisor Services
Full Time Programs...
Over 100 programs leading to certificates, diplomas and degrees. The choice is yours.
Get A Head Start and Apply Now...
Build your future today, at one of Ontario's best post-secondary institutions.
Graduate Studies
Graduate to a job with programs in Business & Management, Health & Human Services, Art & Design or Media & Communication Arts!
Book Your Tour Today!
See for yourself. Ontario's best College experience.
Student Success
We're all about student success. Check out services we offer to help you succeed.
Let us kick start YOUR FUTURE.
What's On Your Mind?
Want to help improve our new site?
CLICK HERE - WE'RE LISTENING!

ACCESS FANSHAWE ONLINE
Search Our Website
Fanshawe College
Visit • Contact • Newsroom • Jobs • Employers • Alumni • Research
Play Video
Featured News...
Small Business Challenge
TD Canada Trust presents Small Business Challenge to Fanshawe students
View Next »
Notices
Admissions
Event - Girls Rock I.T.
Registration Conditions
Summer Term Start-Up
Quick Links
About Fanshawe
Accessibility
AskFanshawe
Athletics
Donate Now!
Campus Locations
Fanshawe Facts
Financial Aid (OSAP)
Graduation
Photo Gallery
President's Blog
Programs
T2202A Tax Forms
Video Gallery
Virtual Library
WebAdvisor Services
Full Time Programs...
Over 100 programs leading to certificates, diplomas and degrees. The choice is yours.
Get A Head Start and Apply Now...
Build your future today, at one of Ontario's best post-secondary institutions.
Graduate Studies
Graduate to a job with programs in Business & Management, Health & Human Services, Art & Design or Media & Communication Arts!
Book Your Tour Today!
See for yourself. Ontario's best College experience.
Student Success
We're all about student success. Check out services we offer to help you succeed.
Let us kick start YOUR FUTURE.
What's On Your Mind?
Want to help improve our new site?
CLICK HERE - WE'RE LISTENING!

ACCESS FANSHAWE ONLINE
Search Our Website
Fanshawe College
Visit • Contact • Newsroom • Jobs • Employers • Alumni • Research
FANSHAWE COLLEGE
Featured News...
Small Business Challenge
TD Canada Trust presents Small Business Challenge to Fanshawe students
View Next »
Notices
Admissions
Event - Girls Rock I.T.
Registration Conditions
Summer Term Start-Up
Quick Links
About Fanshawe
Accessibility
AskFanshawe
Athletics
Donate Now!
Campus Locations
Fanshawe Facts
Financial Aid (OSAP)
Graduation
Photo Gallery
President's Blog
Programs
T2202A Tax Forms
Video Gallery
Virtual Library
WebAdvisor Services
Full Time Programs...
Over 100 programs leading to certificates, diplomas and degrees. The choice is yours.
Get A Head Start and Apply Now...
Build your future today, at one of Ontario's best post-secondary institutions.
Graduate Studies
Graduate to a job with programs in Business & Management, Health & Human Services, Art & Design or Media & Communication Arts!
Book Your Tour Today!
See for yourself. Ontario's best College experience.
Student Success
We're all about student success. Check out services we offer to help you succeed.
Let us kick start YOUR FUTURE.
What's On Your Mind?
Want to help improve our new site?
CLICK HERE - WE'RE LISTENING!

# FASSI SPORT

ITALY

www.fassisport.com

2007

Concept

**A demonstration of how a simple video can enhance the user's view of a new product.** /// Ein simples Video demonstriert, wie man die Betrachtungsweise des Kunden für ein neues Produkt erweitern kann. /// **Une démonstration de la façon dont une simple vidéo peut améliorer l'opinion que le visiteur peut avoir d'un nouveau produit.**

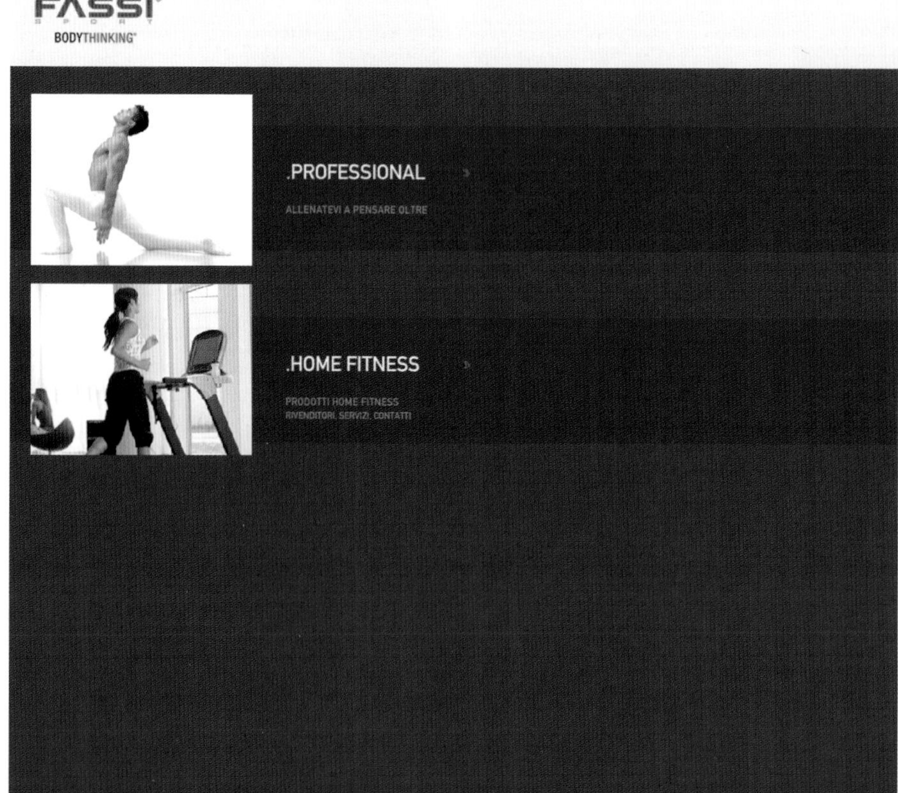


Info

**Design:** Extera <www.extera.com>. /// **Programming:** Extera. /// **Video:** Alberto del Biondi (Industria del Design) <www.albertodelbiondi.com>. /// **Client:** Fassi Sport. /// **Tools:** Flash, Javascript, ASP, CSS.

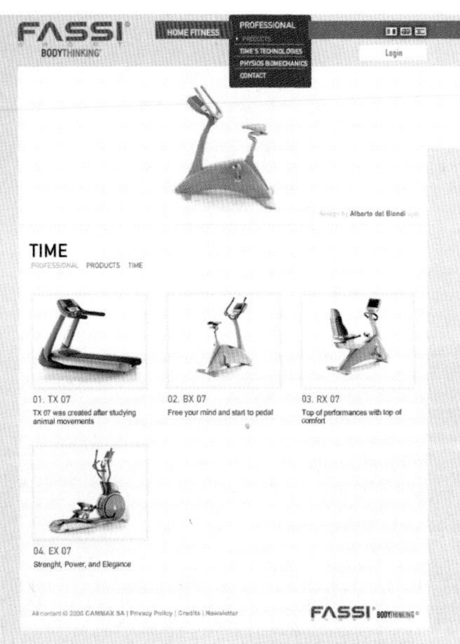
FASSI
BODYTHINKING
HOME FITNESS
PROFESSIONAL
PRODUCTS
TIME'S TECHNOLOGIES
PHYSIOS BIOMECHANICS
CONTACT
Login
Alberto del Biondi
TIME
PROFESSIONAL PRODUCTS TIME
01. TX 07
TX 07 was created after studying animal movements
02. BX 07
Free your mind and start to pedal
03. RX 07
Top of performances with top of comfort
04. EX 07
Strenght, Power, and Elegance
All content © 2006 CAMMAX SA | Privacy Policy | Credits | Newsletter
FASSI BODYTHINKING

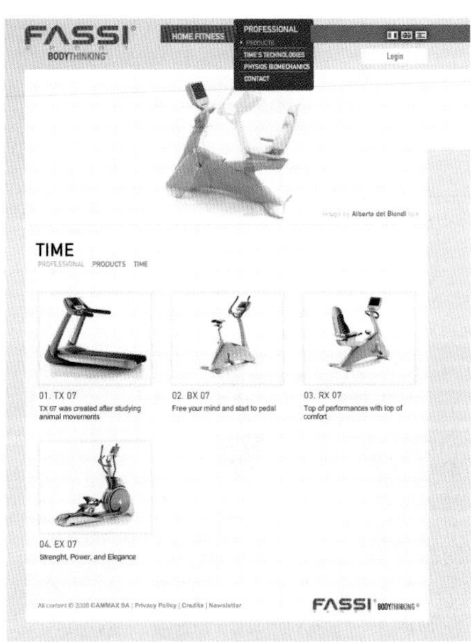
FASSI
BODYTHINKING
HOME FITNESS
PROFESSIONAL
PRODUCTS
TIME'S TECHNOLOGIES
PHYSIOS BIOMECHANICS
CONTACT
Login
Alberto del Biondi
TIME
PROFESSIONAL PRODUCTS TIME
01. TX 07
TX 07 was created after studying animal movements
02. BX 07
Free your mind and start to pedal
03. RX 07
Top of performances with top of comfort
04. EX 07
Strenght, Power, and Elegance
All content © 2006 CAMMAX SA | Privacy Policy | Credits | Newsletter
FASSI BODYTHINKING

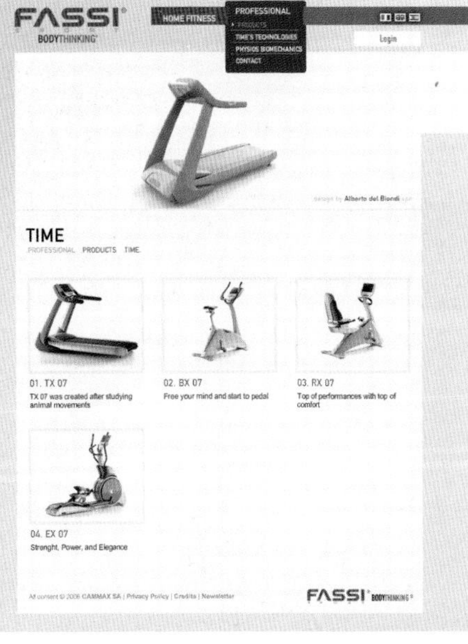
FASSI
BODYTHINKING
HOME FITNESS
PROFESSIONAL
PRODUCTS
TIME'S TECHNOLOGIES
PHYSIOS BIOMECHANICS
CONTACT
Login
Alberto del Biondi
TIME
PROFESSIONAL PRODUCTS TIME
01. TX 07
TX 07 was created after studying animal movements
02. BX 07
Free your mind and start to pedal
03. RX 07
Top of performances with top of comfort
04. EX 07
Strenght, Power, and Elegance
All content © 2006 CAMMAX SA | Privacy Policy | Credits | Newsletter
FASSI BODYTHINKING

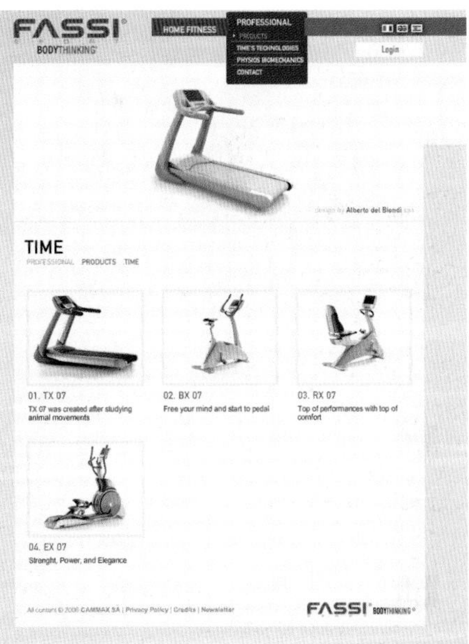
FASSI
BODYTHINKING
HOME FITNESS
PROFESSIONAL
PRODUCTS
TIME'S TECHNOLOGIES
PHYSIOS BIOMECHANICS
CONTACT
Login
Alberto del Biondi
TIME
PROFESSIONAL PRODUCTS TIME
01. TX 07
TX 07 was created after studying animal movements
02. BX 07
Free your mind and start to pedal
03. RX 07
Top of performances with top of comfort
04. EX 07
Strenght, Power, and Elegance
All content © 2006 CAMMAX SA | Privacy Policy | Credits | Newsletter
FASSI BODYTHINKING

# FEEL SOMETHING

AUSTRALIA

www.feelsomething.com.au

2007

Concept

This site was intended to sow the seeds for a fresh brand direction. The concept was to turn the point of view around 180 degrees, so instead of watching what's on FOXTEL we watch people watching FOXTEL, and see how it makes them feel. /// Auf dieser Site soll der Samen für eine neue Ausrichtung der Marke gesät werden. Das Konzept bestand darin, die Perspektive um 180 Grad zu drehen. Man soll also nicht sehen, was auf FOXTEL läuft, sondern Leute betrachten, die gerade FOXTEL schauen, und beobachten, wie sie sich dabei fühlen. /// Ce site a été créé pour donner une nouvelle direction à la marque. Le concept consistait à inverser le point de vue. Au lieu de regarder les émissions de FOXTEL, on voit des gens qui regardent FOXTEL, et ce qu'ils ressentent.

Info

**Design:** Soap Creative <www.soap.com.au>: Bradley Eldridge, Robert Dennis. /// **Programming:** Ashley Ringrose. /// **Video:** Josh Logue, Matthew Willis, Patrick Cook. /// **Others:** Oliver Mistry (Client), Ross Raeburn (Producer), Robert Moss (Music). /// **Client:** FOXTEL. /// **Tools:** Flash. /// **Cost:** 4 weeks.

ESPN
see extreme sports on ESPN

# FRONTLINESHOP TV

GERMANY

www.frontlineshop.tv

2008

Concept

A video concept that brings background information from the worlds of fashion, art and lifestyle to the young target group. The microsite enlarges the affiliated online-store and strengthens the image of the client. /// Dieses Videokonzept vermittelt der jugendlichen Zielgruppe Hintergrundinformationen aus der Welt der Mode, Kunst und Lifestyle. Die Microsite baut den dazugehörigen Online-Shop aus und stärkt das Image des Kunden. /// Un concept vidéo qui fournit des informations de fond sur les mondes de la mode, de l'art et de l'art de vivre à un public jeune. Le microsite est une annexe de la boutique en ligne et renforce l'image du client.

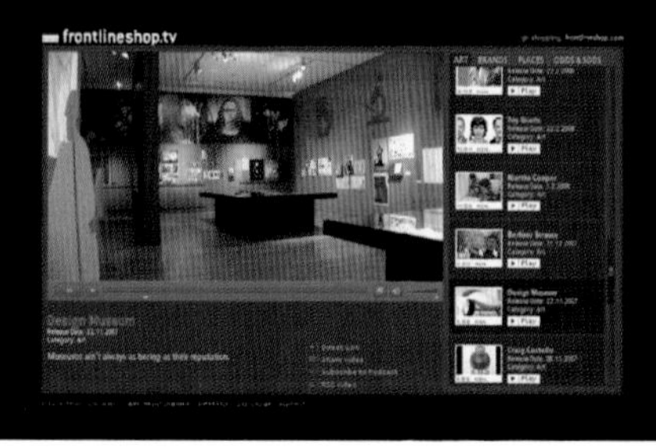


Info

**Design:** H2D2 <www.h2d2.de>: Markus Remscheid, Judith Traudes. /// **Programming:** Dominik Schäfer. /// **Video:** Orendt Studios GmbH. /// **Client:** Frontline GmbH. /// **Tools:** Flash, Photoshop, HTML. /// **Cost:** 200 hours.

frontlineshop.tv
Design Museum

frontlineshop.tv
Design Museum

frontlineshop.tv
Design Museum

frontlineshop.tv
Kidrobot

frontlineshop.tv
Kidrobot

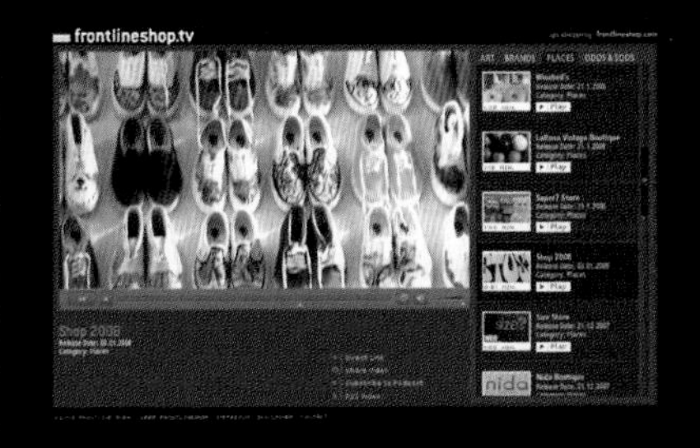
frontlineshop.tv
Shop 2008

frontlineshop.tv
Shop 2008

frontlineshop.tv
Shop 2008

Concept

**Video archive and collection from YouTube, selected by FTC, a skateboarding brand from San Fransisco.** /// Videoarchiv und -sammlung von YouTube, ausgewählt von FTC, einer Skateboard-Marke aus San Francisco. /// **Archives et collection de vidéos de YouTube, sélectionnées par FTC, une marque de skate-board de San Francisco.**

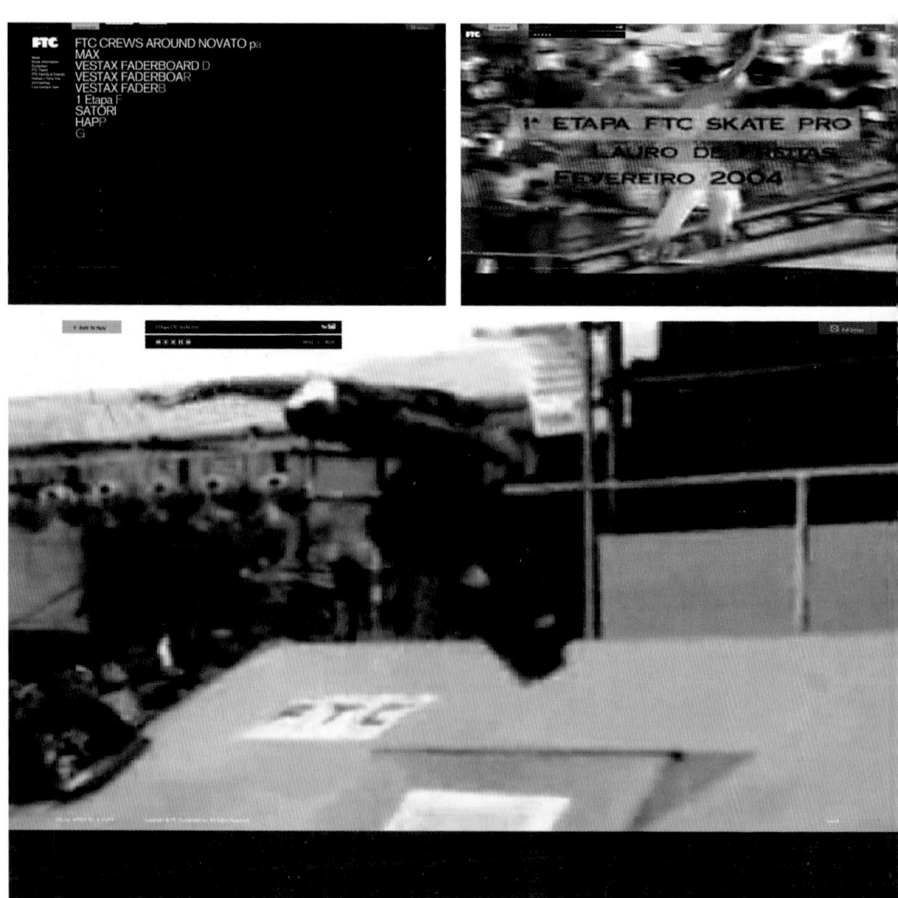


Info

**DESIGN:** artless Inc <www.artless.co.jp>. /// **PROGRAMMING:** org44.com (Flash); Grondbase Inc. /// **CLIENT:** FTC Japan. /// **TOOLS:** Flash, HTML. /// **COST:** 90 days.

FTC

FTC

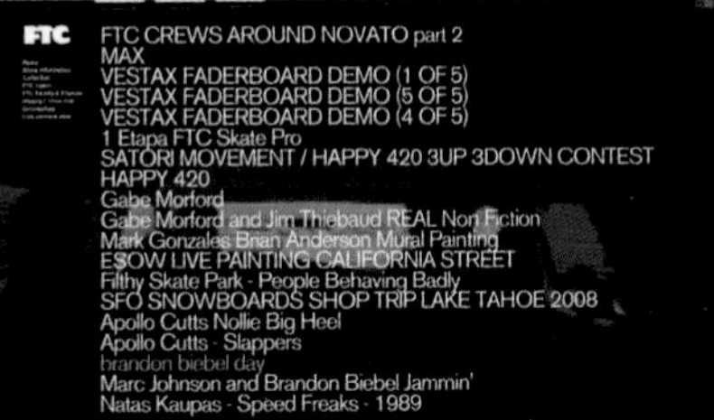
FTC
FTC CREWS AROUND NOVATO part 2
MAX
VESTAX FADERBOARD DEMO (1 OF 5)
VESTAX FADERBOARD DEMO (5 OF 5)
VESTAX FADERBOARD DEMO (4 OF 5)
1 Etapa FTC Skate Pro
SATORI MOVEMENT / HAPPY 420 3UP 3DOWN CONTEST
HAPPY 420
Gabe Morford
Gabe Morford and Jim Thiebaud REAL Non Fiction
Mark Gonzales Brian Anderson Mural Painting
ESOW LIVE PAINTING CALIFORNIA STREET
Filthy Skate Park - People Behaving Badly
SFO SNOWBOARDS SHOP TRIP LAKE TAHOE 2008
Apollo Cutts Nollie Big Heel
Apollo Cutts - Slappers
brandon biebel day
Marc Johnson and Brandon Biebel Jammin'
Natas Kaupas - Speed Freaks - 1989

FTC
FTC CREWS AROUND NOVATO part 2
MAX
VESTAX FADERBOARD DEMO (1 OF 5)
VESTAX FADERBOARD DEMO (5 OF 5)
VESTAX FADERBOARD DEMO (4 OF 5)
1 Etapa FTC Skate Pro
SATORI MOVEMENT / HAPPY 420
HAPPY 420
Gabe Morford
Gabe Morford and Jim
Mark Gonzales Brian
ESOW LIVE PAINTI
Filthy Skate Pa
SFO SNOWBOAR
Apollo Cutt
Apollo Cu
brandon
Marc
Nat

FTC
FTC CREWS AROUND NOVATO part 2
MAX
VESTAX FADERBOARD DEMO (1 OF 5)
VESTAX FADERBOARD DEMO (5 OF 5)
VESTAX FADERBOARD DEMO (4 OF 5)
1 Etapa FTC Skate Pro
SATORI MOVEMENT / HAPPY 420 3UP 3DOWN CONTEST
HAPPY 420
Gabe Morford
Gabe Morford and Jim Thiebaud REAL Non Fiction
Mark Gonzales Brian Anderson Mural Painting
ESOW LIVE PAINTING CALIFORNIA STREET
Filthy Skate Park - People Behaving Badly
SFO SNOWBOARDS SHOP TRIP LAKE TAHOE 2008
Apollo Cutts Nollie Big Heel
Apollo Cutts - Slappers
brandon biebel day
Marc Johnson and Brandon Biebel Jammin'
Natas Kaupas - Speed Freaks - 1989

FTC
FTC CREWS AROUND NOVATO part 2
MAX
VESTAX FADERBOARD DEMO (1 OF 5)
VESTAX FADERBOARD DEMO (5 OF 5)
VESTAX FADERBOARD DEMO (4 OF 5)
1 Etapa FTC Skate Pro
SATORI MOVEMENT / HAPPY 420 3UP 3DOWN CONTEST
HAPPY 420
Gabe Morford
Gabe Morford and Jim Thiebaud REAL Non Fiction
Mark Gonzales Brian Anderson Mural Painting
ESOW LIVE PAINTING CALIFORNIA STREET
Filthy Skate Park - People Behaving Badly
SFO SNOWBOARDS SHOP TRIP LAKE TAHOE 2008
Apollo Cutts Nollie Big Heel
Apollo Cutts - Slappers
brandon biebel day
Marc Johnson and Brandon Biebel Jammin'
Natas Kaupas - Speed Freaks - 1989

FTC
CALIFORNIA STREET
in
TOKYO, JAPAN

FTC

# FWA THEATER

WORLDWIDE

www.fwatheater.com

2008

Concept

This site enables FWA Theater to be dynamically branded and adaptable with multiple video formats, while supporting strong and captivating user interactions in an easily navigable environment. /// Durch diese Site, die mit verschiedenen Videoformaten arbeitet, präsentiert sich FWA Theater als dynamische Marke. Gleichzeitig unterstützt sie starke und fesselnde User-Interaktionen in einer leicht navigierbaren Umgebung. /// Ce site permet à FWA Theater d'avoir une stratégie de marque dynamique et flexible, grâce à plusieurs formats vidéo, tout en proposant une interactivité solide et captivante dans un environnement où la navigation est sans complication.

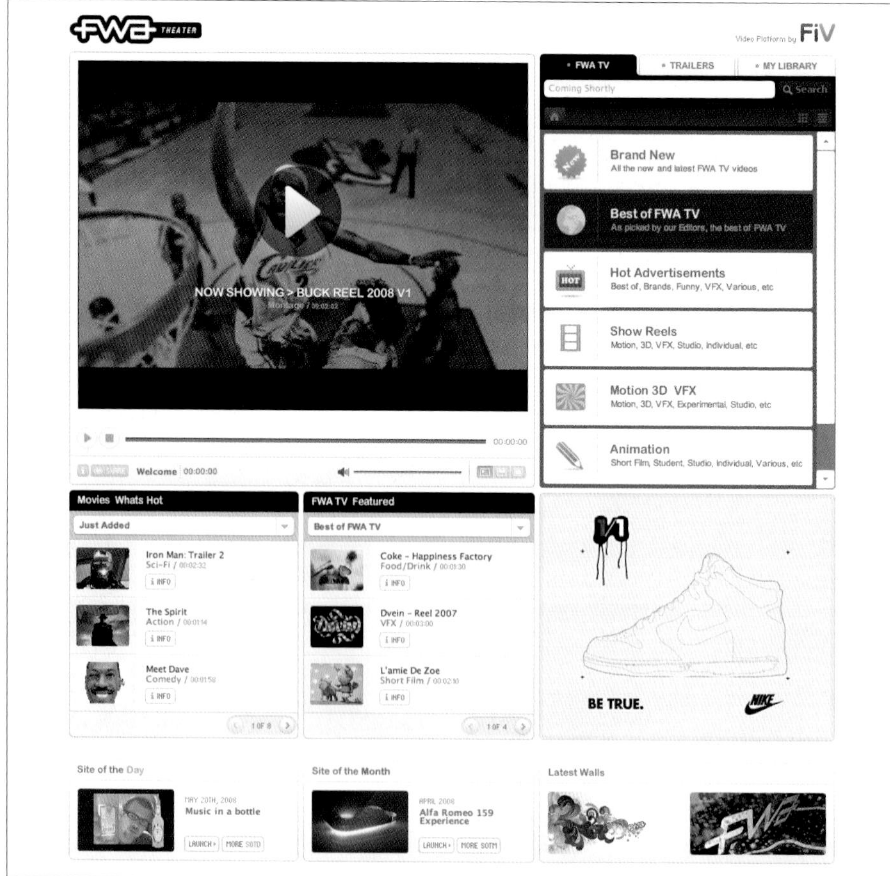


Info

**Design:** Fantasy Interactive <www.f-i.com>: David Martin (Creative Director); M. David Low (Producer); Younghee Joo (Lead Senior Designer). /// **Programming:** Firdosh Tangri (Lead Senior Application Developer); Filip Michalowski (Interactive Developer); Robert Pohl (Senior Application Developer). /// **Others:** Rob Ford (Favourite Website Awards). /// **Client:** Favourite Website Awards <www.thefwa.com>. /// **Tools:** Adobe Flex, Flash AS3, HTML, JavaScript. /// **Cost:** Work in progress.

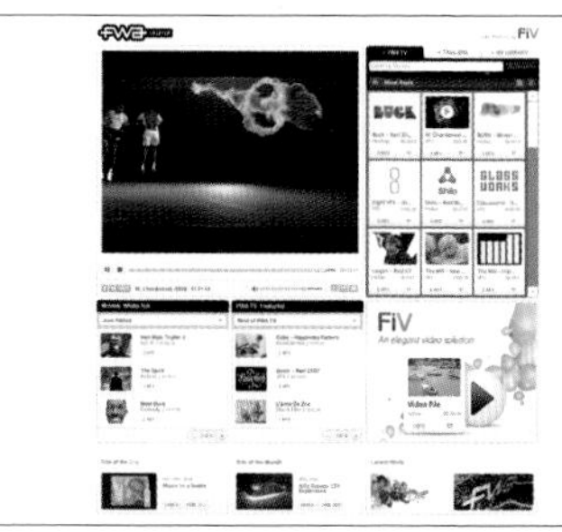

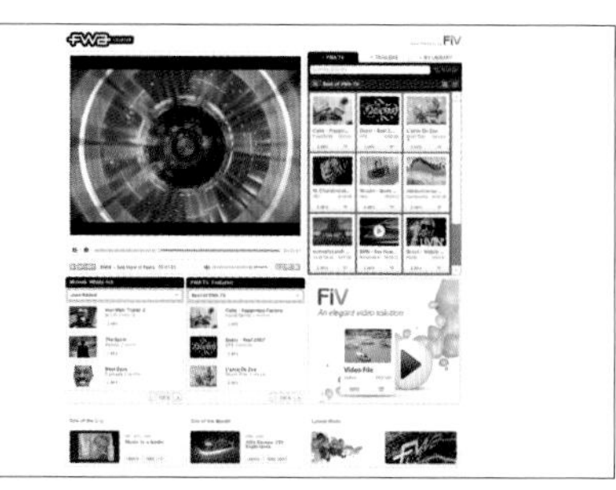

FWA THEATER

Video Platform by FiV

FWA TV · TRAILERS · MY LIBRARY

Coming Shortly · Search

Show Reels

Buck – Reel 20... Montage 00:02:02 · i INFO

M. Chardonnet... VFX 00:01:49 · i INFO

BORN – Winter ... Motion 00:01:09 · i INFO

Eight VFX – Sh... VFX 00:02:26 · i INFO

Shilo – Reel Wi... Motion 00:07:18 · i INFO

Glassworks – S... VFX 00:01:20 · i INFO

Logan – Reel 07 Motion 00:01:17 · i INFO

The Mill – New ... VFX 00:05:31 · i INFO

The Mill – Hist... VFX 00:03:11 · i INFO

00:00:19

SHARE · Glassworks – Showreel 00:01:20

Movies Whats Hot

Just Added

Iron Man: Trailer 2 Sci-Fi / 00:02:32 · i INFO

The Spirit Action / 00:01:14 · i INFO

Meet Dave Comedy / 00:01:58 · i INFO

1 OF 8

FWA TV Featured

Best of FWA TV

Coke – Happiness Factory Food/Drink / 00:01:30 · i INFO

Dvein – Reel 2007 VFX / 00:03:00 · i INFO

L'amie De Zoe Short Film / 00:02:10 · i INFO

1 OF 4

D&G DOLCE & GABBANA

Site of the Day

MAY 20TH, 2008 · Music in a bottle · LAUNCH › · MORE SOTD

Site of the Month

APRIL 2008 · Alfa Romeo 159 Experience · LAUNCH › · MORE SOTM

Latest Walls

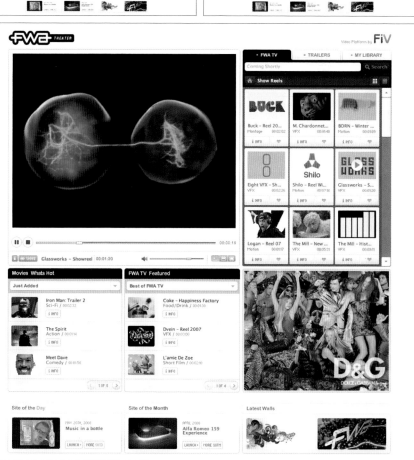

# GO FAST! SPORTS

# THE NETHERLANDS

www.gofastsports.nl

2008

Concept

Go Fast! Sports needed a new online identity to represent its forward-thinking approach. Based on the experience of the Go Fast! Energy Drink, this is a project with lots of spots for streaming video files of all the Go Fast! Sports events. /// Go Fast! Sports brauchte eine neue Online-Identität, die dessen vorausschauende Denkweise repräsentiert. Basierend auf dem Erleben des Go Fast! Energy Drinks ist es ein Projekt mit vielen Streaming Videos für alle Go Fast! Sport-Events. /// Go Fast! Sports avait besoin d'une nouvelle identité Internet pour représenter sa démarche avant-gardiste. À partir de l'expérience de la boisson énergisante Go Fast!, ce projet met en jeu une multitude de points d'accès aux fichiers vidéo de tous les événements Go Fast! Sports.

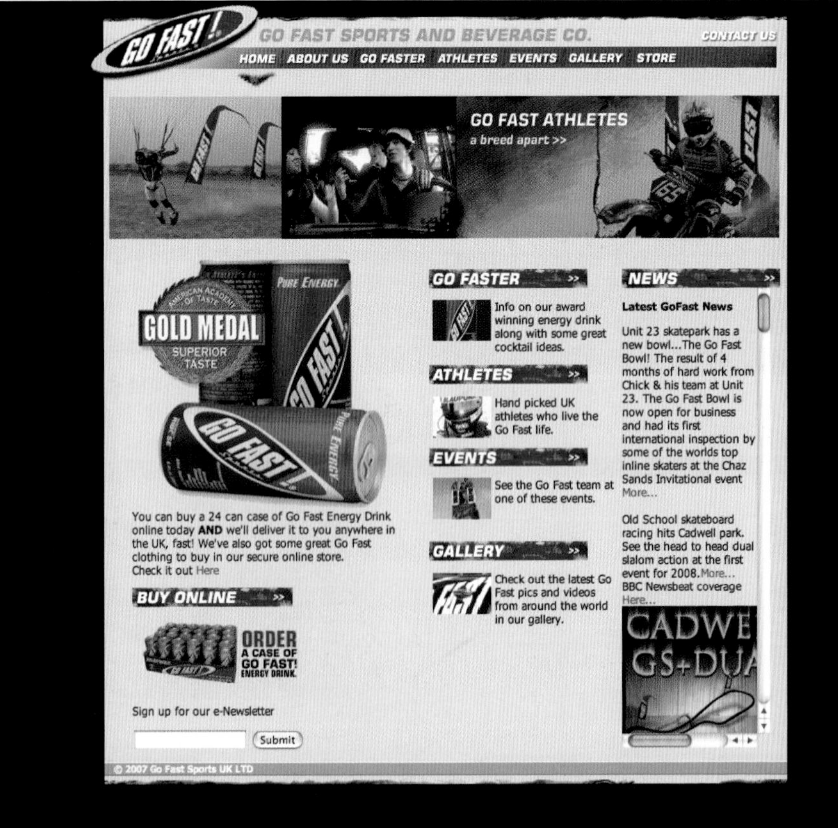


Info

**DESIGN:** THEPHARMACY <www.thepharmacymedia.com>: Willem van der Krieken. /// **PROGRAMMING:** Jan-Willem Reuling, Dirk van Hout. /// **VIDEO:** Go Fast! Sports. /// **CLIENT:** Go Fast! Sports. /// **TOOLS:** Flash, Photoshop, Illustrator, PHP, MySQL. /// **COST:** 110 hours.

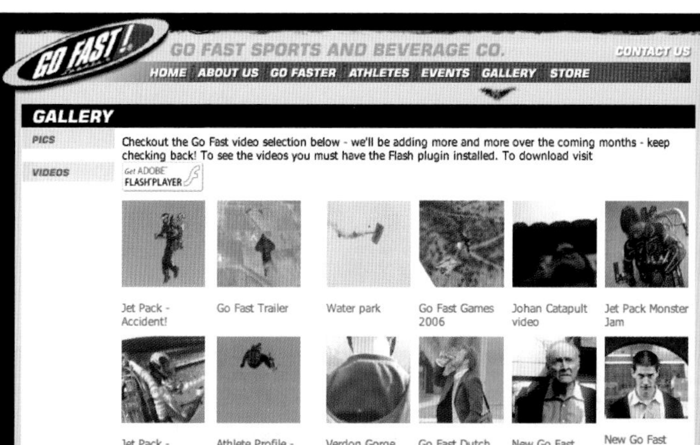
GO FAST!
GO FAST SPORTS AND BEVERAGE CO.
CONTACT US
HOME ABOUT US GO FASTER ATHLETES EVENTS GALLERY STORE
GALLERY
PICS
VIDEOS
Checkout the Go Fast video selection below - we'll be adding more and more over the coming months - keep checking back! To see the videos you must have the Flash plugin installed. To download visit
Get ADOBE FLASH PLAYER
Jet Pack - Accident!
Go Fast Trailer
Water park
Go Fast Games 2006
Johan Catapult video
Jet Pack Monster Jam
Jet Pack - Stadium Flight
Athlete Profile - Tara Dakides
Verdon Gorge low pull!
Go Fast Dutch Advert
New Go Fast Advert (30')
New Go Fast Advert (60')
© 2007 Go Fast Sports UK LTD

GO FAST!
GO FAST SPORTS AND BEVERAGE CO.
CONTACT US
HOME ABOUT US GO FASTER ATHLETES EVENTS GALLERY STORE
GALLERY
PICS
VIDEOS
seven
Jet Pack Monster Jam
Jet Pack - Stadium Flight
Athlete Profile - Tara Dakides
Verdon Gorge low pull!
Go Fast Dutch Advert
New Go Fast Advert (30')
New Go Fast Advert (60')
© 2007 Go Fast Sports UK LTD

# GUIDING LIGHT

USA

http://gl.freedominteractivedesign.com

2007

Concept

**"Guiding Light" is the oldest show in daytime television history, and celebrated its 70th anniversary in 2007. Its first official website prominently features daily episodic recaps, and user-uploaded video submissions to become Fan of the Month.** /// „Guiding Light" ist die älteste Sendung in der Geschichte des Fernsehens; sie hat 2007 ihren 70. Geburtstag gefeiert. Die erste offizielle Website präsentiert vor allem Zusammenfassungen von Episoden und Beiträgen für den Fan des Monats, die von Usern hochgeladen wurden. /// **« Guiding Light » est l'émission qui a le plus d'ancienneté dans l'histoire des programmes de télévision de la journée, et a fêté son 70e anniversaire en 2007. Son premier site web officiel présente avant tout des récapitulations d'épisodes, et des entrées vidéo que les utilisateurs soumettent pour devenir Fan du mois.**

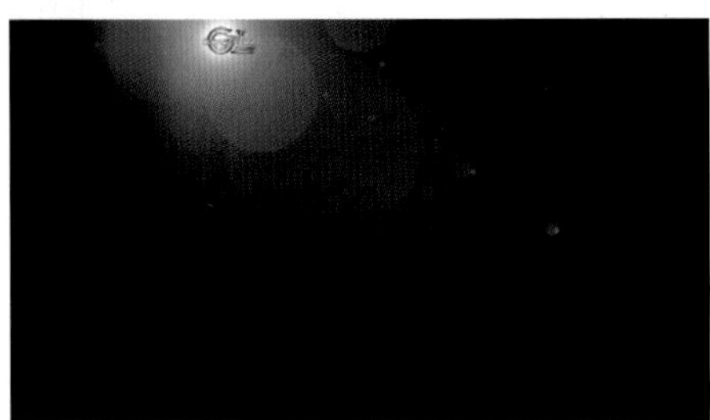

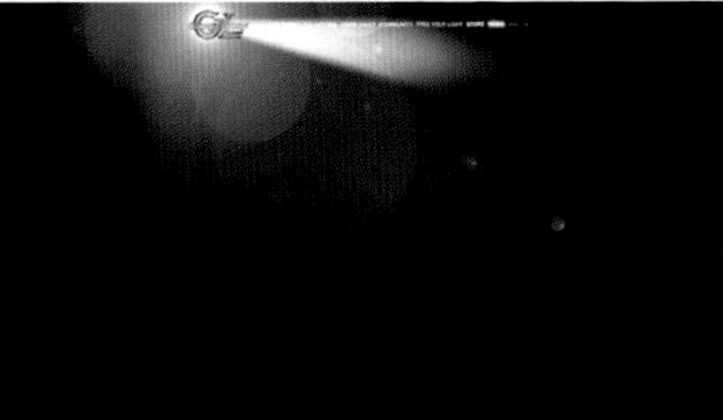

Info

**Design:** Freedom Interactive Design <www.freedominteractivedesign.com>: Mark Ferdman (Creative Director); Matt Sundstrom (Senior Art Director). /// **Programming:** Shea Gonyo (Tech Director); Brian Kadar (Senior Action Script Developer); Caleb Brown (Senior NET Developer). /// **Video:** Nick Kircos, Sophia Leang (Video Compression). /// **Others:** Danny Chang (Production Artist). /// **Client:** Procter & Gamble Productions. /// **Tools:** Flash, Microsoft ASP.net. /// **Cost:** 1300 hours.

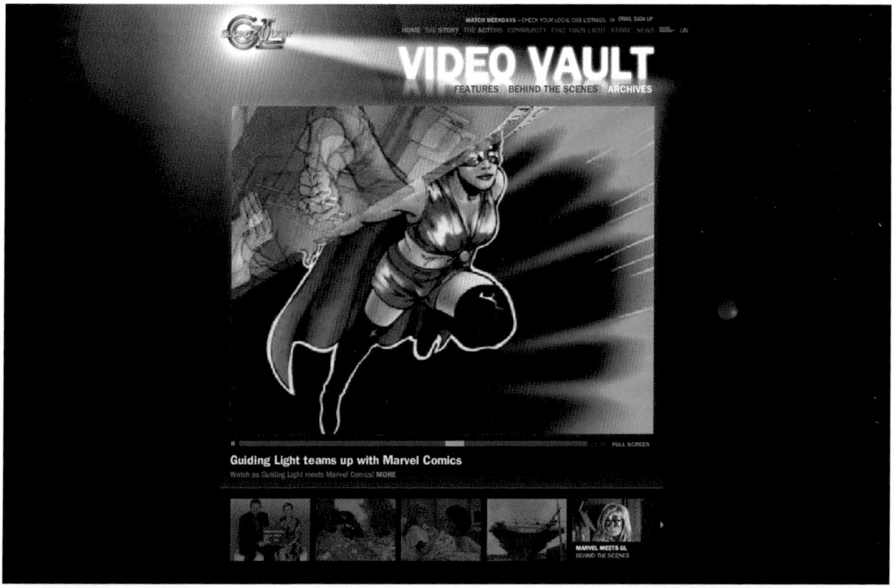

WATCH WEEKDAYS – CHECK YOUR LOCAL CBS LISTINGS. EMAIL SIGN UP
HOME THE STORY THE ACTORS COMMUNITY FIND YOUR LIGHT STORE NEWS ON

VIDEO VAULT

FEATURES BEHIND THE SCENES ARCHIVES

FULL SCREEN

**Guiding Light teams up with Marvel Comics**

Watch as Guiding Light meets Marvel Comics! **MORE**

MARVEL MEETS GL
BEHIND THE SCENES

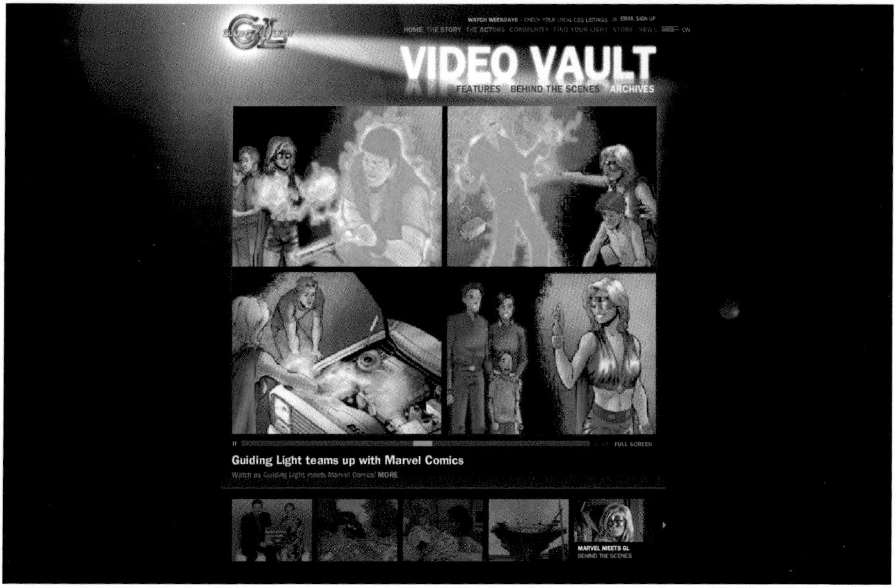

WATCH WEEKDAYS – CHECK YOUR LOCAL CBS LISTINGS. EMAIL SIGN UP
HOME THE STORY THE ACTORS COMMUNITY FIND YOUR LIGHT STORE NEWS ON

VIDEO VAULT

FEATURES BEHIND THE SCENES ARCHIVES

FULL SCREEN

**Guiding Light teams up with Marvel Comics**

Watch as Guiding Light meets Marvel Comics! **MORE**

MARVEL MEETS GL
BEHIND THE SCENES

# HAZE

FRANCE

www.hazegame.com

2008

Concept

**This promotional hot site for Haze explores all the limits of using video full screen, introducing a narrative that captures the attention of the audience.** /// Diese Promowebsite für Haze erforscht die Grenzen eines bildschirmfüllenden Videos und bannt mit einer eigenen Geschichte die Aufmerksamkeit des Publikums. /// **Ce site promotionnel temporaire pour Haze explore toutes les limites de la vidéo en plein écran, et utilise un style narratif innovant qui capte l'attention du public.**

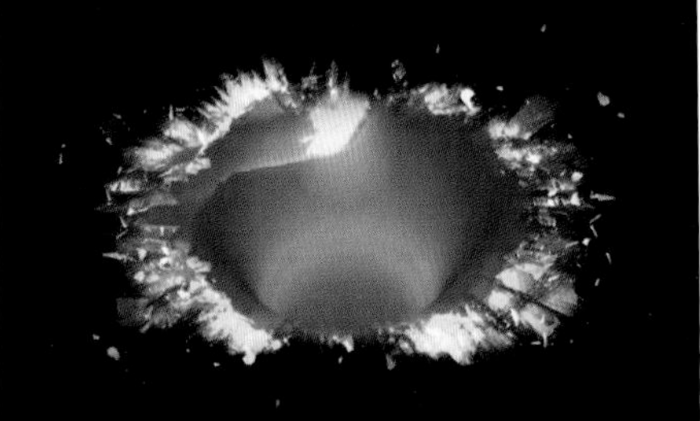

Info

**Design:** Soleil Noir <www.soleilnoir.net>. /// **Client:** Ubisoft. /// **Tools:** Photoshop, Flash, After Effects, 3D Studio Max, XML. /// **Cost:** 2 months.

B72
ASSAULT RIFLE
Mantels Soldaten haben die B72

SK 3
FRAGMENTATION
GRENADE
Diese Granate mit Zeitzünder ist ideal,
um gewaltige Zerstörung zu verursachen.

IN 2048
GOVERNMENTS CONTRACT
PRIVATE ARMIES
TO FIGHT THE WARS
rekrutieren Regierungen Privatarmeen für
ihre Kriege

Am jenem Tag

# HDI – WAS AUCH KOMMT

GERMANY

www.wasauchkommt.de

2007

Concept

**To illustrate the service range of an insurance company, the shopping carts leave the video player and wreak havoc on the site itself. ///** Um das vielfältige Angebot einer Versicherungsgesellschaft zu veranschaulichen, gehen die Einkaufswagen aus dem Videoplayer stiften und richten verheerende Verwüstungen an der Site selbst an. /// **Pour illustrer la gamme de services d'une compagnie d'assurance, les chariots sortent de la fenêtre vidéo et sèment la pagaille sur le site.**

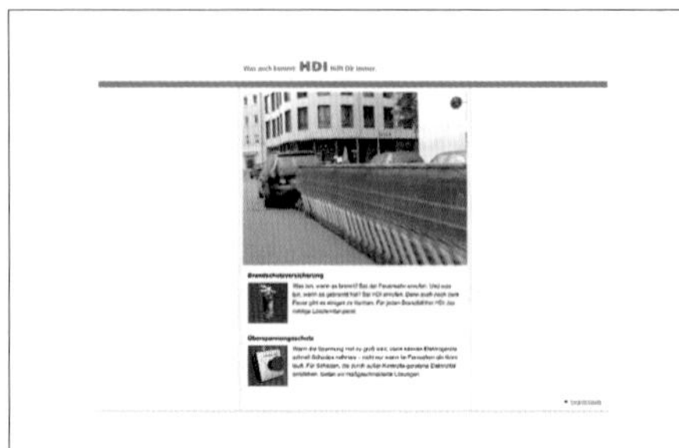

Info

**DESIGN:** blackbeltmonkey, digital advertising agency <www.blackbeltmonkey.com>: Mike John Otto, Oliver Bentz (Creative Director); Mike John Otto (Art Director), Marcellus Gau (Project Manager); blackbeltmonkey, Gudella Barche (Concept). /// **PROGRAMMING:** Mellow Message; Robert Mentzel (Flash). /// **VIDEO:** Silberlink Film (Film-production); Andre Haupt (3D); Deli pictures (Post-production). /// **OTHERS:** Detlef Buck (Director); Studio Funk, V8 Studio (Sound). /// **CLIENT:** HDI Versicherungen. /// **TOOLS:** Photoshop, Cinema 4D, Flash, After Effects, Combustion. /// **AWARDS:** Designaside, Lookom, Styleboost, FWA (Site of the Day). /// **COST:** 1,5 month.

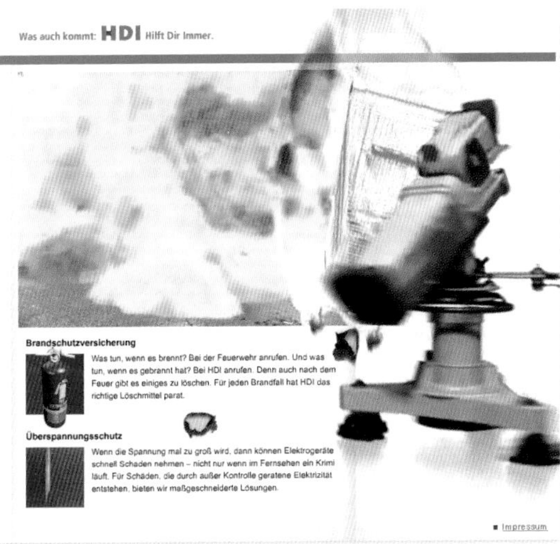
Was auch kommt: HDI Hilft Dir Immer.
Brandschutzversicherung
Was tun, wenn es brennt? Bei der Feuerwehr anrufen. Und was tun, wenn es gebrannt hat? Bei HDI anrufen. Denn auch nach dem Feuer gibt es einiges zu löschen. Für jeden Brandfall hat HDI das richtige Löschmittel parat.
Überspannungsschutz
Wenn die Spannung mal zu groß wird, dann können Elektrogeräte schnell Schaden nehmen – nicht nur wenn im Fernsehen ein Krimi läuft. Für Schäden, die durch außer Kontrolle geratene Elektrizität entstehen, bieten wir maßgeschneiderte Lösungen.
Impressum

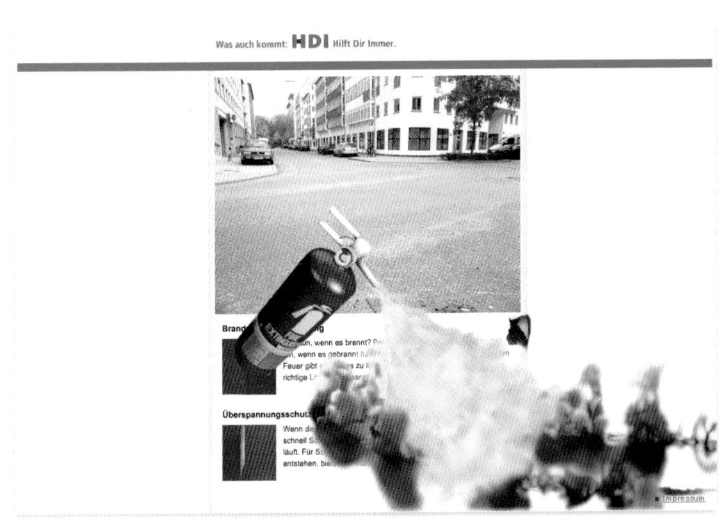
Was auch kommt: HDI Hilft Dir Immer.
Überspannungsschutz
Impressum

# HUIS CLOS

BRAZIL

www.huisclos.com.br

2008

Concept

The project used to launch the Winter 2008 Huis Clos collection website. /// Mit diesem Projekt wurde die Website der Huis Clos Collection für Winter 2008 gelauncht. /// Ce projet lançait le site web de la collection hiver 2008 de Huis Clos.

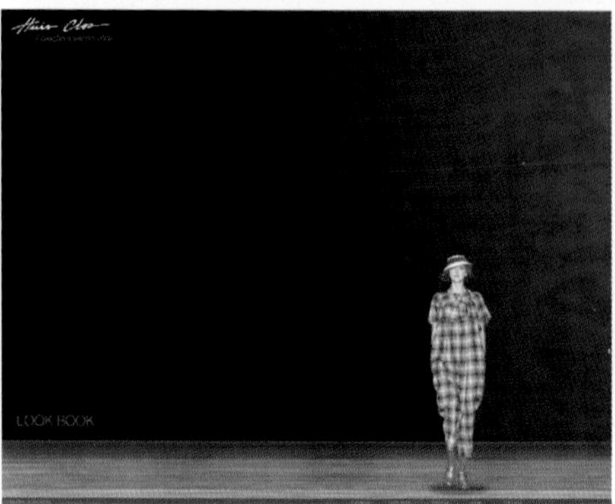

Info

**DESIGN:** 6D Estúdio <www.6d.com.br>: Stéphane Munnier. /// **PROGRAMMING:** Davi Fontenele, Stéphane Munnier. /// **VIDEO:** Client's archives. /// **CLIENT:** Huis Clos. /// **TOOLS:** Photoshop, Illustrator, Final Cut Pro, Flash, HTML, PHP. /// **COST:** 100 hours.

Huis Clos
Coleção Inverno 2008
LOOK BOOK

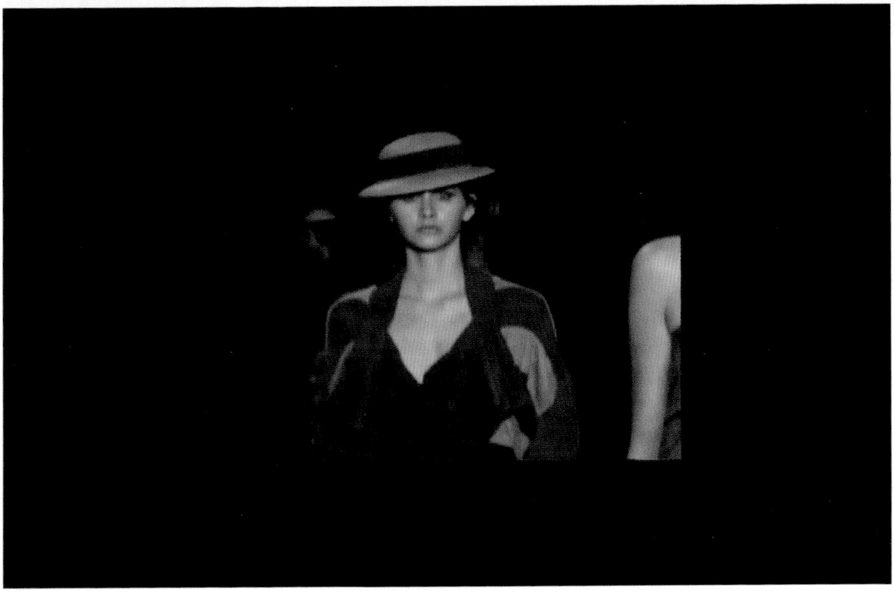

# ILHABELA

BRAZIL

www.vaiprocurarsuaturma.com.br/hellbabe/webserie.aspx

2007

Concept

For the first time in Brazil, a sitcom was shown only via the internet. Its cast was selected through a competition on the website, which is the main communication tool between the brand Ilhabela and its customers. /// In Brasilien wurde eine Sitcom zum ersten Mal nur über das Internet ausgestrahlt. Das Casting der Schauspieler erfolgte über einen Wettbewerb auf der Website, die das wichtigste Kommunikationsinstrument der Marke Ilhabela und ihrer Kunden ist. /// Pour la première fois au Brésil, une sitcom était diffusée exclusivement sur Internet. Ses acteurs ont été sélectionnés par concours sur le site, qui est le principal outil de communication entre la marque Ilhabela et ses clients.

Info

**DESIGN:** W3Haus <www.w3haus.com.br>: Chico Baldini, Diego Chiarelli. /// **PROGRAMMING:** Julio Fortis, Matias Causa. /// **VIDEO:** Zeppelin Filmes. /// **OTHERS:** Karoline Dal Soto (Account Executive); LiveAd (Buzz Marketing); Escala (Ads). /// **CLIENT:** Grendene. /// **TOOLS:** Photoshop, Flash, ASP.net, HTML, XML. /// **AWARDS:** Most Original Website (Peixe Grande Competition); Best Internet Campaign (3rd Fórum de Internet Corporativa/Associação Gaúcha de Agências Digitais). /// **COST:** 600 hours.

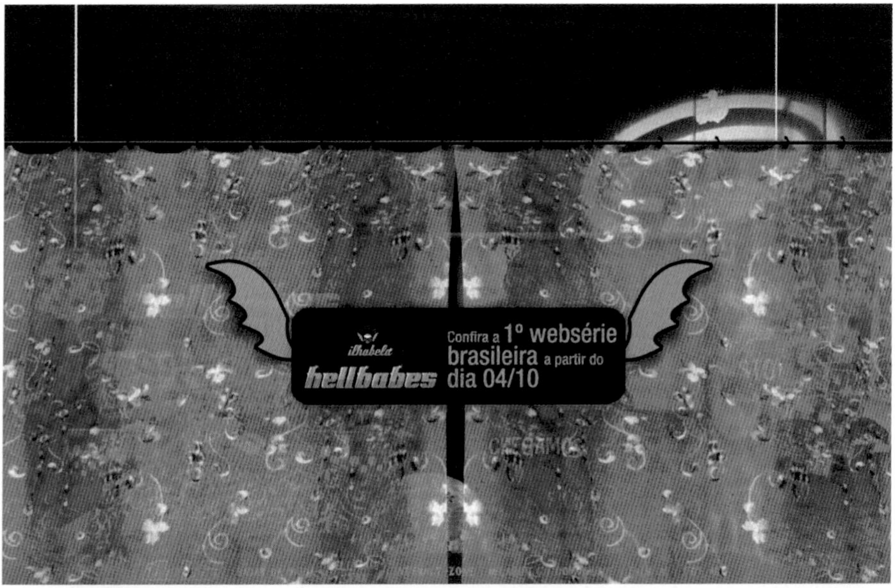
ilhabela
hellbabes
Confira a 1° websérie brasileira a partir do dia 04/10

ilhabela
hellbabes
Confira o 1° episódio
de HELLBABES WEBSÉRIE!
SEÇÃO SECRETA
ilhabela
O QUE É HELLBABES
VIDEOFOTOLOG
HELLBABES WEBSÉRIE
CÚMPLICES
FICHAS CRIMINAIS
SALA DE IMPRENSA
ilhabela RADAR DA MODA | HELL BABE STAR | INTERACT-ZONE | BELAGIFTS | COMUNIDADE | FALA AÍ | TOY ART

# ISSEY MIYAKE : BRAND SITE

JAPAN

www.isseymiyake.com/isseymiyake.html

2007

Concept

**This website presents the Issey Miyake Paris Collection Show movie and styling book archives.** /// Diese Website präsentiert den Film für die Issey Miyake Paris Collection Show und die Archive mit den Styling-Büchern. /// **Ce site web présente le film de l'Issey Miyake Paris Collection Show et des archives de carnets de stylisme.**

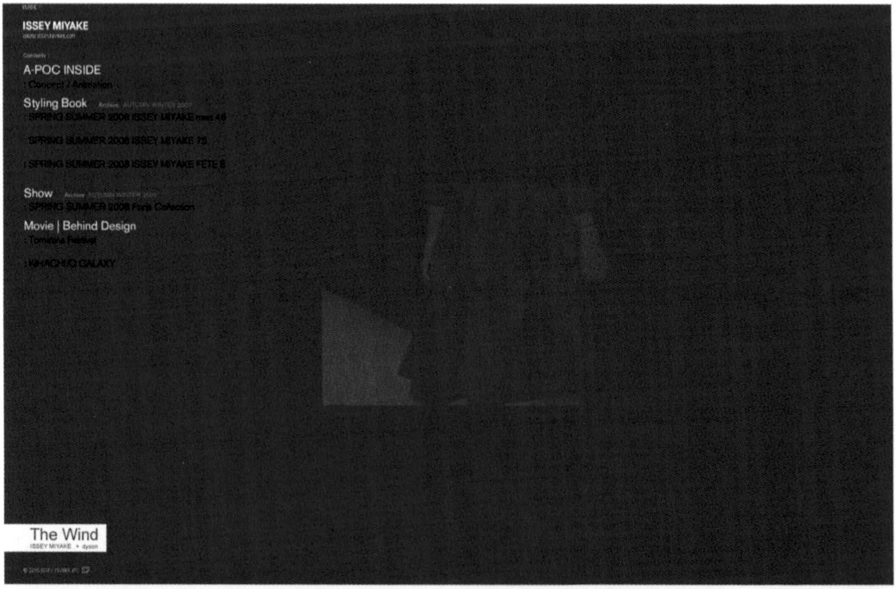

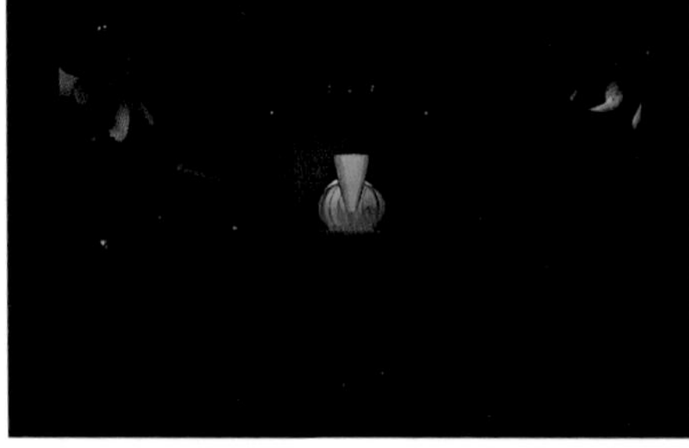

Info

**Design:** artless Inc. <www.artless.co.jp>. /// **Programming:** Wataru Sumita (3da). /// **Video:** Issey Miyake Inc. /// **Client:** Issey Miyake Inc. /// **Tools:** Flash, HTML. /// **Awards:** FWA. /// **Cost:** 90 days.

# JUST JACKS

CANADA

www.justjacks.com

2008

Concept

Online marketing presence showing the "Live The Dream" video spot and promoting the end result of attending the Just Jacks Poker Camps. /// Diese Online-Marketing-Präsenz zeigt den Videospot „Live The Dream" und wirbt für die Teilnahme an den Just Jacks Poker Camps. /// Projet de marketing en ligne avec le spot « Live the Dream », qui montre le résultat que l'on obtient lorsqu'on participe à un « camp de poker » Just Jacks.

Info

**Design:** Velocity Studio & Associates <www.velocitystudios.com>: Marco Di Carlo, Shane Stuart. /// **Programming:** Alex Davies. /// **Video:** Marco Di Carlo, Daniel Beckerman. /// **Others:** Christian Kennerney (Voice-over). /// **Client:** Just Jacks Poker Academy. /// **Tools:** Flash, After Effects, Cold Fusion, Ajax, CSS.

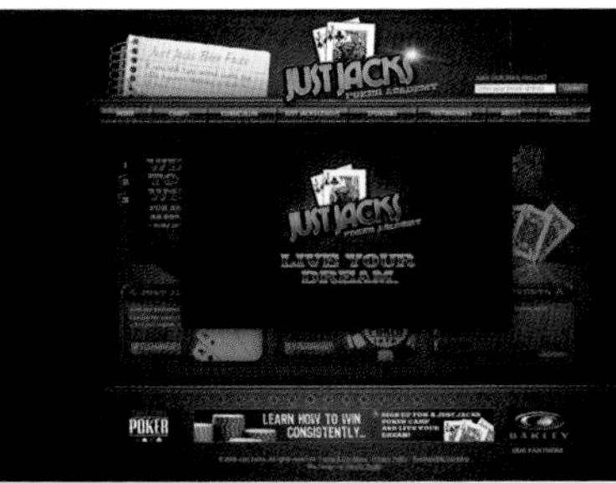

JUST JACKS
POKER ACADEMY
LIVE YOUR DREAM.
LEARN HOW TO WIN CONSISTENTLY...
OAKLEY
JUST JACKS
POKER ACADEMY
WIN A SEAT TO THE WSOP
LIVE YOUR DREAM.
JUST JACKS LEAGUE
THE GRAND PRIZE
UPCOMING EVENTS
LEARN HOW TO WIN CONSISTENTLY...
OAKLEY
POKER
JUST JACKS LEAGUE
OAKLEY
JUST JACKS
POKER ACADEMY
POKER
JUST JACKS LEAGUE
OAKLEY
Just Jacks Poker Facts
Anytime opponents are either too loose or too tight, you can profit by playing more hands
JUST JACKS
POKER ACADEMY
JOIN OUR MAILING LIST
Enter your Email Address
SUBMIT
HOME
CAMPS
CURRICULUM
JUST JACKS LEAGUE
SPONSORS
TESTIMONIALS
ABOUT
CONTACT
1
2
3
LEARN MORE
LEARN MORE
POKER
JUST JACKS LEAGUE
CLICK HERE FOR MORE JUST JACKS LEAGUE INFORMATION
OAKLEY
OUR PARTNERS
© 2008 Just Jacks. All rights reserved. Terms & Conditions | Privacy Policy | Responsible Gambling
Site Design by Velocity Studio

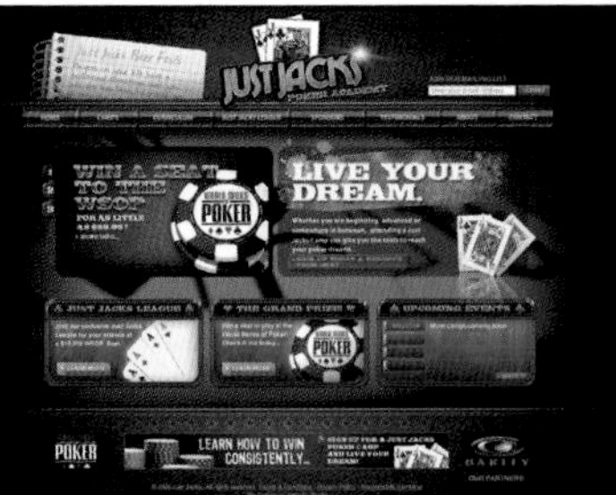

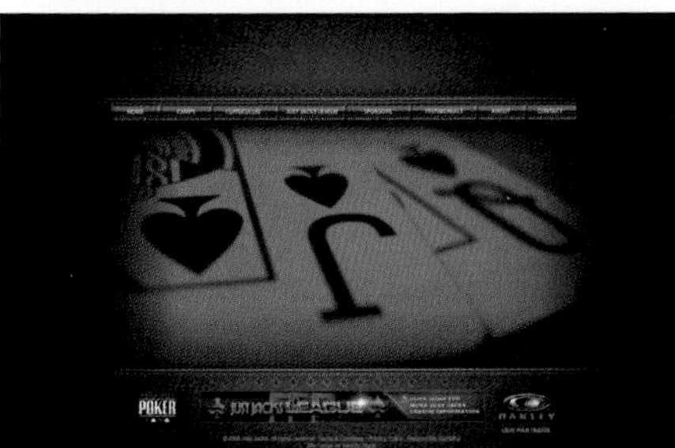

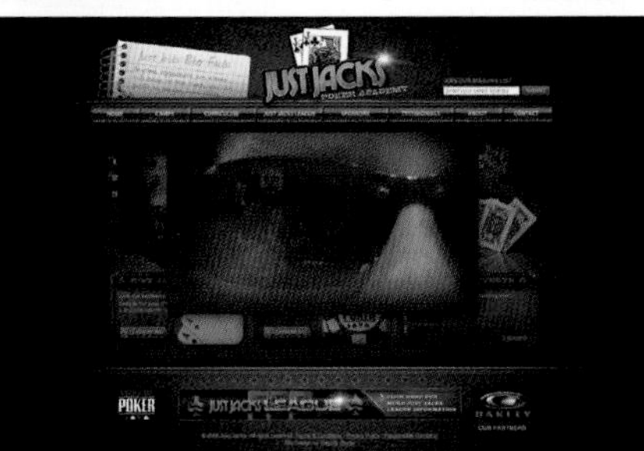

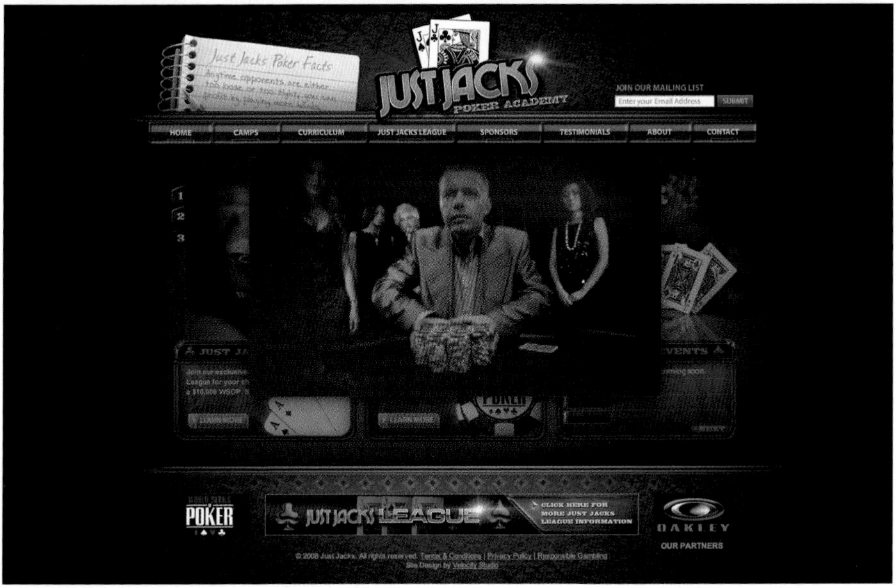

# KFC FLAVOR STATION

USA

http://clients.fcb.com/webby/kfc

2007

Concept

The challenge of this project was to show KFC's customers that they have the freedom to choose their own sauce at the Flavor Station, leading to the website ChooseYourSauce.com, where half a million viewers could engage with the online story created. /// Die Herausforderung dieses Projekts bestand darin, den Kunden von KFC zu zeigen, dass sie an der Flavor Station eigene Saucen wählen können. Dadurch kommen sie zur Website ChooseYourSauce.com. Über eine halbe Million Besucher können bei der dort stattfindenden Online-Story eingreifen. /// Pour ce projet, le défi était de montrer aux clients de KFC qu'ils ont la liberté de choisir leur propre sauce à la Flavor Station. Le résultat est le site web ChooseYourSauce.com, où un demi-million de visiteurs ont pu se plonger dans l'histoire créée pour l'occasion.

Info

**Design:** Diet Strychnine Corp. <www.dietstrychnine.com>: Alex Zamiar, Derek Noonan (Art Director), Alex Fuller (Design); FCBi. /// **Programming:** Stephen Strong (Lead Tech); Jack Doyle, Jason Mitton, Graham Cousens. /// **Video:** David Jones (Creative Director); Matt Horton (Group Creative Director); Jonathan Richman (Copy); Kohl Norville – ZGroup Films (Film Director). /// **Others:** Ivo Knenezivic, Zoe Garci, Stephen Strong (Agency Producers). /// **Client:** Kentucky Fried Chicken. /// **Awards:** Webbie Awards. /// **Cost:** $280,000.00.

KFC'S NEW FLAVOR STATION

FLAVOR STATION MEDIA PLAYER

Press the right arrow key on your keyboard to advance to the end of the scene.

→ START OVER

I ♥ CHICKEN

→ HOME

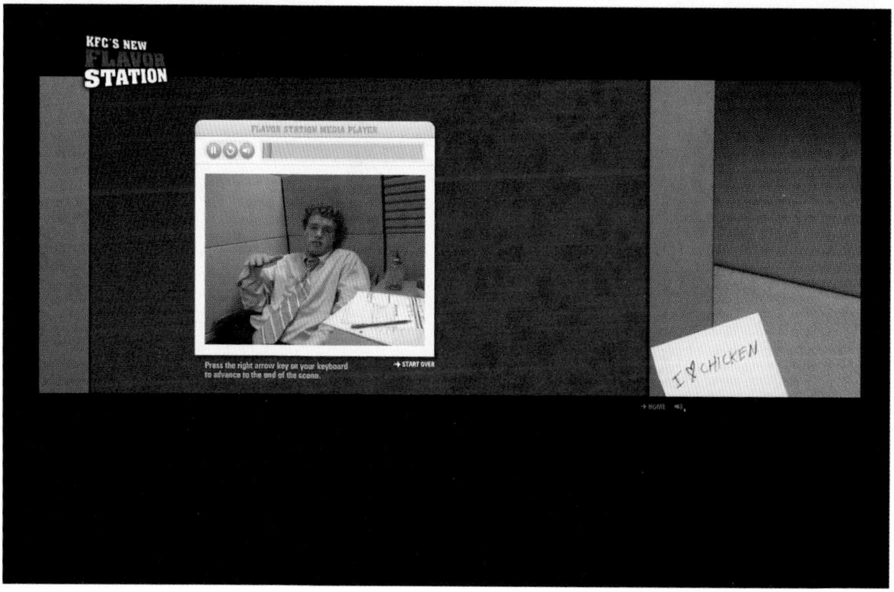

KFC'S NEW FLAVOR STATION

FLAVOR STATION MEDIA PLAYER

Press the right arrow key on your keyboard to advance to the end of the scene.

→ START OVER

I ♥ CHICKEN

→ HOME

# K-SWISS FREE RUNNING

EUROPE

www.kswissfreerunning.com

2008

Concept

K-Swiss Free Running is the launch campaign for the K-Swiss Ariake, designed especially for the acrobatic urban sport of Free Running. The campaign site builds on a simple mechanic in which visitors create and send video messages. /// K-Swiss Free Running ist die Kampagne für den Launch von K-Swiss Ariake – einem speziell für den akrobatischen, urbanen Sport Free Running entworfenen Sportschuh. Die Site der Kampagne enthält einen einfachen Mechanismus, über den die Besucher Videobotschaften erstellen und versenden können. /// K-Swiss Free Running est la campagne de lancement de l'Ariake de K-Swiss, une chaussure conçue tout spécialement pour le sport urbain acrobatique du free running. Le site de la campagne s'appuie sur une mécanique toute simple : les visiteurs créent et envoient des messages vidéo.

"Free running is all about self expression.
Express yourself with a message and
watch me free run it."
K-SWISS
Sébastien Foucan
Founder, Free Running

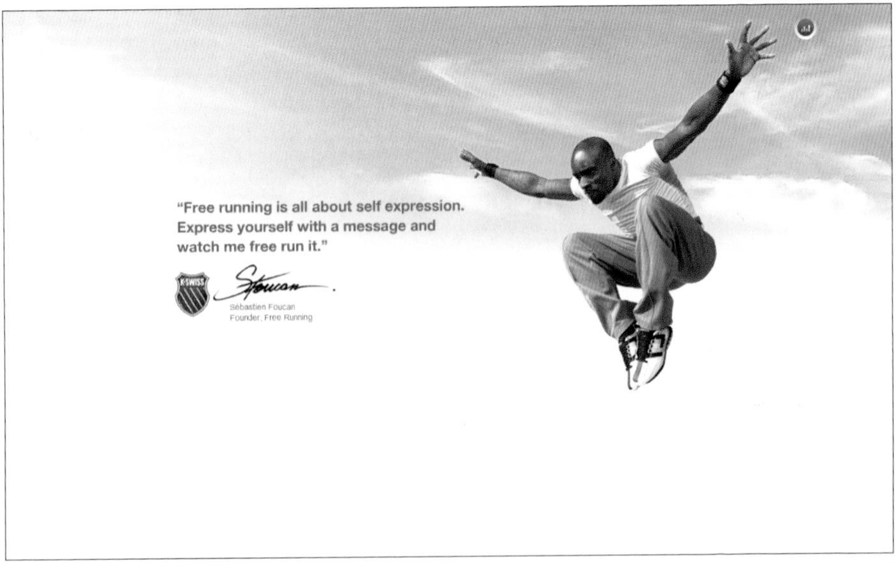

Express yourself
TYPE HERE

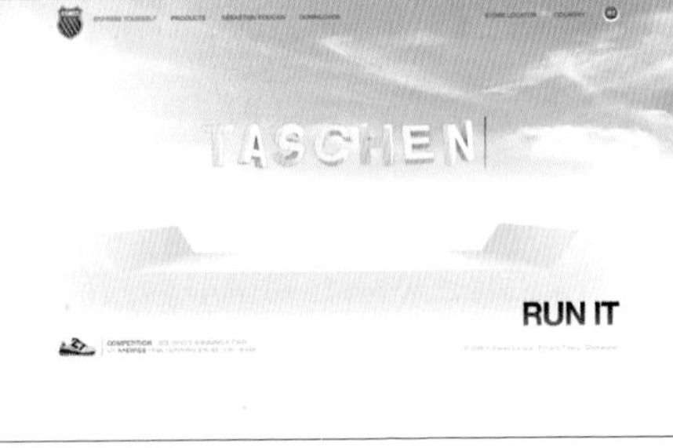
TASCHEN
RUN IT

Info

**DESIGN:** Perfect Fools <www.perfectfools.com>: Mark Chalmers, Tony Högqvist (Creative Director); Christian Mezöfi (Lead Art Director); Oscar Asmoarp (Art Director); Christian Johansson, Vinh Kha (Concept). /// **PROGRAMMING:** Björn Kummeneje (Lead Tech), David Genelid (Tech). /// **VIDEO:** Acne Film. Ensrette: Linnéa Bergman Sjöstrand, Daniel Skoglund (Film Directors). /// **OTHERS:** Karl Nord (Genius Intern); Fredrik Heghammar, Kathrin Spaak (Producers); James Goode (Account Lead), Patrick Gardner (Account Lead/Copy). /// **CLIENT:** K-Swiss Europe. /// **TOOLS:** Flash.

PAUSE
/ PASS IT ON
RUN IT AGAIN / NEW MESSAGE / DOWNLOAD MOVIE

PAUSE
/ PASS IT ON
RUN IT AGAIN / NEW MESSAGE / DOWNLOAD MOVIE

PAUSE
/ PASS IT ON
RUN IT AGAIN / NEW MESSAGE / DOWNLOAD MOVIE

PAUSE
/ PASS IT ON
RUN IT AGAIN / NEW MESSAGE / DOWNLOAD MOVIE

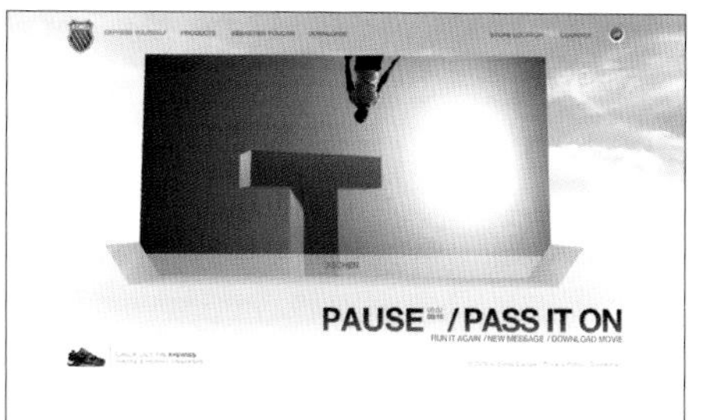

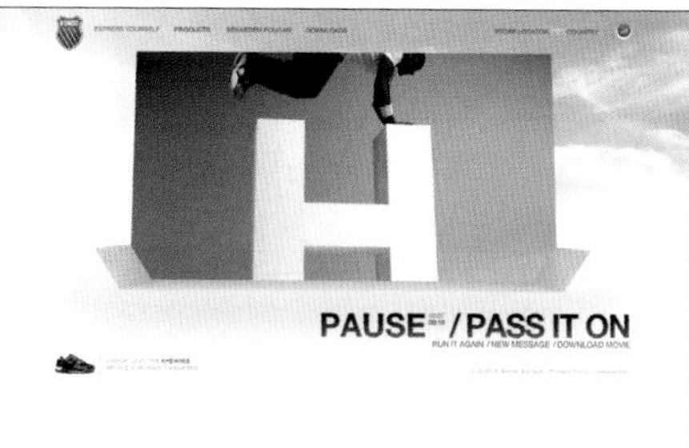

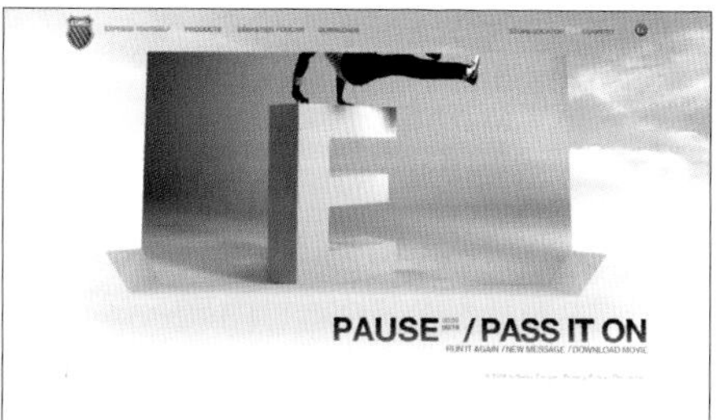

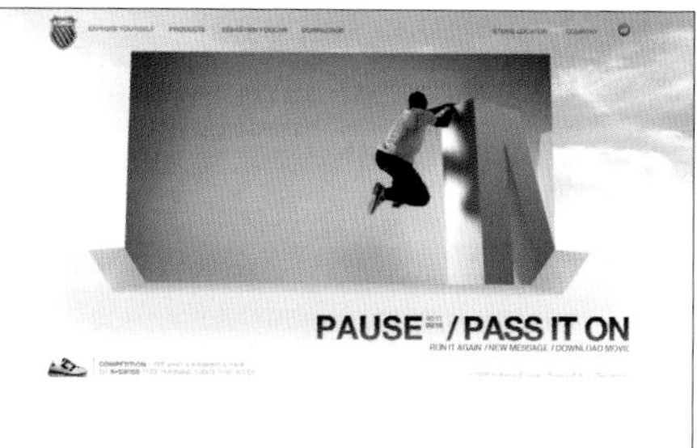

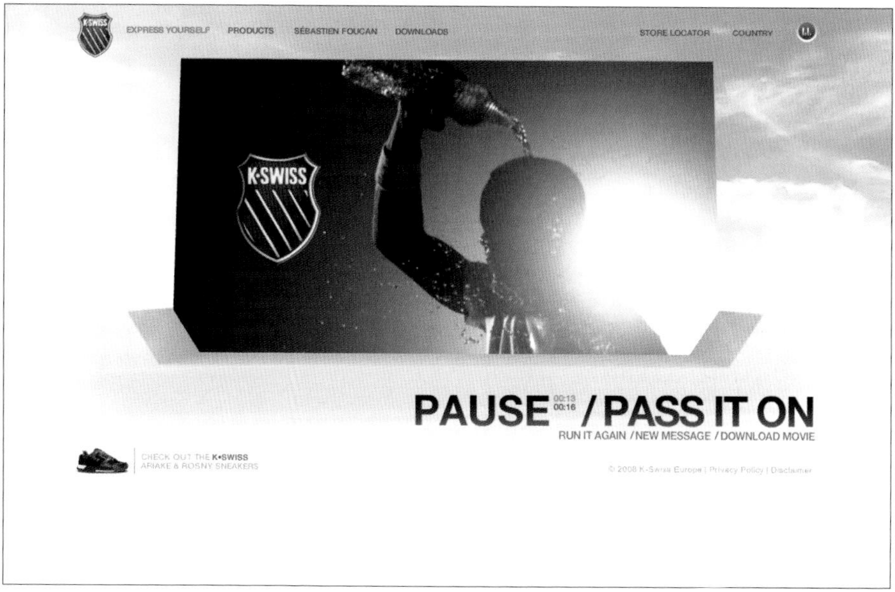

K-SWISS
EXPRESS YOURSELF
PRODUCTS
SÉBASTIEN FOUCAN
DOWNLOADS
STORE LOCATOR
COUNTRY
K-SWISS
PAUSE
00:13
00:16
/ PASS IT ON
RUN IT AGAIN / NEW MESSAGE / DOWNLOAD MOVIE
CHECK OUT THE K•SWISS
ARIAKE & ROSNY SNEAKERS
© 2008 K-Swiss Europe | Privacy Policy | Disclaimer

# LOBO

BRAZIL

www.lobo.cx

1996

Concept

A simple yet elegant portal on to Lobo's fine portfolio of films and animations. /// Ein einfaches, aber elegantes Portal zum ausgezeichneten Lobo-Portfolio mit Filmen und Animationen. /// Un portail simple mais élégant qui présente le magnifique portfolio de films et d'animations de Lobo.

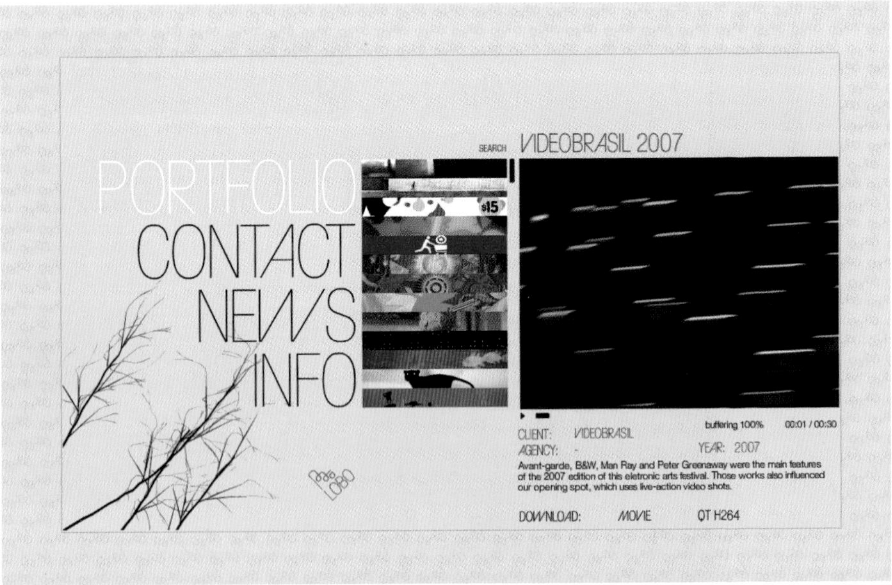

SEARCH
VIDEOBRASIL 2007
PORTFOLIO
CONTACT
NEWS
INFO
buffering 100%
00:01 / 00:30
CLIENT: VIDEOBRASIL
AGENCY: -
YEAR: 2007
Avant-garde, B&W, Man Ray and Peter Greenaway were the main features of the 2007 edition of this eletronic arts festival. Those works also influenced our opening spot, which uses live-action video shots.
DOWNLOAD: MOVIE QT H264

WORK
PORTFOLIO
CONTACT
NEWS
INFO

WORK
PORTFOLIO
CONTACT
NEWS
INFO

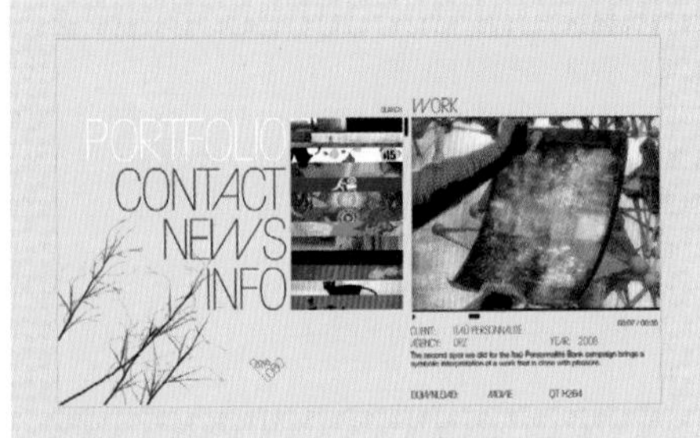

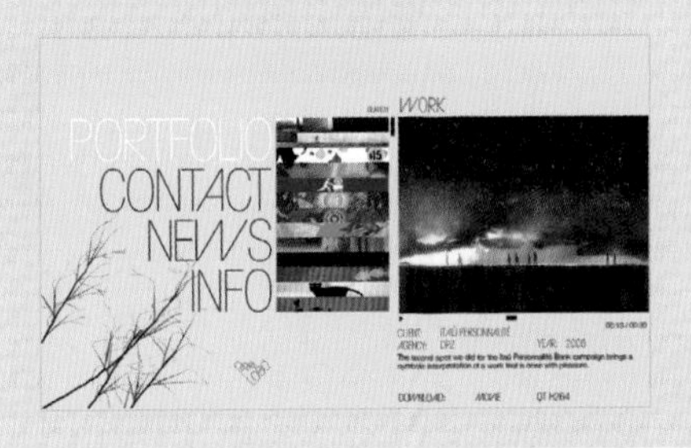

Info

**Design:** 14bits <http://14bits.com.br>: Mateus de Paula Santos, Rico Villas Boas. /// **Programming:** Jayme Cavalcanti Neto, Rico Villas Boas. /// **Video:** Lobo. /// **Client:** Lobo. /// **Tools:** Flash. /// **Cost:** 500 hours.

SEARCH
KODAK
PORTFOLIO
CONTACT
NEWS
INFO
00:04 / 00:30
CLIENT: KODAK
AGENCY: OGILVY NY
YEAR: 2007
Done in a very tight schedule, this spot launched a new Kodak printer with cheap cartridges. The CMYK colors were adopted by the brand, so our job was using them in an interesting way in the animations.
DOWNLOAD: MOVIE QT H264

SEARCH
2-DAY RACE
MORE
PORTFOLIO
CONTACT
NEWS
INFO
00:16 / 00:30
CLIENT: TARGET
AGENCY: BBDO NY
YEAR: 2007
A campaign for Target with 4 TV spots plus 23 chapters of an interactive game. Watch the TV spot clicking "more" on the top right. For the game, please go to the news section.
DOWNLOAD: MOVIE QT H264

# MAXIME PERELMUTER

BRAZIL

www.maximeperelmuter.com.br

2006

Concept

The main concern of this project was to bring the atmosphere of the fashion house backstage to the website. /// Das Hauptanliegen dieses Projekts war, die Backstage-Atmosphäre dieses Modehauses auf die Website zu übertragen. /// Ce projet avait pour objectif principal de recréer l'atmosphère des coulisses de cette maison de mode sur le site web.

Info

**DESIGN:** 6D Estúdio <www.6d.com.br>: Bruno Fraga. /// **PROGRAMMING:** Marlus Araújo. /// **VIDEO:** Marcos Tola. /// **CLIENT:** Maxime Perelmuter. /// **TOOLS:** Photoshop, Illustrator, Final Cut Pro, After Effects, Flash, HTML. /// **COST:** 160 hours.

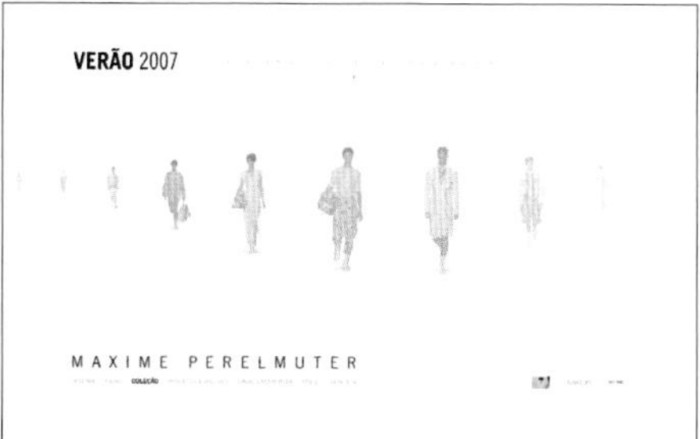
VERÃO 2007
MAXIME PERELMUTER

VERÃO 2007
MAXIME PERELMUTER

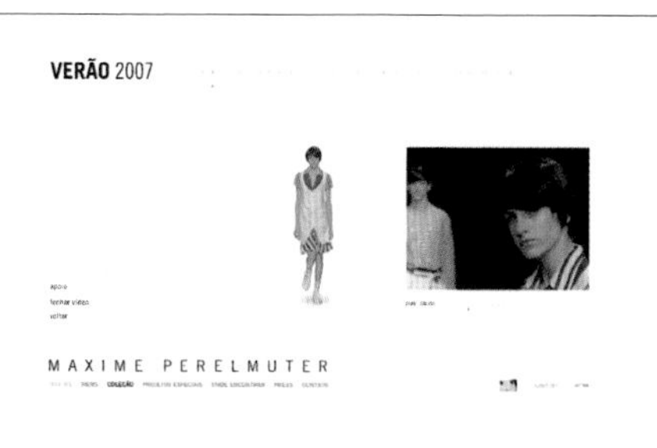
VERÃO 2007
MAXIME PERELMUTER

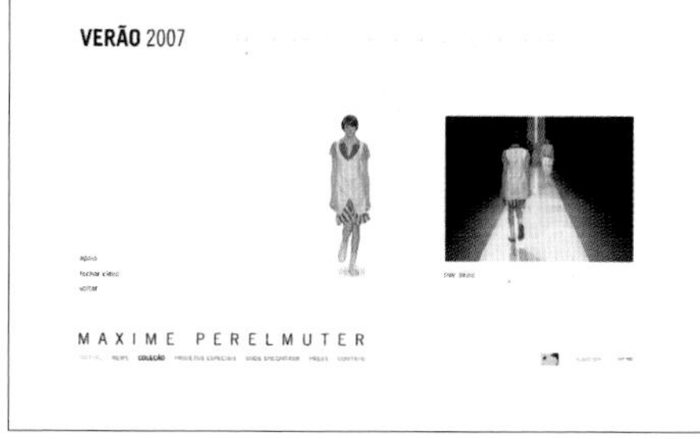
VERÃO 2007
MAXIME PERELMUTER

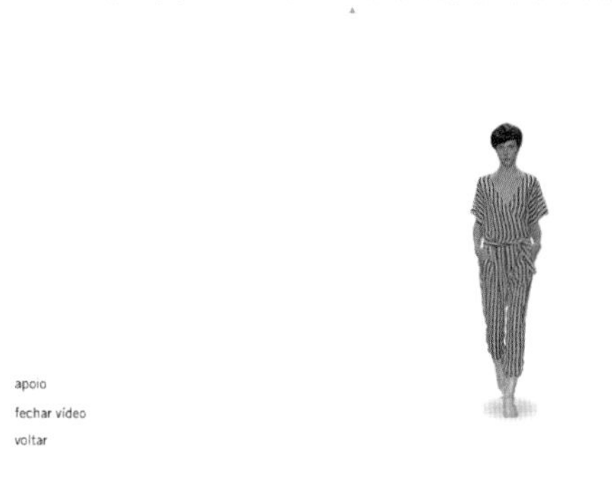
VERÃO 2007
apoio
fechar video
voltar
MAXIME PERELMUTER
MAXIME NEWS COLEÇÃO PROJETOS ESPECIAIS ONDE ENCONTRAR PRESS CONTATO

play pause

# MEDICI.TV

FRANCE

www.medici.tv

2008

Concept

Video-on-demand and live-events site with a particular focus on a large catalog of film and documentaries about classical music. Subscription and download-based purchases. /// Diese Website mit Video on Demand und Live-Events legt den Schwerpunkt vor allem auf den großen Katalog mit Filmen und Dokumentationen über klassische Musik. Abonnements und Kauf durch Download hier möglich. /// Site de vidéos à la demande et d'événements en direct, avec un catalogue très complet de films et de documentaires sur la musique classique. Les achats se font par téléchargement, après paiement d'un abonnement.

LES PIANOS DE LA NUIT
© IDÉALE AUDIENCE / ARTE France - France 2004

STEPHEN KOVACEVICH
LA ROQUE D'ANTHÉRON 2004

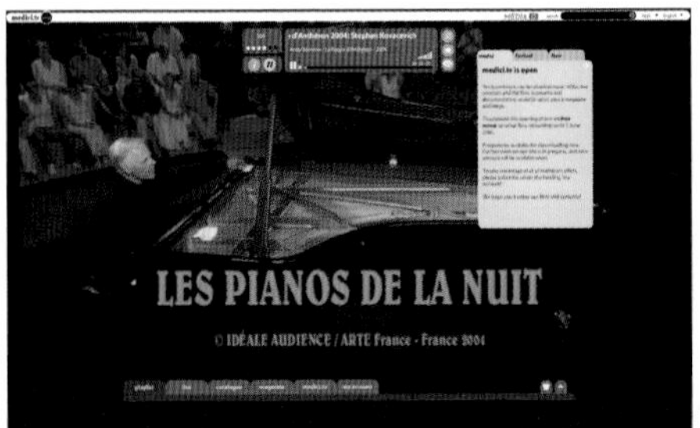

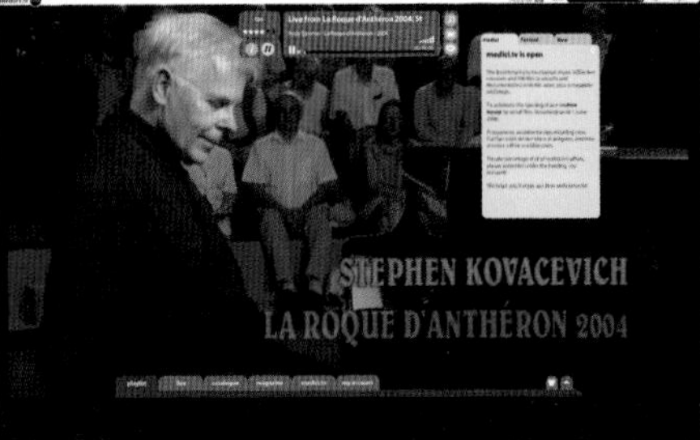

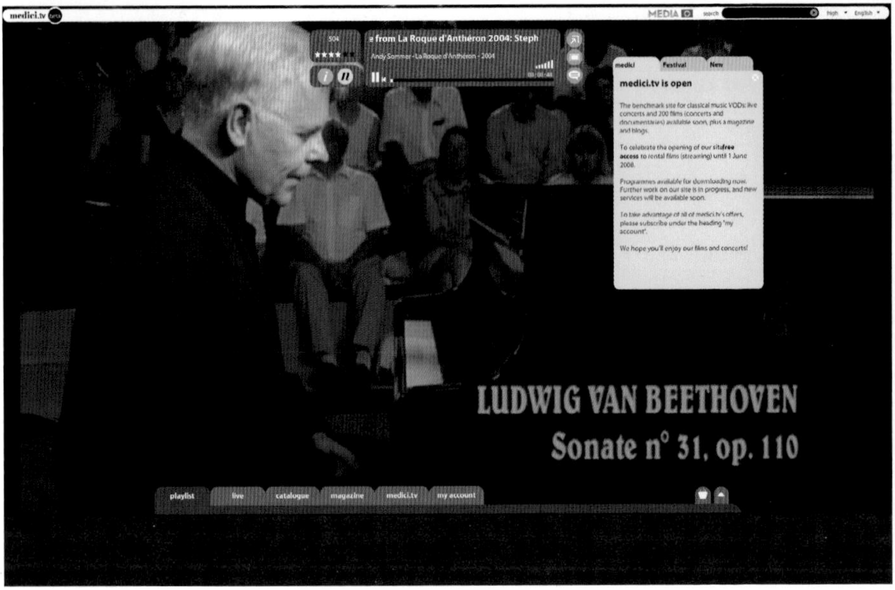

medici.tv
MEDIA
search
High
English
504
e from La Roque d'Anthéron 2004: Steph
Andy Sommer - La Roque d'Anthéron - 2004
medici
Festival
New
medici.tv is open
The benchmark site for classical music VODs: live concerts and 200 films (concerts and documentaries) available soon, plus a magazine and blogs.
To celebrate the opening of our site free access to rental films (streaming) until 1 June 2008.
Programmes available for downloading now. Further work on our site is in progress, and new services will be available soon.
To take advantage of all of medici.tv's offers, please subscribe under the heading 'my account'.
We hope you'll enjoy our films and concerts!
LUDWIG VAN BEETHOVEN
Sonate n° 31, op. 110
playlist
live
catalogue
magazine
medici.tv
my account

Info

**Design:** Spill <www.spill.net>: Liz Stirling, Nicholas Mir Chaikin, Virginie Nguyen Tan Hon, Jonathan Da Costa. /// **Programming:** Christophe Le Bars, Jonathan Da Costa, Marion Bouguet. /// **Video:** Medici Arts, Ideale Audience, EuroArts. /// **Others:** Hervé Boissiére (Executive Producer); Juliette Mage for Spill with Aurélie Mydlarz for Medici (Design Coordination/Producer). /// **Client:** Medici.tv. /// **Tools:** Flash, PHP, MySQL, Catalyst/PERL. /// **Cost:** 1100 hours.

medici.tv beta
MEDIA
search
High
English
Bernstein: Shostakovich, Symphony No.1
4th movement Finale (excerpt)
Horant H. Hohlfeld - 1988
medici
Festival
New
medici.tv is open
The benchmark site for classical music VODs: live concerts and 200 films (concerts and documentaries) available soon, plus a magazine and blogs.
To celebrate the opening of our site **free access** to rental films (streaming) until 1 June 2008.
playlist
live
catalogue
magazine
medici.tv
my account
catalogue
Catalogue
Music on film
Concerts
Operas & Voices
Portraits
Dance
Archives
The 'inclassiques'
Documentaries
Essays
Performers
Conductors
Singers
Violinists
Cellists
Pianists
Chamber music
Directors
Bruno Monsaingeon
Frank Scheffer
Alexander Sokurov
Johan van der Keuken
Collections
Classic Archive
The Art of
Berliner Philharmoniker
Lucerne Festival
La Roque d'Anthéron
Juxtapositions
New
Claudio Abbado: Beethoven, Sy
Berliner Philharmoniker
Bob Coles - 2001
Maurizio Pollini: Beethoven, Pia
Maurizio Pollini (piano)
Michael Beyer - 2004
Anna Netrebko: St. Petersburg G
Victor Tretiakov (violin) - Elisso Vir
Michael Beyer - 2003
Maya Plisetskaya: Diva of Dance
Bolshoi Theatre,1945-1977
Wolf Seesemann - 2004
Leonard Bernstein: Shostakovich
Lenny in rehearsal and performanc
Horant H. Hohlfeld - 1988
André Navarra & John Barbirolli
Hallé Orchestra
Classic Archive - 1962
Christian Ferras: Franck, Violin S
Pierre Barbizet - Jean Fournet
Classic Archive - 1963,1967
Dietrich Fischer-Dieskau: Mahler
Gerald Moore
Classic Archive - 1959,1960,1962
Sir Simon Rattle: Mozart Gala
Magdalena Kozena - Emanuel Ax -
Manfred Wittelsberger - 2005
Claudio Abbado: Beethoven, Sy
Berliner Philharmoniker
Bob Coles - 2001
Claudio Abbado: Beethoven, Sy
Berliner Philharmoniker
Bob Coles - 2001
Claudio Abbado: Beethoven, Sy
Berliner Philharmoniker
Bob Coles - 2001
1/8

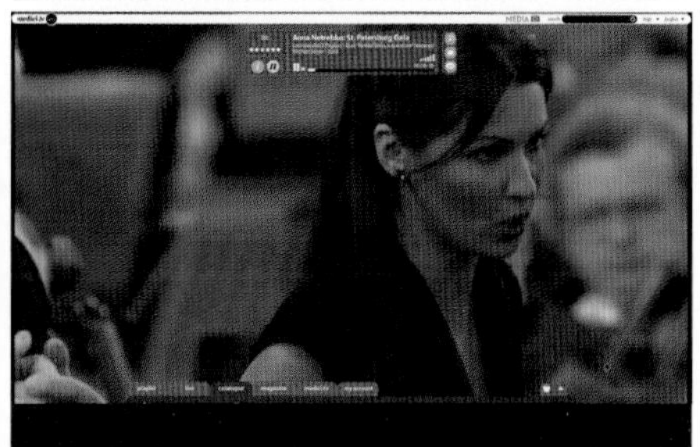

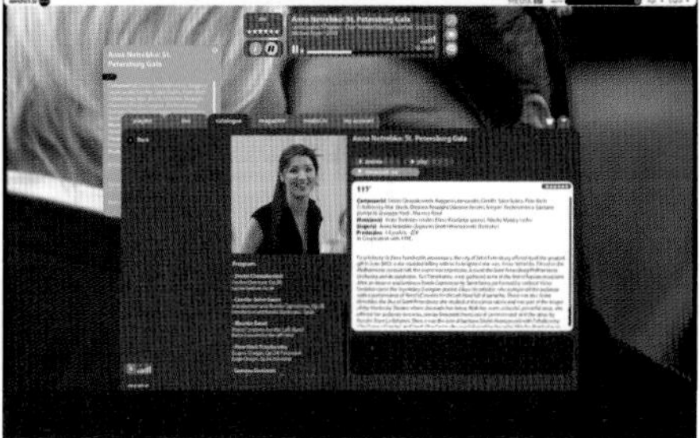

# MERCEDES-BENZ.TV

GERMANY

www.mercedes-benz.tv

2007

Concept

Mercedes-Benz.tv combines the advantages of a classical TV format with the interactivity and diversity of online TV. Large-format video pictures, a plain and distinct design, easy navigation elements and excellent technical performance. /// Mercedes-Benz.tv kombiniert die Vorteile eines klassischen Fernsehformats mit der Interaktivität und Vielfalt von Online-TV mit großformatigen Videobildern, einem klaren und eindeutigen Design, einfachen Navigationselementen und einer ausgezeichneten technischen Performance. /// Mercedes-Benz.tv combine les avantages d'un format de télévision classique à l'interactivité et la diversité de la télévision sur Internet. Les vidéos sont affichées en grand format, le style du site est simple et original, la navigation est fluide et la performance technique est excellente.

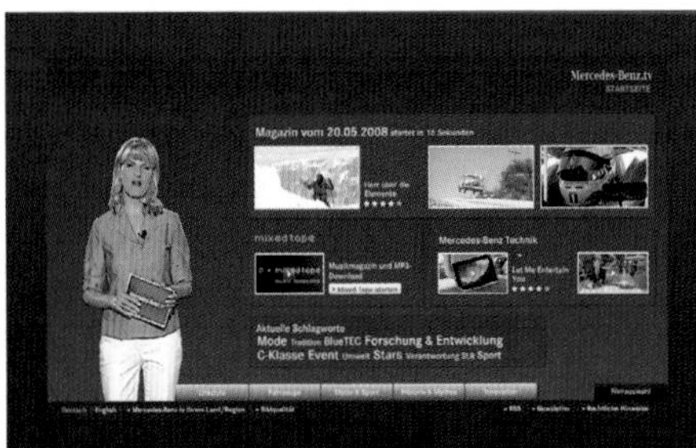

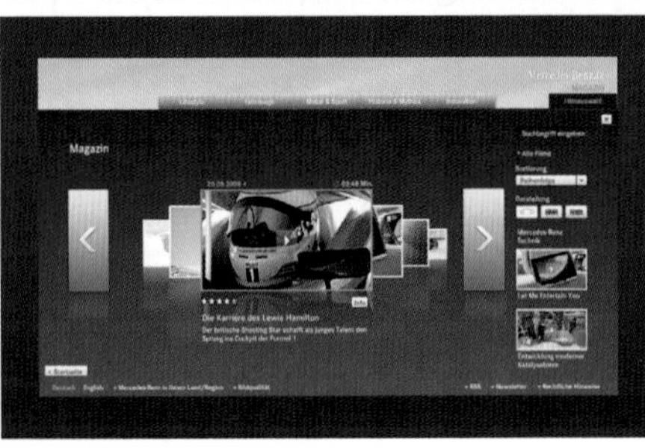

Info

**DESIGN:** Scholz & Volkmer <www.s-v.de>: Katja Rickert (Creative Direction); Mario Jilka (Art Direction); Barbara Seng (Screen Design). /// **PROGRAMMING:** Thorsten Kraus (Tech Direction); Philippe Just, Mario Dold (Flash); Florian Hermann (Programming). /// **VIDEO:** FischerAppelt, TV Media GmbH (Content Production). /// **OTHERS:** Robert Blahudka (Project Management); Georg Cockburn (Concept); Boris Lakowski, Thomas Nolle (Consulting); Jens Fischer (Sound). /// **CLIENT:** Mercedes-Benz. /// **TOOLS:** Flash, XML, HTML, DTHML. /// **AWARDS:** FWA (Site of the Day), German IPTV Award (Most Creative Design), Annual Advertising Yearbook.

Mercedes-Benz.tv
MAGAZIN
< 25.03.2008 >
John Maeda über „Simplicity"
< Startseite
Lifestyle
Fahrzeuge
Motor & Sport
Historie & Mythos
Innovation
Filmauswahl
Deutsch | English | Mercedes-Benz in Ihrem Land/Region | Bildqualität
RSS | Newsletter | Rechtliche Hinweise

Mercedes-Benz.tv
MAGAZIN
Jetzt bewerten
18 Stimmen
Info
Film versenden
URL
John Maeda über „Simplicity"
< Startseite
Lifestyle
Fahrzeuge
Motor & Sport
Historie & Mythos
Innovation
Filmauswahl
Deutsch | English | Mercedes-Benz in Ihrem Land/Region | Bildqualität
RSS | Newsletter | Rechtliche Hinweise

# MOVE ME

UK

www.move-me.com

2006

Concept

**The purpose of this project is to expose people to contemporary choreographic practice, to give people a chance to be creative, engage with audiences and create an expanding database of short original dance videos.** /// Bei diesem Projekt sollen sich Menschen mit zeitgenössischer Choreographie-Praxis beschäftigen. Hier sind sie kreativ, kommen mit dem Publikum in Kontakt und erstellen eine sich ständig erweiternde Datenbank mit kurzen und originellen Tanzvideos. /// **Ce projet a pour objectif d'exposer les gens aux pratiques chorégraphiques contemporaines, de stimuler la créativité, de créer un lien avec le public et de mettre en place et faire croître une base de données de clips de danse originaux.**

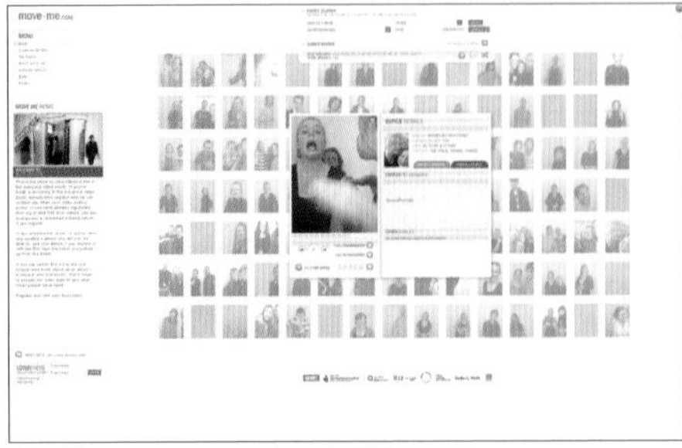

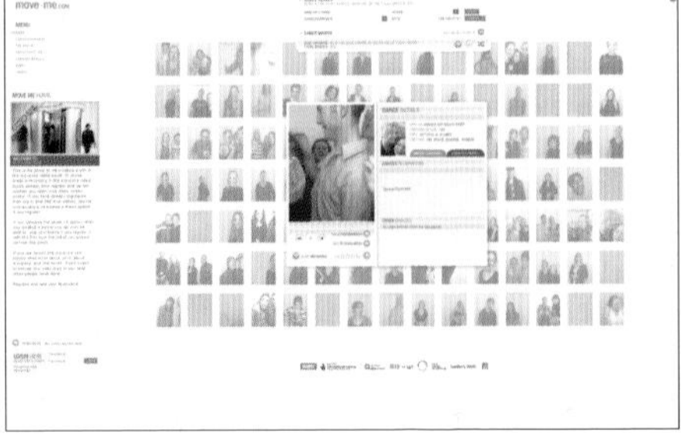

Info

**Design:** Amberfly <www.amberfly.com>: Peter Barr, Douglas Noble. /// **Programming:** Peter Barr, Douglas Noble. /// **Video:** Amberfly, Goat Media, Richochet Dance. /// **Client:** Goat Media. /// **Tools:** Flash, PHP. /// **Awards:** FWA (Site of the Day), Netscape Cool (Site of the Day), Webby Awards (Nomination). /// **Cost:** 200 hours.

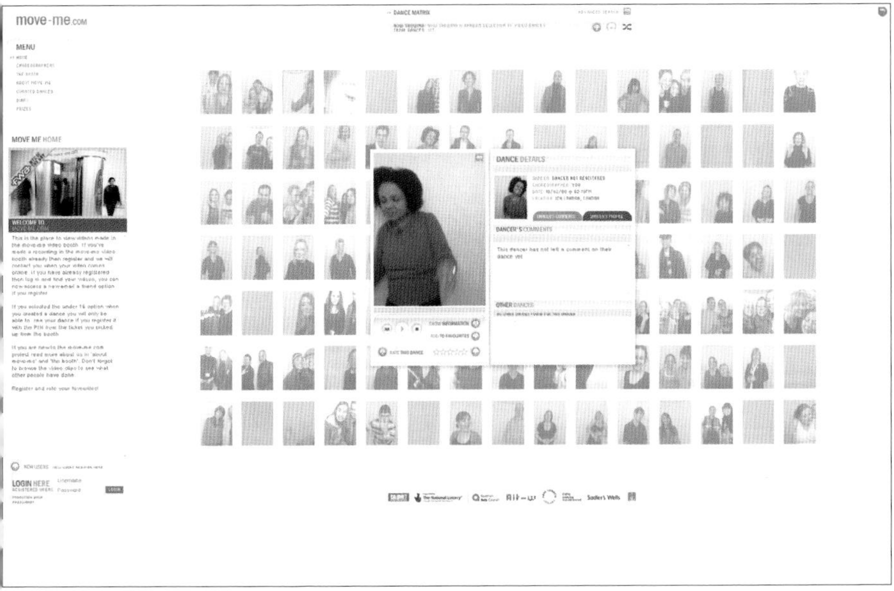

move-me.com
MENU
DANCE MATRIX
MOVE ME HOME
WELCOME TO
DANCE DETAILS
DANCER'S COMMENTS
This dancer has not left a comment on their dance yet
OTHER DANCES
NEW USERS
LOGIN HERE
Sadler's Wells

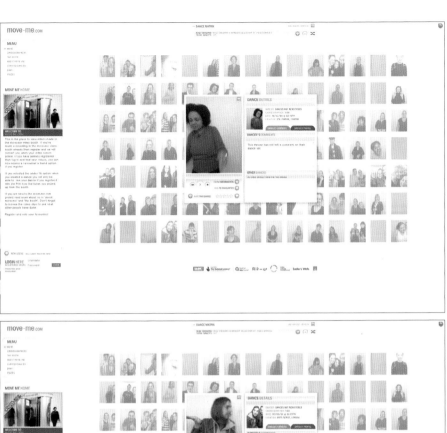

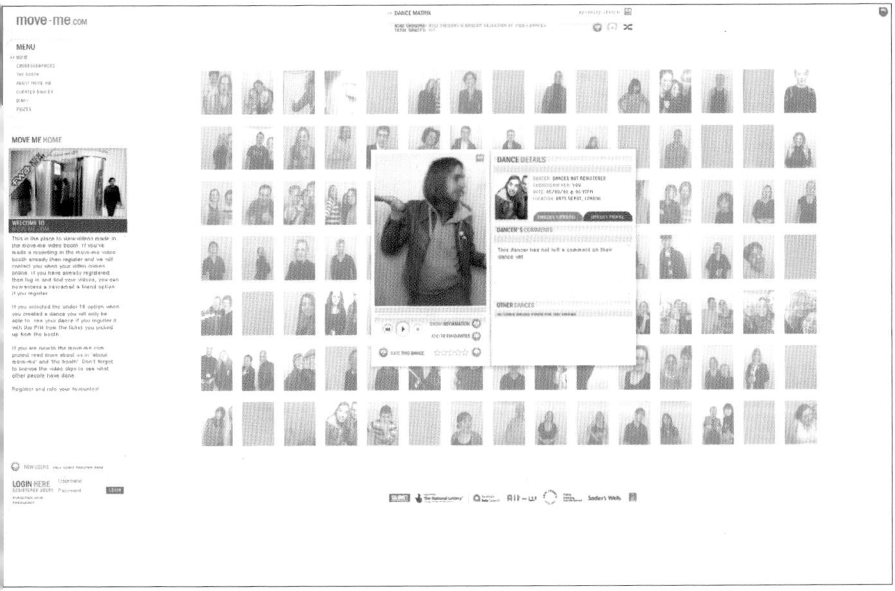

# MUSE – HAARP

SOUTH AFRICA

www.muselive.co.za

2008

Concept

An album promo site based around the live aspect of the release using full-screen video backgrounds on the Home and Videos sections. /// Eine Promosite für die CD, die um den Live-Aspekt des Releases herum aufgebaut ist und in den Bereichen *Home* und *Videos* mit bildschirmfüllenden Videohintergründen arbeitet. /// Un site de promotion d'album qui joue sur le fait qu'il s'agit d'un enregistrement en direct, avec de la vidéo en plein écran comme toile de fond pour les pages d'accueil et de vidéo.

Info

**DESIGN:** Prezence <www.prezence.co.za>: Wesley Reyneke. /// **PROGRAMMING:** Wesley Reyneke. /// **CLIENT:** Warner Music Gallo Africa. /// **TOOLS:** Photoshop, Flash. /// **COST:** 30 hours.

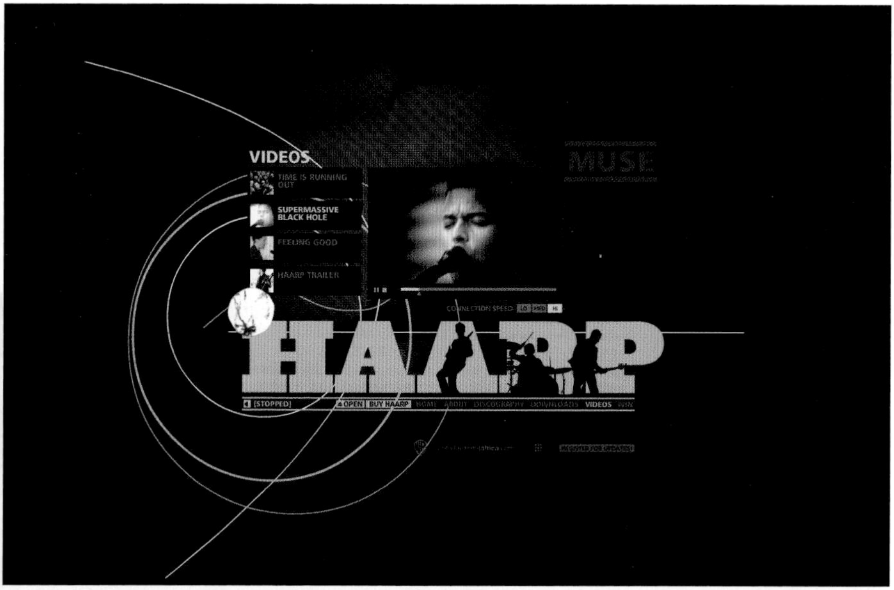
VIDEOS
TIME IS RUNNING OUT
SUPERMASSIVE BLACK HOLE
FEELING GOOD
HAARP TRAILER
MUSE
CONNECTION SPEED: LO MED HI
HAARP
[STOPPED]
OPEN
BUY HAARP
HOME
ABOUT
DISCOGRAPHY
DOWNLOADS
VIDEOS

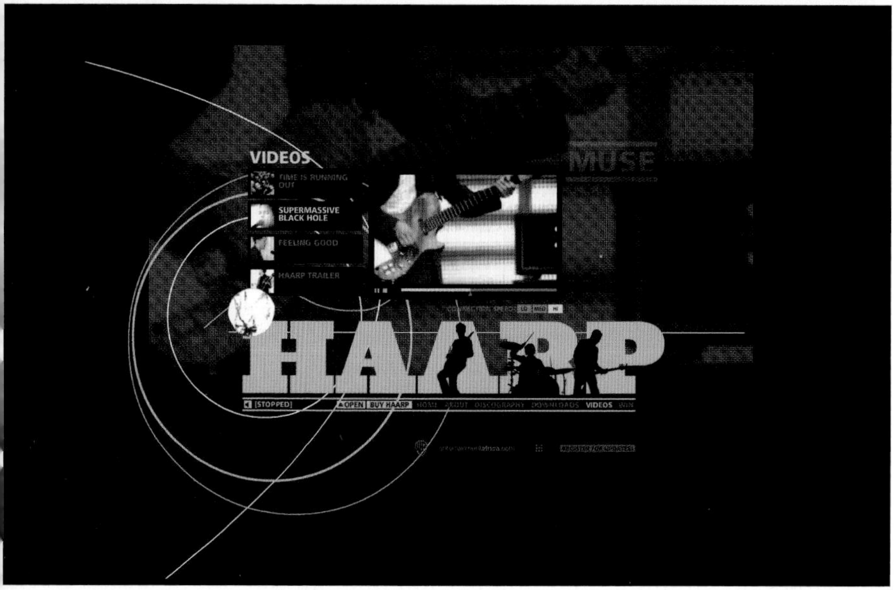
VIDEOS
TIME IS RUNNING OUT
SUPERMASSIVE BLACK HOLE
FEELING GOOD
HAARP TRAILER
MUSE
CONNECTION SPEED: LO MED HI
HAARP
[STOPPED]
OPEN
BUY HAARP
HOME
ABOUT
DISCOGRAPHY
DOWNLOADS
VIDEOS

# NEOGAMA BBH

BRAZIL

http://neogamabbh.com.br/#/pt/profile

2007

Concept

The NEOGAMA BBH office in São Paulo reflects the company's reputation for excellent design and art direction. The website shows details of the architecture and atmosphere in the agency. /// NEOGAMA BBH in São Paulo setzen auch in ihrem Büro den Ruf des Unternehmens um, ein hervorragendes Design und Art Direction zu bieten. Die Website zeigt Details der Architektur und die Atmosphäre in der Agentur. /// Les bureaux de NEOGAMA BBH à São Paulo reflètent l'excellente réputation que la société s'est forgée dans les domaines du design et de la direction artistique. Le site web montre des détails de l'architecture et de l'atmosphère de l'agence.

Info

**Design:** 14bits <http://14bits.com.br>: Andrei Gurgel, Marcio Ribas. /// **Programming:** Caio Chassot, Henrique Matias, Jayme Cavalcanti Neto, Rico Villas Boas. /// **Video:** Tiago Vassão. /// **Others:** Leo Beraldo (Photo). /// **Client:** NEOGAMA BBH. /// **Tools:** Flash. /// **Cost:** 700 hours.

NEOGAMA·BBH

**Porque uma ovelha negra como simbolo?**

Esta é uma agência com personalidade, crenças e prática de comunicação muito próprias. Tão próprias, que nosso logotipo é uma ovelha negra e nossa assinatura é "Se o mundo faz zig, faça zag".

Não se trata de ser do contra, mas sim de ser fiel a si mesmo, trilhando um caminho próprio e criativo sem nunca perder de vista as convicções que geraram a NEOGAMA e a BBH.

**Somos especialistas em posicionamento de**

CLIENTES NOVIDADES RESULTADOS PORTFOLIO PONTOS DE VISTA NEOGAMABBH CONTATO
PERFIL SERVIÇOS E EXPERTISE PRINCIPAIS EXECUTIVOS ESTRUTURA TRAJETÓRIA DEPOIMENTOS ARQUITETURA

NEOGAMA·BBH

**Porque uma ovelha negra como simbolo?**

Esta é uma agência com personalidade, crenças e prática de comunicação muito próprias. Tão próprias, que nosso logotipo é uma ovelha negra e nossa assinatura é "Se o mundo faz zig, faça zag".

Não se trata de ser do contra, mas sim de ser fiel a si mesmo, trilhando um caminho próprio e criativo sem nunca perder de vista as convicções que geraram a NEOGAMA e a BBH.

**Somos especialistas em posicionamento de**

CLIENTES NOVIDADES RESULTADOS PORTFOLIO PONTOS DE VISTA NEOGAMABBH CONTATO
PERFIL SERVIÇOS E EXPERTISE PRINCIPAIS EXECUTIVOS ESTRUTURA TRAJETÓRIA DEPOIMENTOS ARQUITETURA

# NIKE SOCCER TAPE

USA

www.nikesoccer.com/tape

2003

Concept

The Soccer Tape campaign website for Nike USA, created in association with Odopod and Wieden + Kennedy. /// Die Website von Nike USA für die Kampagne „Soccer Tape“ wurde zusammen mit Odopod und Wieden + Kennedy erstellt. /// Le site web de la campagne Soccer Tape de Nike USA a été créé en association avec Odopod et Wieden + Kennedy.

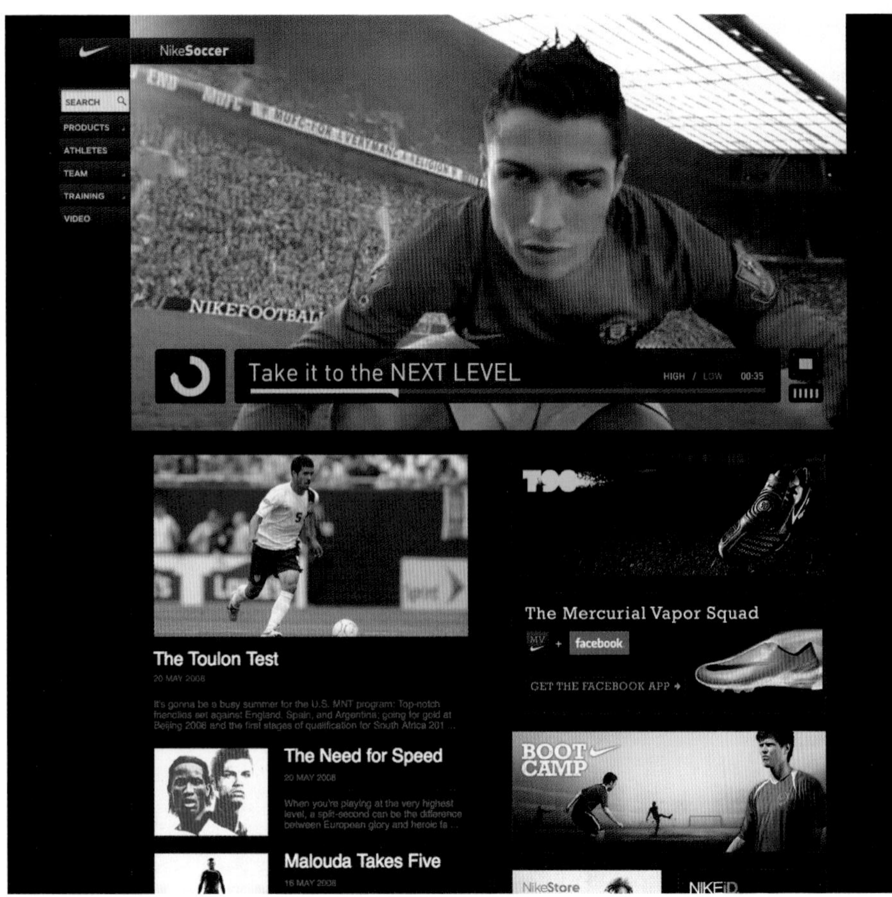


Info

**DESIGN:** Ever Growing Studio <www.evergrowing.net>: Arron Bleasdale. /// **PROGRAMMING:** Josh On. /// **VIDEO:** Wieden + Kennedy. /// **OTHERS:** Arron Bleasdale (Photo). /// **CLIENT:** Nike. /// **TOOLS:** Photoshop, Illustrator, Flash, Final Cut Pro, After Effects, JavaScript, PHP, HTML, ActionScript. /// **AWARDS:** Communication Arts, Macromedia (Site of the Day). /// **COST:** 300 hours.

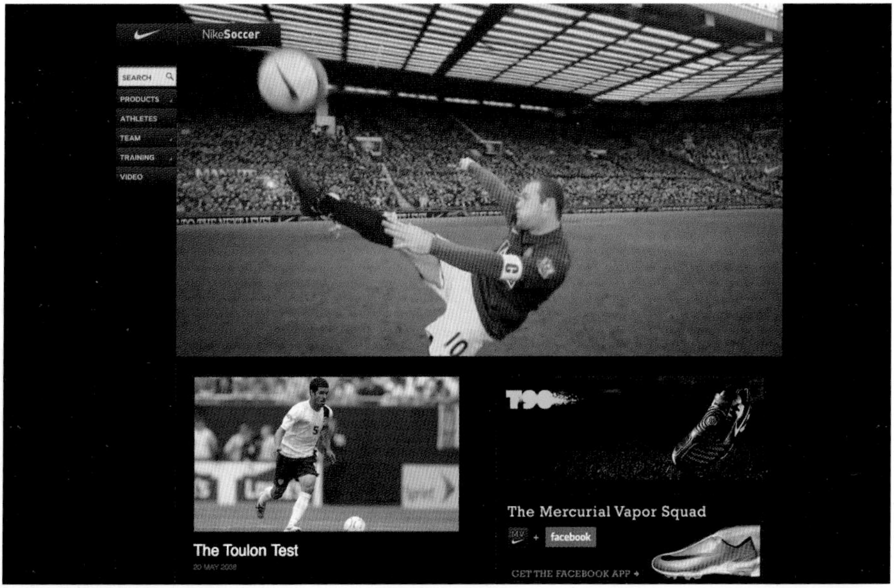

NikeSoccer

SEARCH
PRODUCTS
ATHLETES
TEAM
TRAINING
VIDEO

The Toulon Test
20 MAY 2008

T90

The Mercurial Vapor Squad
MV + facebook
GET THE FACEBOOK APP →

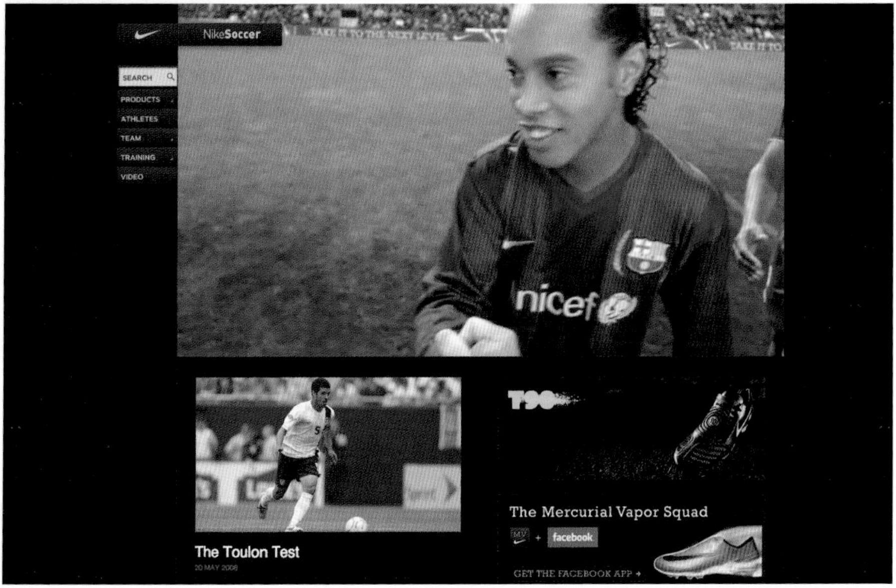

NikeSoccer

SEARCH
PRODUCTS
ATHLETES
TEAM
TRAINING
VIDEO

The Toulon Test
20 MAY 2008

T90

The Mercurial Vapor Squad
MV + facebook
GET THE FACEBOOK APP →

# NOKIA N95 VIDEO PLAYLIST SOUTH AFRICA

www.entertainmentafrica.com/index.php?video_jukebox=nokia 2007

Concept

The Video Playlist (Jukebox) on EntertainmentAfrica.com redesigned to look and work like a Nokia N95 handset where all videos viewed by users during the promotional period would play through the virtual phone. /// Die Abspielliste der Video Jukebox auf EntertainmentAfrica.com wurde neu gestaltet, damit sie wie ein Nokia N95 aussieht und bedienbar ist. Alle von den Usern während der Werbephase betrachteten Videos werden über das virtuelle Handy abgespielt. /// La Video Playlist (Jukebox) d'EntertainmentAfrica.com a été remodelée de façon à ressembler à un téléphone Nokia N95. Pendant la période promotionnelle, les utilisateurs ont visionné toutes les vidéos sur ce téléphone virtuel.

Info

**DESIGN:** Prezence <www.prezence.co.za>: Neil Aves. /// **PROGRAMMING:** Neil Aves. /// **CLIENT:** Nokia. /// **TOOLS:** Photoshop, Flash. /// **COST:** 8 hours.

3 MERCY BY DUFFY
4 THE LOOK OF LOVE MADISON PARI
5 NEW YORK GIRLS BY MORNINGWO
6 ALL THIS BEAUTY BY THE WEEPIES
7 I LIKE THE WAY BY KASKADE
8 AMAZING LIFE BY JEM
9 HOW DEEP IS YOUR LOVE BY THE B
10 THE HEART OF THE MATTER BY INI
CHART LEGEND
Charlie Sheen marries again Actor Charlie Sheen has now married his fiancé Brooke Mueller in a intimate private Los Angeles ceremony.
50 Cent's house burns down The mansion that 50 Cent and his ex girlfriend are fighting over suspiciously burnt down but no one
DON KING PRESENTS PRIZE FIGHTER
Don King Presents: Prizefighter soundtrack announced 2K Sports announced today the artists featured in the soundtrack and ring
Liv Tyler prepared for 'Hulk' role by giving birth Actress Liv Tyler claims that giving
Ashlee Simpson-Wentz cancels tour dates Ashlee Simpson- Wentz has announced that she
Enemey Territory: Quake Wars for consoles Set in the year 2065, 'Enemy Territory:
Yves Saint Laurent dies Iconic fashion designer Yves Saint Laurent has passed away after an
Kaiser Chiefs loved working with Mark Ronson Kaiser Chief is proud to have had super
XBLA game not what we imagined hearing its name 'Double D Dodgeball' is in fact an
David Beckham the sexiest man David Beckham has been voted the sexiest man
Kurt Cobain's ashes stolen The late legendary rocker Kurt Cobain's ashes have
Raving Rabbids party hearty with the Wii Balance Board Ubisoft have announced the
PREV NEXT 4 / 5285 ALL
PREV NEXT 4 / 6881 ALL
PREV NEXT 4 / 1244 ALL
STOP PIRACY CLICK HERE TO REPORT PIRACY, DONT SUPPORT IT!
MUSIC OUT NOW
MOVIES OUT NOW
GADGETS COOL STUFF
Just Me R&B icon Keith Sweat keeps it comin' with 'Just Me', his debut album for Atco and his first studio
Sex and The City: The Movie As Carrie Bradshaw plans her long-anticipated wedding to Mr. Big with
RoboReptile A highly interactive, seeing and hearing cyber-reptilian, Roboreptile is one of the most
The Best of 'Radiohead: The Best of' is a compilation album by English
El Cantante El Cantante is about legendary Puerto Rican salsa singer Hector Lavoe, a
Emergency Light - UltraTec The Ultratech Emergence/Camping light has a large & bright
Payment of Existence 'Payment of Existence' is the third full length album by Norwegian
Rogue An idyllic wildlife cruise disintegrates into terror when a party of tourists are
Everlight - Twist Torches The world novelty, EVERLight "Twist" amazes through
PREV NEXT 3 / 2164 ALL
PREV NEXT 3 / 56 ALL
PREV NEXT 3 / 386 ALL
MUSIC PROMOS
MOVIES PROMOS
COMPETITIONS WIN!
Lenny Kravitz: It Is Time For A Love
The Spiderwick Chronicles Play the
Carte Blanche Cool Earth DVD Give-aways
Colbie Caillat Take a listen to Coibi Caillat's
First Sunday Win DVD's with exclusive movie
Win with Warner and Lock and Load!
One Republic Catch the fireflies and stand a
Made Of Honor Win 1 of 2 Made Of Honor
Win a copy of the PS3 exclusive 'Haze'
Atom : Famous Atom brings you their latest
21 Win a Sony Playback Walkman for you and a
Win with Hed Kandi and Just Music
PREV NEXT 4 / 155 ALL
PREV NEXT 4 / 94 ALL
PREV NEXT 4 / 5 ALL
VIDEO PLAYLIST SPONSORED BY NOKIA N95
Video Playlist
Forgetting Sarah
Definitely Maybe
Counterfeiters
Be Kind Rewind
Race Driver GRID
Tzozo en Professor and
Win a N95!
N95 Features
Win a Nokia N95!
Click to View Features
brought to you by
Telkom Media
prezencesouthafrica MUSIC | MOVIES | GAMES | GADGETS | EVENTS | COMPETITIONS | REGISTER | MY PROFILE
For any web related queries, please contact us at: info@entertainmentafrica.co.za
Copyright © 2008 EntertainmentAfrica.com. Reproduction without permission is prohibited. All rights reserved.
STOP PIRACY
STER-KINEKOR MOBILE
WATCH TRAILERS
CLICK HERE TO GET IT!

# RELEARN TO DRIVE

USA

www.relearntodrive.com

2007

Concept

The Relearn to Drive section of the site is unbranded and designed to peak users' interest before revealing BMW's association. The Performance Center section features videos of driving instructors, course footage and customer testimonials. /// Im Bereich *Relearn to Drive* dieser Website ist die Marke nicht erkennbar. So wird erst das Interesse des Users angestachelt, bevor der Zusammenhang mit BMW erkennbar wird. Im Abschnitt *Performance Center* werden Videos mit Fahrlehrern, Aufnahmen der Strecke und Kundenempfehlungen gezeigt. /// La page Relearn to Drive du site ne porte pas de marque, et est conçue pour piquer l'intérêt des visiteurs avant de révéler la participation de BMW. La page Performance Center présente des vidéos de professeurs de conduite, de cours et de témoignages de clients.

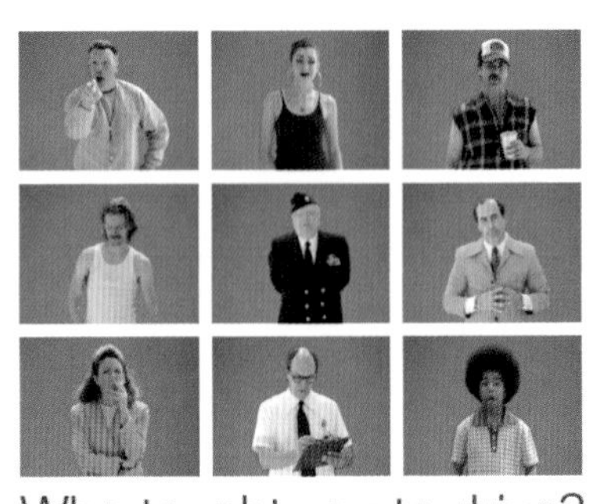
Who taught you to drive?
Undo the damage.

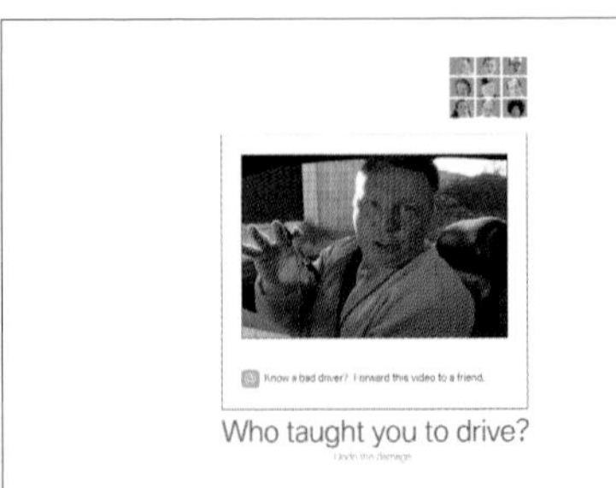
Who taught you to drive?

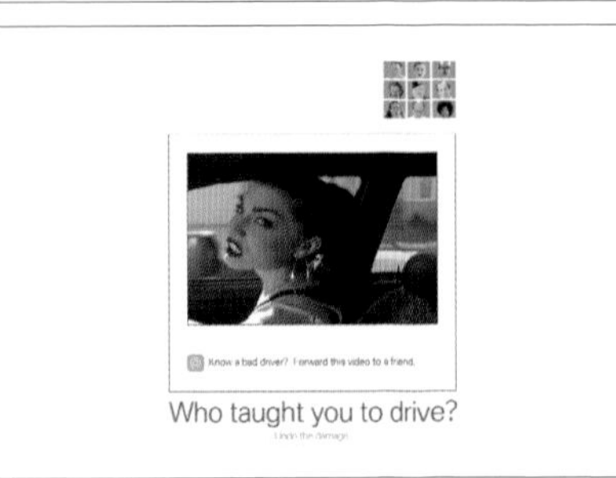
Who taught you to drive?

Info

**Design:** JUXT Interactive <www.juxtinteractive.com>: Mark Ray, Chad Laughlin, Scott Staab, Ryan Martindale, Aaron Kovan, Jeff Bond, Kelly Harris, Nick Gesualdi, Lani DeGuire. /// **Programming:** Justin Bernard, Victor Allen, Khanh Ngyuen, Eric Lim, Todd Purgason. /// **Video:** GSD&M/Idea City. /// **Client:** BMW. /// **Tools:** Flash, Maya, Final Cut, After Effects. /// **Awards:** Gold Addy, Effie, Webby Award (Finalist), Pixel Award (Finalist), Communications Arts (Site of the Week). /// **Cost:** 500 hours.

Know a bad driver? Forward this video to a friend.

Who taught you to drive?

Undo the damage.

Know a bad driver? Forward this video to a friend.

Who taught you to drive?

Undo the damage.

# REXONA MILLION BALL

AUSTRALIA

www.rickysmillionballmission.com

2008

Concept

**Test your ball skills against the iconic captain of the Australian cricket team, Ricky Ponting, while you register for your free ball. ///** Messen Sie Ihre Ballfähigkeiten gegen Ricky Ponting, den Kult-Captain des australischen Cricket-Teams, und registrieren Sie sich, um einen kostenlosen Ball zu bekommen. /// **Testez vos talents face à l'emblématique capitaine de l'équipe australienne de cricket, Ricky Ponting, et profitez-en pour obtenir une balle gratuite.**

Info

**DESIGN:** Soap Creative <www.soap.com.au>: Robert Dennis, Bradley Eldridge. /// **PROGRAMMING:** Shane McCartney. /// **VIDEO:** Darren Bailey, Patrick Cook. /// **OTHERS:** Ross Raeburn (Strategy); Sarah Ford (Client); Naked (Offline Concept). /// **CLIENT:** FOXTEL. /// **TOOLS:** Flash, After Effects, Photoshop, Illustrator. /// **COST:** 4 weeks.

Yes I did, I am on a mission to give away a million balls to get guys sweating more.
SKIP >

0,988,594
REXONA BALLS DELIVERED

RICKY'S MISSION STATEMENT
GET YOUR HANDS ON A BALL
REXONA MENS RANGE
CAMPAIGN UPDATE
BEHIND THE SCENES
TELL A FRIEND
Rexona MEN
BEHIND THE SCENES
MISSION LAUNCH
Day: 1
Ricky's Idea
Rexona MEN

# RINASCIMENTO

ITALY

www.rinascimento.info

2008

Concept

A fashion website full of videos to be enjoyed. /// Eine Website voller Mode-Videos. /// Un site web de mode qui regorge de vidéos.

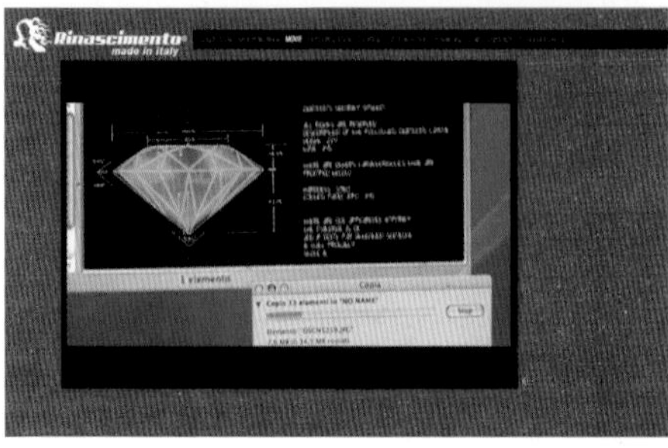

Info

**Design:** Extera <www.extera.com>. /// **Programming:** Extera. /// **Video:** Thomas Cicognani. /// **Client:** Teddy. /// **Tools:** Flash, Javascript, ASP, CSS.

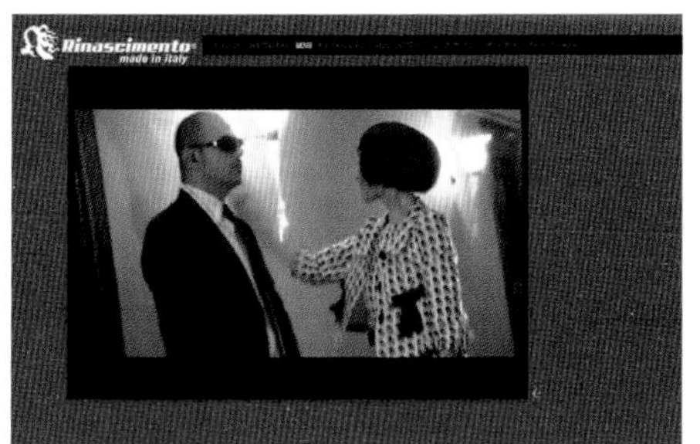

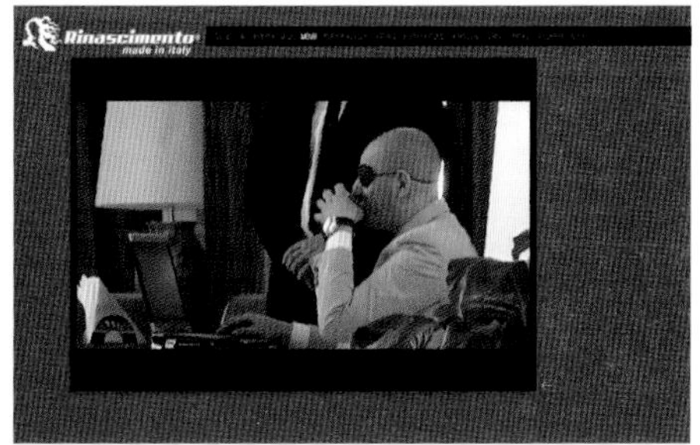

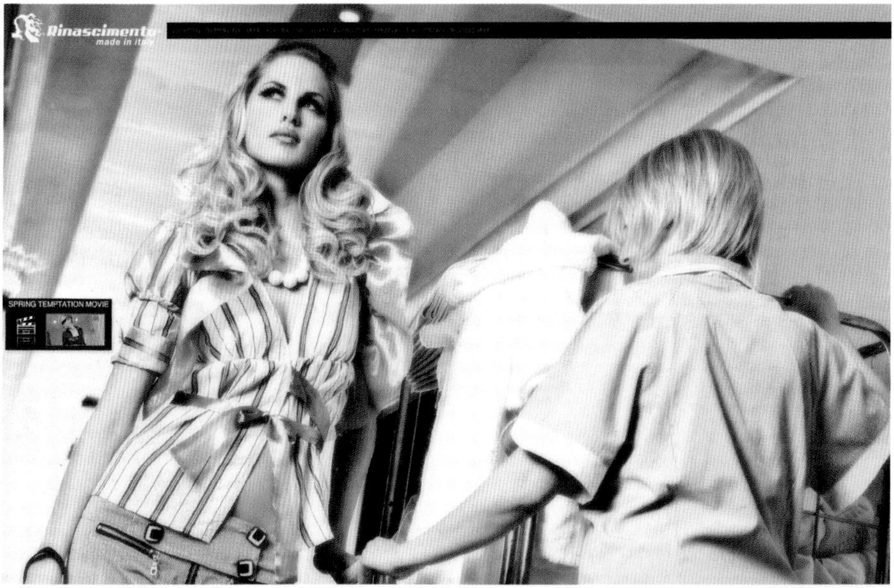

Rinascimento
made in italy
Rinascimento
made in italy
Rinascimento
made in italy
SPRING TEMPTATION MOVIE
Rinascimento
made in italy
Rinascimento
made in italy

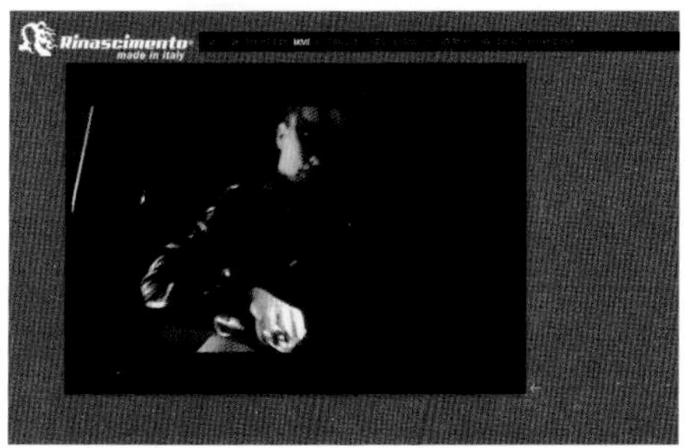

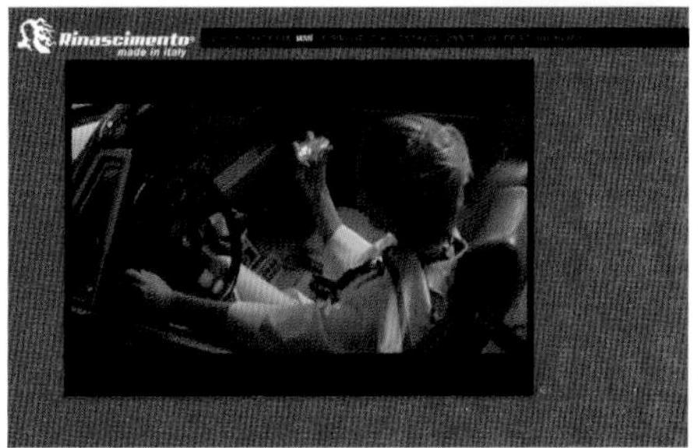

# SAAB 60 YEARS

WORLDWIDE

www.saab.com/microsites/60years/GLOBAL/en/index2.shtml

2007

Concept

**Celebrating Saab's 60th anniversary, it seemed appropriate to pause briefly and take a look back over the decades, and see just where all the company's great innovations have come from.** /// Für den 60. Geburtstag von Saab besann man sich und warf einen Blick auf die vergangenen Jahrzehnte, um zu schauen, woher all die großartigen Innovationen der Firma stammen. /// **Pour le 60e anniversaire de Saab, il semblait approprié de faire une courte pause pour contempler les décennies écoulées, et connaître ainsi l'origine des grandes innovations de l'entreprise.**

Info

**DESIGN:** Lowe Brindfors <www.lowebrindfors.se>: Magnus Wretblad (Creative Director); Rickard Villard, Jakob Swedenborg, Pelle Lundquist, Niklas Wallberg (Art Directors); Perfect Fools <www.perfectfools.com>: Tony Högqvist (Creative Director). /// **PROGRAMMING:** Perfect Fools: Björn Kummeneje (Techl Director). /// **VIDEO:** Kalle Haglund. /// **OTHERS:** Perfect Fools: Fredrik Heghammar (Producer); Lowe Brindfors: Espen Bekkebråten, Jens Odelbring, Johanna Hibbs, Anna Axelsson; Open Communications, Per Sundin (Copy). /// **CLIENT:** Saab Automobile. /// **TOOLS:** Flash. /// **AWARDS:** Swedish Golden Eggs (Silver).

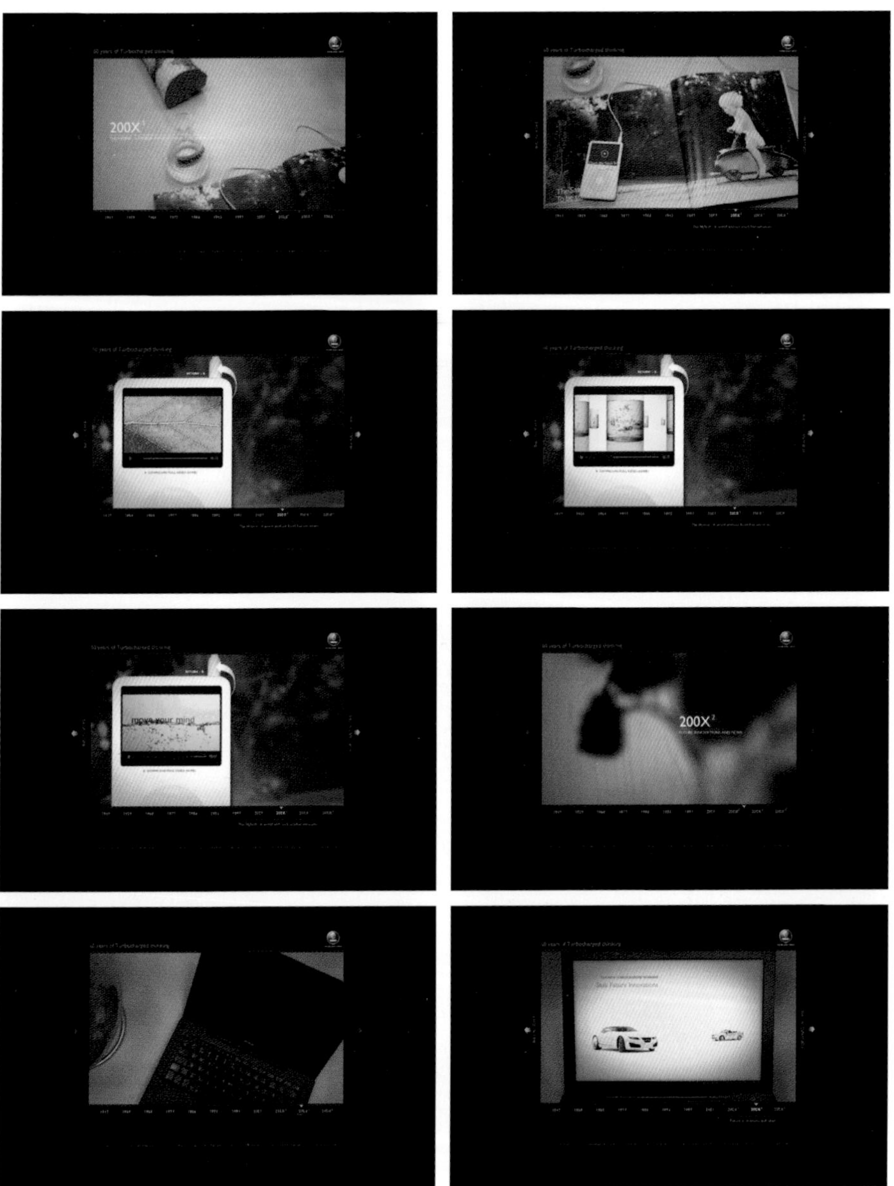

# SAAB PILOTS WANTED

WORLDWIDE

www.saab.com/microsites/pilotswanted/GLOBAL/en/index2.shtml

2006

Concept

What would happen if you combined an airfield of red-hot Saabs with Saab's 5-man Performance Team? This site is packed with fast-paced video, and the Saab Pilots Wanted campaign lets visitors test drive a new Saab with impressive realism. /// Was würde passieren, wenn Sie ein ganzes Flugfeld brandaktueller Saabs mit dem 5-Mann-Performance-Team von Saab kombinieren? Diese Site steckt voller temporeicher Videos. Bei der Kampagne *Saab Pilots Wanted* machen Besucher eine beeindruckend realistische Testfahrt mit einem neuen Saab. /// Que se passerait-il si l'on combinait un terrain d'aviation, des Saab d'un rouge torride et les 5 membres de l'équipe Performance de Saab ? Ce site est rempli de vidéos au rythme effréné, et la campagne Saab Pilots Wanted permet aux visiteurs de tester une nouvelle Saab avec un réalisme impressionnant.

Info

**Design:** Lowe Brindfors <www.lowebrindfors.se>: Niklas Wallberg (Creative Director); Tim Sheibel, Johan Tesch (Art Directors); Michael Fox (Head of Art); Alex Kerber (Assistant); Mårten Ivert (Director); Perfect Fools <www.perfectfools.com>: Tony Högqvist (Creative Director). /// **Programming:** Perfect Fools: Björn Kummeneje (Tech Director). /// **Video:** Mårten Ivert (Director). /// **Others:** Perfect Fools: Stefan Dufgran, Fredrik Heghammar (Producers); Lowe Brindfors: Johanna Hibbs, Linda Karlsson, Espen Bekkebråten, Patrick O'Neill. /// **Client:** Saab Automobile. /// **Tools:** Flash. /// **Awards:** Cannes Cyber Lion (Bronze), New York Festivals (Silver), Eurobest (Bronze), Clio (Shortlist).

HOME
TEST PILOT
EVENTS
BOOK TEST-DRIVE
PERFORMANCE TEAM
ICE EXPERIENCE
REAR CAMERA
FRONT
COCKPIT
SIDE
REAR
NOSE-TO-NOSE
318 METERS
move your mind

HOME
TEST PILOT
EVENTS
BOOK TEST-DRIVE
PERFORMANCE TEAM
ICE EXPERIENCE
REAR CAMERA
FRONT
COCKPIT
SIDE
REAR
CHASE
438 METERS
move your mind

# SAMSON & ARMSTRONG

UK

www.samsonandarmstrong.com

2008

Concept

The project briefing was a viral animation campaign — a series of short animations created for online promotion. /// Im Briefing für dieses Projekt wurde eine virale Kampagne mit Animation gefordert – eine Serie kurzer Trickfilme, die als Online-Werbung erstellt wurden. /// Le client voulait une campagne virale composée d'une série de courts-métrages d'animation créés pour la promotion sur Internet.

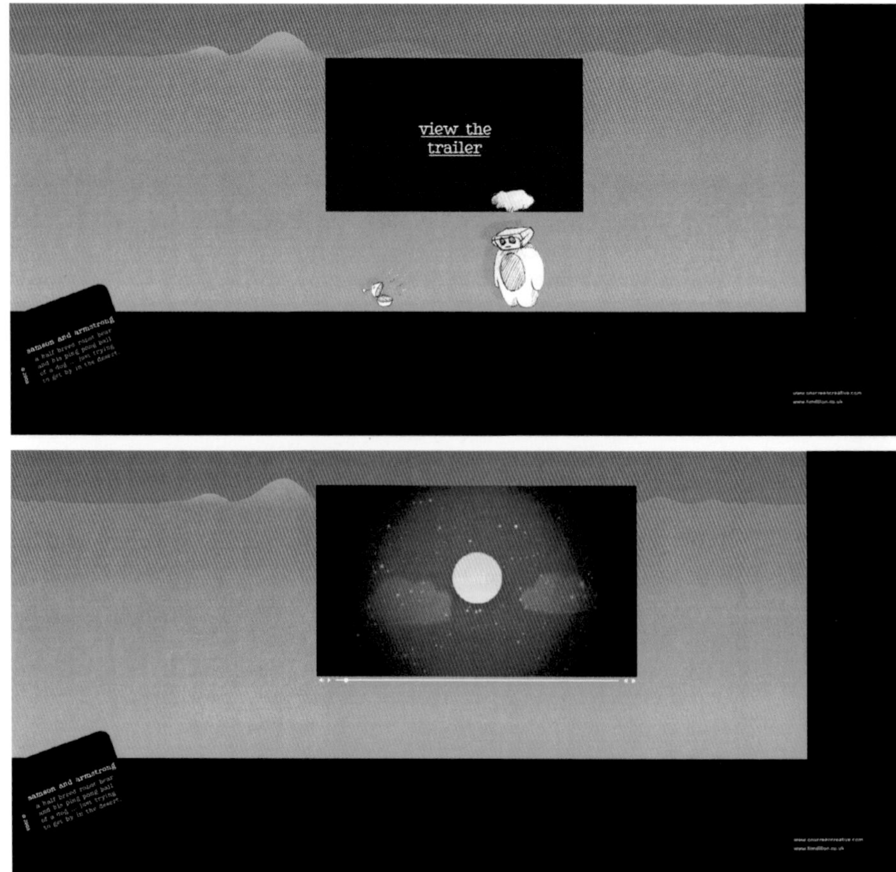


Info

**DESIGN:** Onscreen Creative <www.onscreencreative.com>: Tim Dillon. /// **CLIENT:** Onscreen Creative. /// **TOOLS:** After Effects, Flash, HTML, Photoshop, Illustrator.

a half breed
robot bear ...

and his ping pong
ball of a dog ...

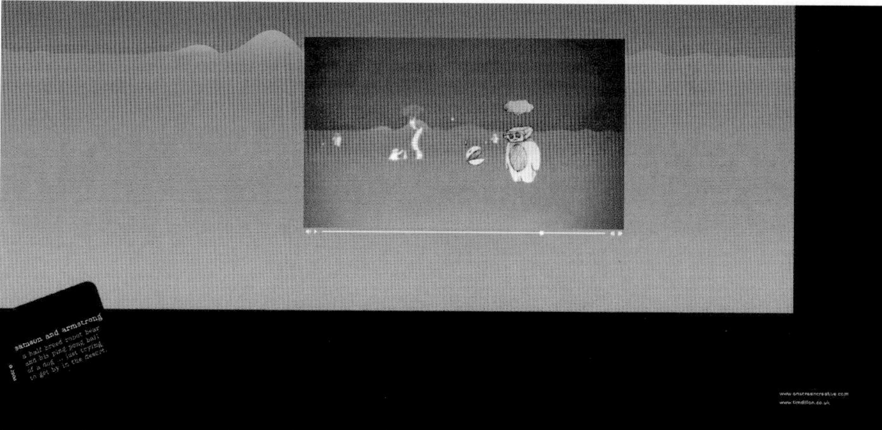
samson and armstrong
a half breed robot bear
and his ping pong ball
of a dog ... just trying
to get by in the desert.
www.onscreencreative.com
www.timdillon.co.uk

samson &
armstrong
coming soon
samson and armstrong
a half breed robot bear
and his ping pong ball
of a dog ... just trying
to get by in the desert.
www.onscreencreative.com
www.timdillon.co.uk

# SAMSUNG - HIGHLIFE

FRANCE

www.highlife.fr

2007

Concept

**This project wanted the user to imagine the future at home with the whole Samsung digital experience.** /// Bei diesem Projekt soll sich der User ausmalen, wie sein Zuhause in der Zukunft mit dem gesamten digitalen Angebot von Samsung gestaltet werden kann. /// **Pour ce projet, on voulait que le visiteur imagine son foyer doté de tout l'équipement numérique Samsung.**

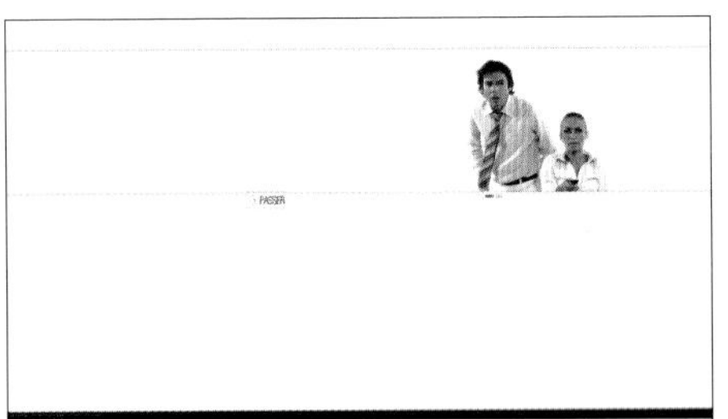

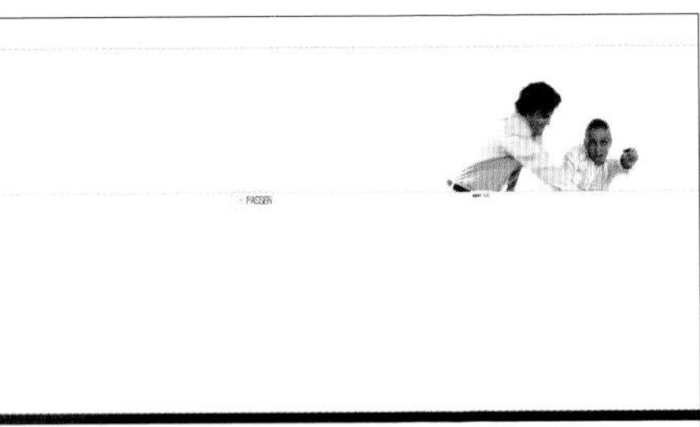

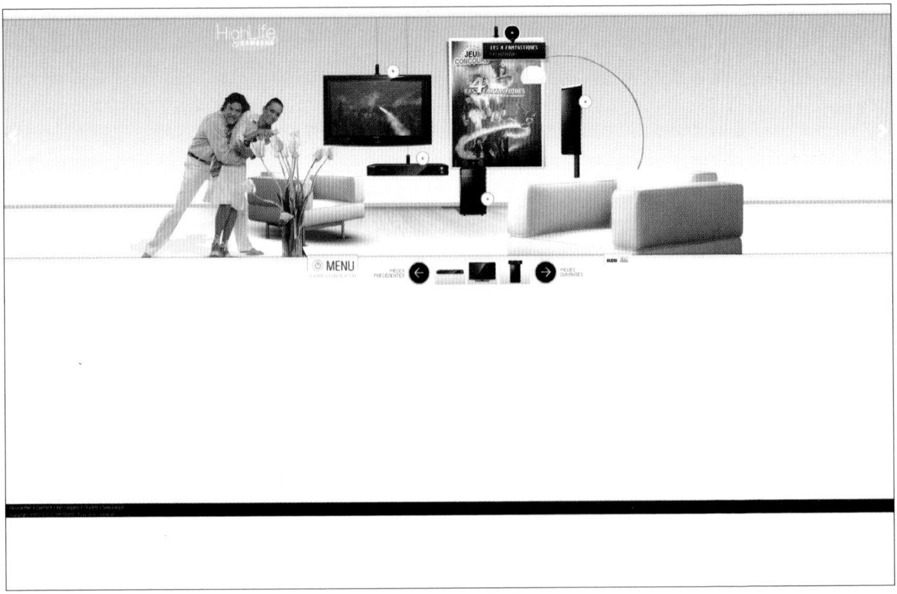

Info

**DESIGN:** Soleil Noir <www.soleilnoir.net>. /// **CLIENT:** Samsung Electronic France. /// **TOOLS:** Photoshop, Flash, After Effects. /// **AWARDS:** FWA (Site of the Day). /// **COST:** 3 months.

XBOX 360 LIVE
Vivez l'expérience HD !
MENU

ECOVER
JEU CONCOURS
MENU

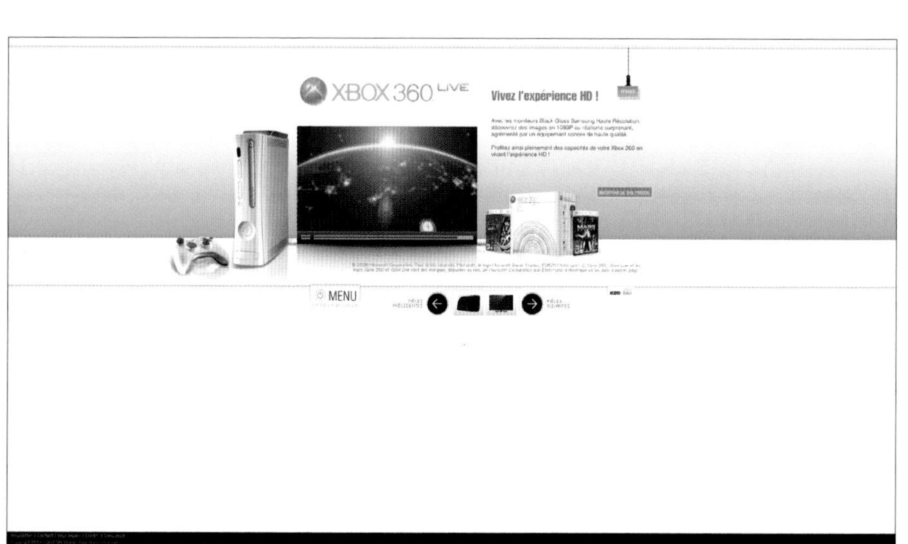

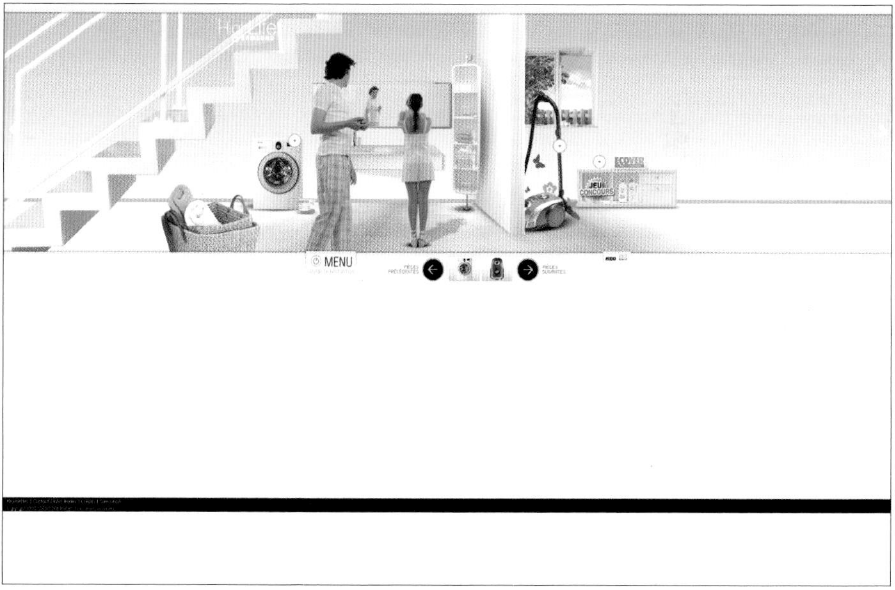

# SEARS WISECRACK WEED

USA

http://www.pointroll.com/PointRoll/AdDemo/DomaniTests/300x250_weed_v3Md47.asp

2008

Concept

The weed responds, via conditional video, according to how you interact with the banner and the lawn tool that you select to destroy him. /// Das Unkraut reagiert mit situationsabhängigen Videoclips darauf, wie Sie mit dem Banner und dem Rasenmäher umgehen, die Sie zur Unkrautvernichtung gewählt haben. /// La mauvaise herbe vous répond par le truchement de vidéos qui s'adaptent à la façon dont vous interagissez avec le bandeau et à l'outil de jardinage que vous choisissez pour la détruire.

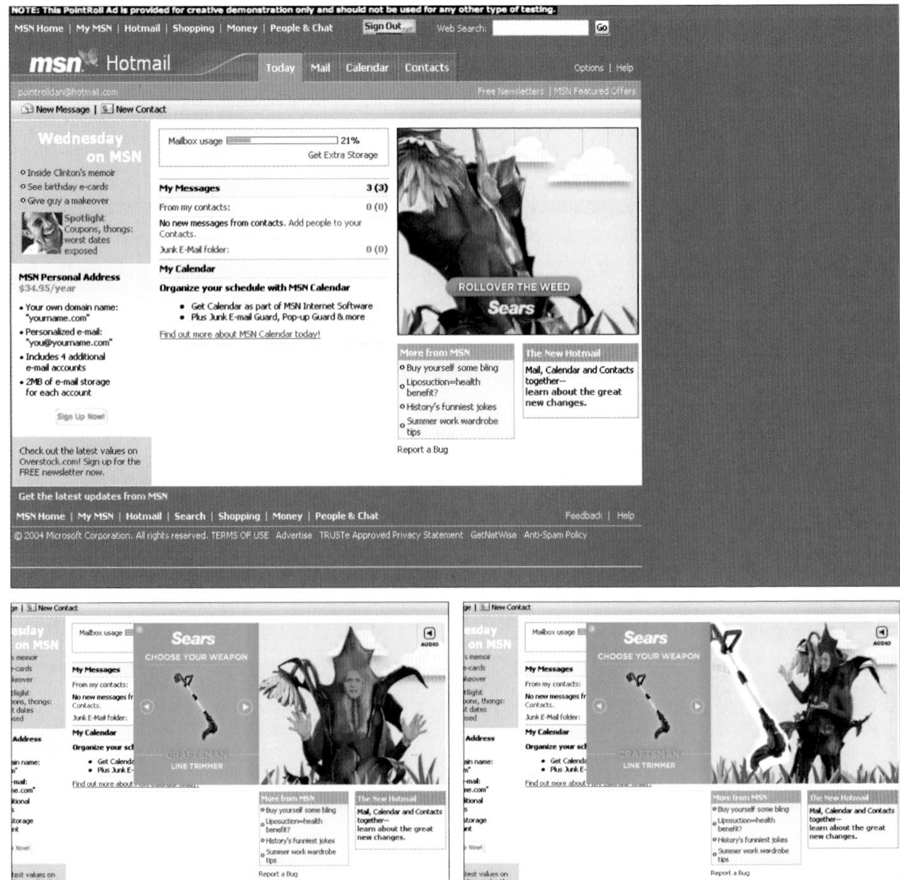


Info

**Design:** Domani Studios <http://domanistudios.com>. /// **Client:** Y&R; Sears. /// **Tools:** Flash, FCP, After Effects, Photoshop.

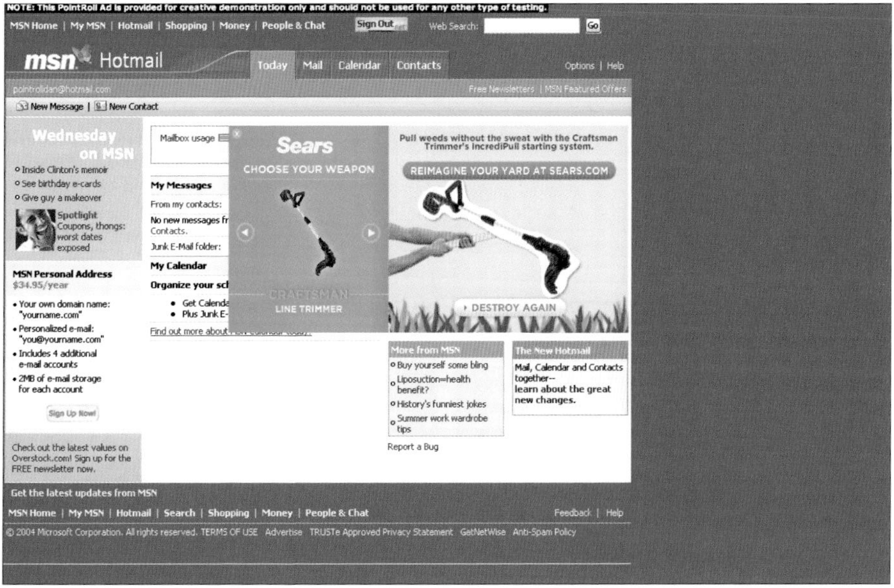

NOTE: This PointRoll Ad is provided for creative demonstration only and should not be used for any other type of testing.

MSN Home | My MSN | Hotmail | Shopping | Money | People & Chat

Sign Out

Web Search: Go

msn Hotmail

Today Mail Calendar Contacts

Options | Help

pointrolldan@hotmail.com

Free Newsletters | MSN Featured Offers

New Message | New Contact

Wednesday on MSN

- Inside Clinton's memoir
- See birthday e-cards
- Give guy a makeover

Spotlight
Coupons, thongs: worst dates exposed

MSN Personal Address
$34.95/year

- Your own domain name: "yourname.com"
- Personalized e-mail: "you@yourname.com"
- Includes 4 additional e-mail accounts
- 2MB of e-mail storage for each account

Sign Up Now!

Check out the latest values on Overstock.com! Sign up for the FREE newsletter now.

Mailbox usage

My Messages

From my contacts:

No new messages fr
Contacts.

Junk E-Mail folder:

My Calendar

Organize your sc

- Get Calenda
- Plus Junk E-

Find out more about

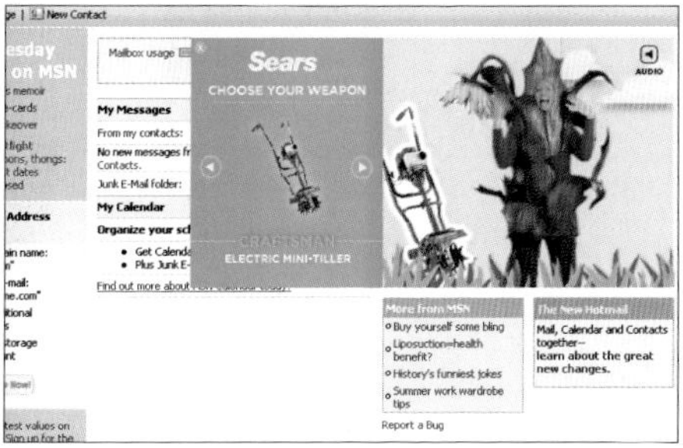

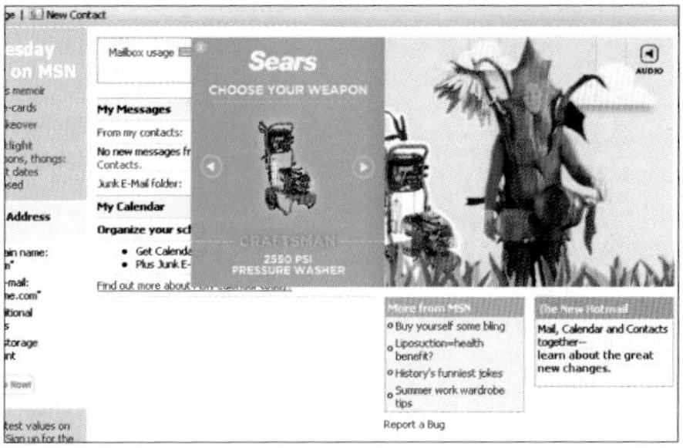

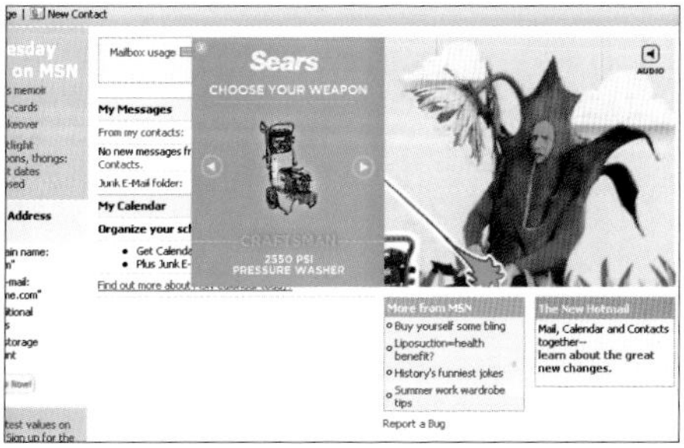

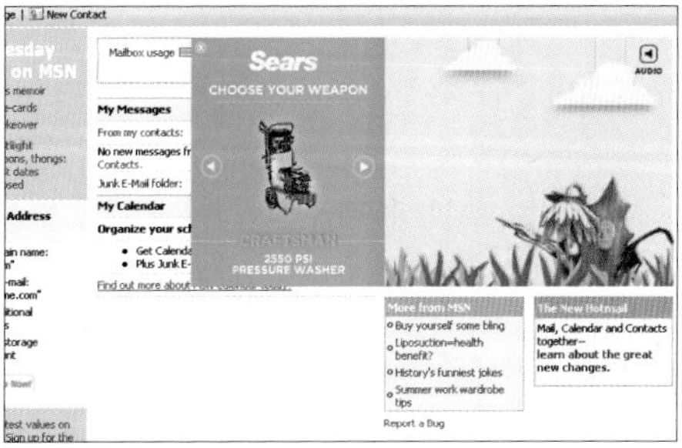

Sears
CHOOSE YOUR WEAPON
CRAFTSMAN
LINE TRIMMER

Pull weeds without the sweat with the Craftsman Trimmer's IncrediPull starting system.

REIMAGINE YOUR YARD AT SEARS.COM

DESTROY AGAIN

More from MSN

- Buy yourself some bling
- Liposuction=health benefit?
- History's funniest jokes
- Summer work wardrobe tips

The New Hotmail

Mail, Calendar and Contacts together--
learn about the great new changes.

Report a Bug

Get the latest updates from MSN

MSN Home | My MSN | Hotmail | Search | Shopping | Money | People & Chat

Feedback | Help

© 2004 Microsoft Corporation. All rights reserved. TERMS OF USE Advertise TRUSTe Approved Privacy Statement GetNetWise Anti-Spam Policy

# SEGA LABS – FULL AUTO

USA

www.segalabs.com

2006

Concept

Campaign website for Sega's award-winning Xbox 360 game "Full Auto". The site features six highly-explosive films created and directed by Mekanism. /// Die Website für die Kampagne von Sega für das Xbox 360 Spiel „Full Auto". Auf der Site werden sechs höchst explosive Filme unter der Regie von Mekanism vorgestellt. /// Site web publicitaire pour le jeu primé « Full Auto » de Sega pour la Xbox 360. Le site présente six films explosifs créés et réalisés par Mekanism.

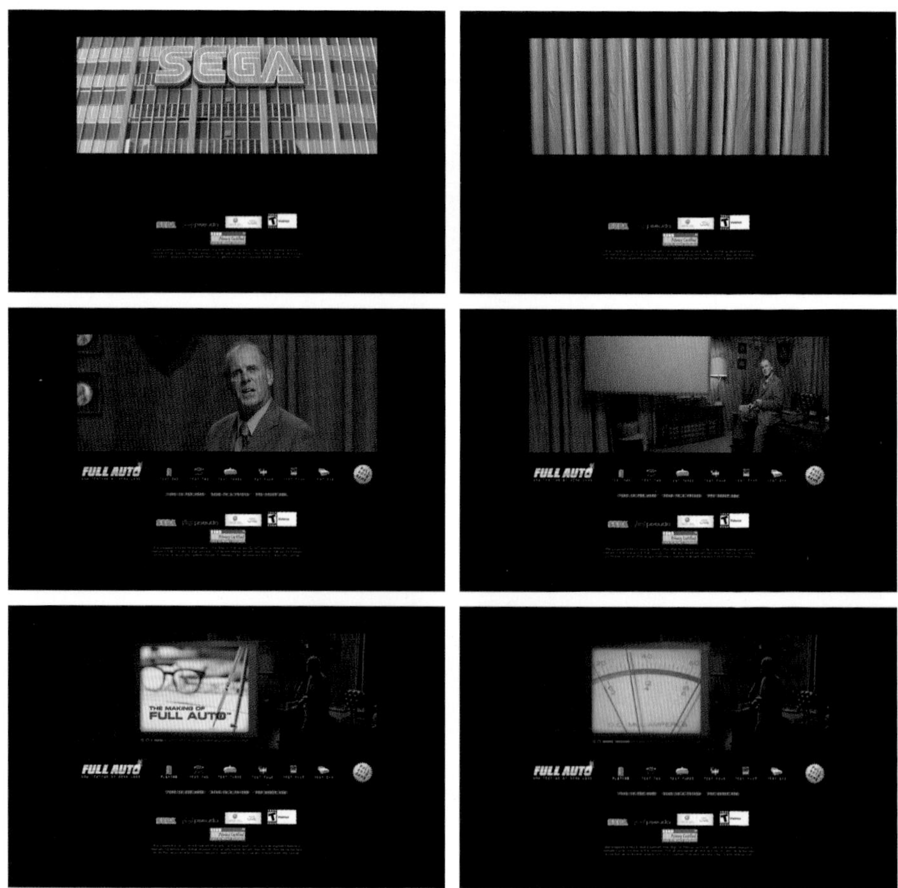


Info

**Design:** Ever Growing Studio <www.evergrowing.net>: Arron Bleasdale. /// **Programming:** Michael Kosacki. /// **Video:** Tommy Means, Ian Kovalik (Mekanism). /// **Client:** Sega. /// **Tools:** Photoshop, Flash, Final Cut Pro, After Effects, JavaScript, PHP, HTML, ActionScript. /// **Awards:** One Show Interactive (Viral and Email), Clio. /// **Cost:** 300 hours.

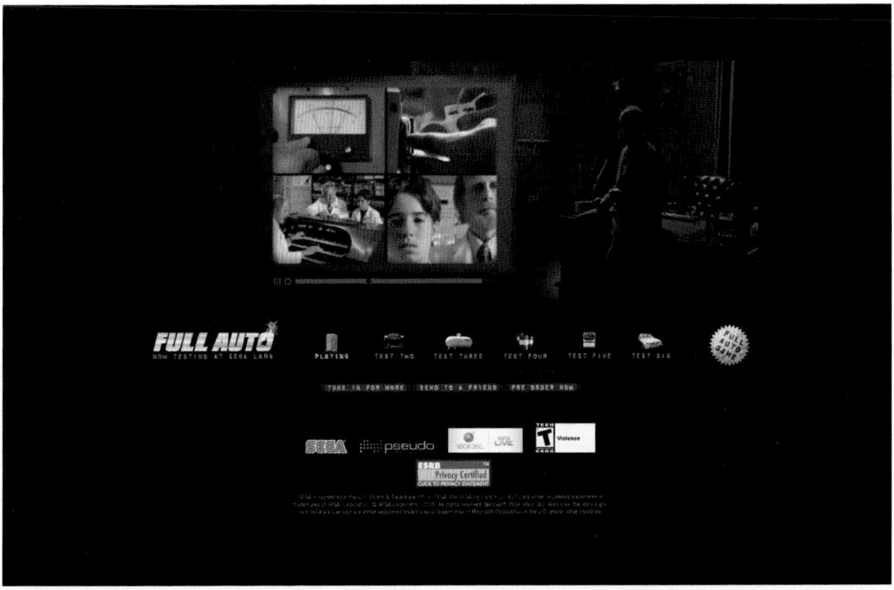

FULL AUTO
NOW TESTING AT SEGA LABS
PLAYING
TEST TWO
TEST THREE
TEST FOUR
TEST FIVE
TEST SIX
FULL AUTO GAME
TUNE IN FOR MORE
SEND TO A FRIEND
PRE-ORDER NOW
SEGA
pseudo
XBOX 360
XBOX LIVE
TEEN
T
ESRB
Violence
ESRB
Privacy Certified
CLICK TO PRIVACY STATEMENT

SEGA LABS
FULL AUTO

FULL AUTO

episode 2
THE SOUND OF
DESTRUCTION
FULL AUTO

FULL AUTO

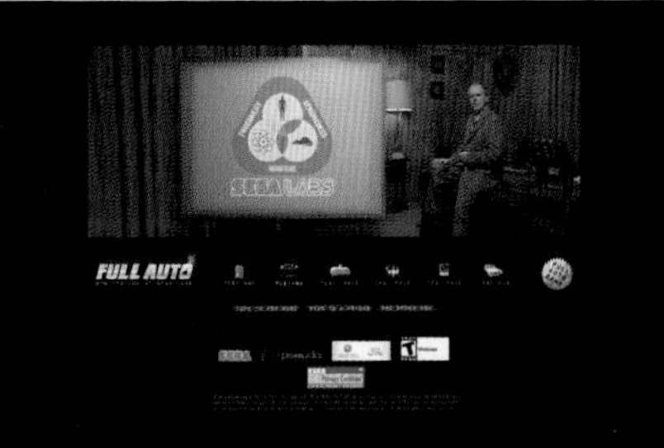

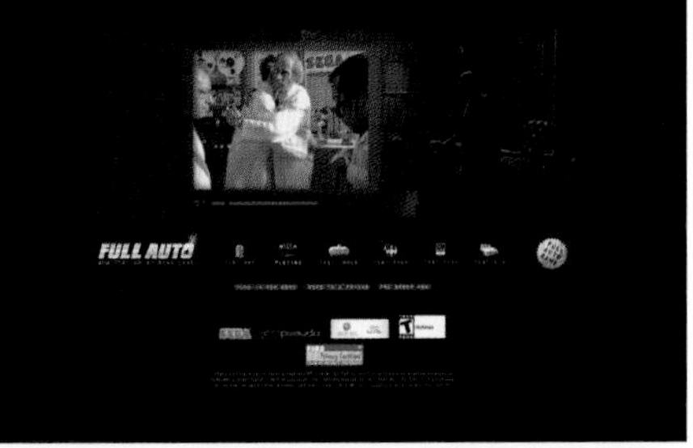

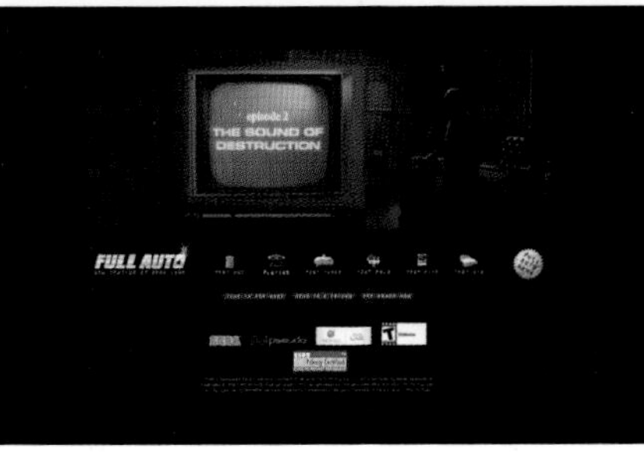

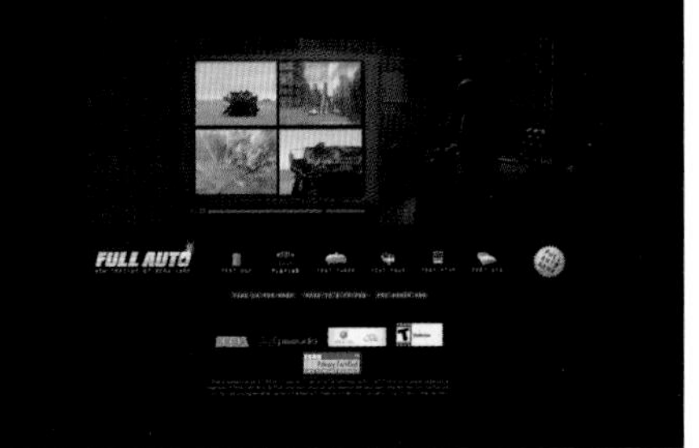

# SIGNE 2 CHANCE

FRANCE

www.signe2chance.com

2007

Concept

**Visitors to this site are invited to take part in a highly amusing interactive adventure game. They have to accomplish a series of steps to collect lucky signs on their way to the Super Jackpot.** /// Die Besucher dieser Site werden zur Teilnahme an einem höchst amüsanten interaktiven Adventure-Spiel eingeladen. Sie müssen verschiedene Stufen vollenden, um auf Ihrem Weg zum Super Jackpot Glückszeichen zu sammeln. /// **Les visiteurs de ce site sont invités à prendre part à un jeu d'aventure interactif très divertissant. Ils doivent réussir une série d'étapes pour collectionner les symboles porte-bonheur sur le chemin du Super Jackpot.**

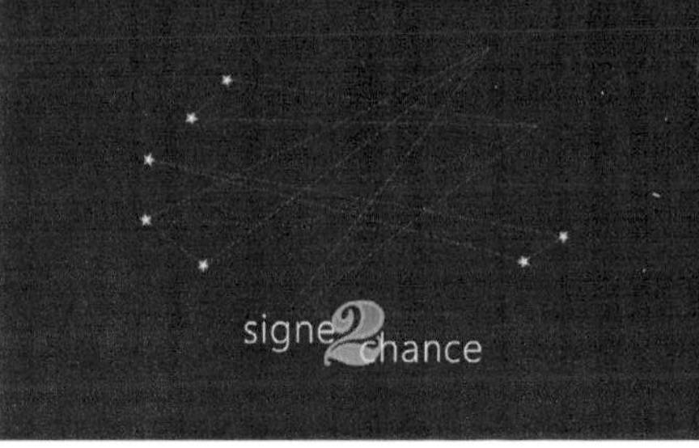


Info

**DESIGN:** Les Chinois <www.leschinois.com>: Pierre-Yves Roudy. /// **PROGRAMMING:** Alexandre C. (Lead Developer). /// **VIDEO:** Prime Touch. /// **CLIENT:** Groupe Lucien Barrière. /// **TOOLS:** Flash, Photoshop, After Effects. /// **COST:** 2,5 months.

MACHINES A SOUS

signe 2 chance

passer l'introduction

En savoir plus

Meilleurs scores

Envoyer à un ami

Goodies

A gagner

Aujourd'hui n'est pas
un jour comme les autres !

Des signes de chance se multiplient
autour de vous et un médium
vous propose une consultation...

Entrez dans l'aventure et suivez les
Signes 2 Chance, vous pourrez peut-être
gagner un séjour pour 2 personnes dans
l'un des prestigieux Hôtels Barrière... et
bien d'autres choses encore !

Mentions légales

Règlement

ENTRER DANS
L'AVENTURE

signe 2 chance

# SOKO COLT

GERMANY

www.soko-colt.de

2007

Concept

**With several video messages playing on the VCR in his office, the chief inspector invites the user to help the task force solving the case.** /// Durch verschiedene Videonachrichten, die der Videorekorder in seinem Büro abspielt, lädt der Chefinspektor den User ein, seiner Soko bei der Lösung des Falls zu helfen. /// **Pendant que plusieurs messages vidéo passent sur le magnétoscope de son bureau, l'inspecteur en chef invite le visiteur à aider l'équipe chargée de résoudre l'affaire.**

Info

**Design:** blackbeltmonkey, digital advertising agency <www.blackbeltmonkey.com>: Oliver Bentz, Mike John Otto (Creative Director); blackbeltmonkey, Santa Maria Werbeagentur (Art Direction); Marcellus Gau (Project Manager). /// **Programming:** Mellow Message. /// **Video:** Markenfilm. /// **Others:** V8 Studio (Sound). /// **Client:** Mitsubishi. /// **Tools:** Photoshop, Flash. /// **Awards:** Designaside, Lookom, Styleboost. /// **Cost:** 1 month.

FOLGEN SIE DEN
ANWEISUNGEN AUF
DEN SCHILDERN.
HIER KLICKEN
HIER KLICKEN
HIER KLICKEN
HIER KLICKEN
HIER KLICKEN
HIER KLICKEN
Hilfe | Impressum
Ton aus

ZURÜCK

ZURÜCK

ZURÜCK

ZURÜCK

# SPACE MOUNTAIN: MISSION 2

FRANCE

www.mission2.com

2005

Concept

"Recruiting interplanetary exploronauts!" Disneyland Paris chose this theme to launch its new "Space Mountain: Mission 2" attraction. The website takes users inside the exploronaut recruitment center. /// „Exploronauten gesucht!" Disneyland Paris entschied sich für dieses Thema als Werbung für die neue Attraktion „Space Mountain: Mission 2". Die Website nimmt die User mit in das Rekrutierungszentrum der Exploronauten. /// « Nous recrutons des exploronautes interplanétaires ! » Disneyland Paris a choisi ce thème pour lancer sa nouvelle attraction « Space Mountain : Mission 2 ». Le site web fait entrer les visiteurs dans le centre de recrutement des exploronautes.

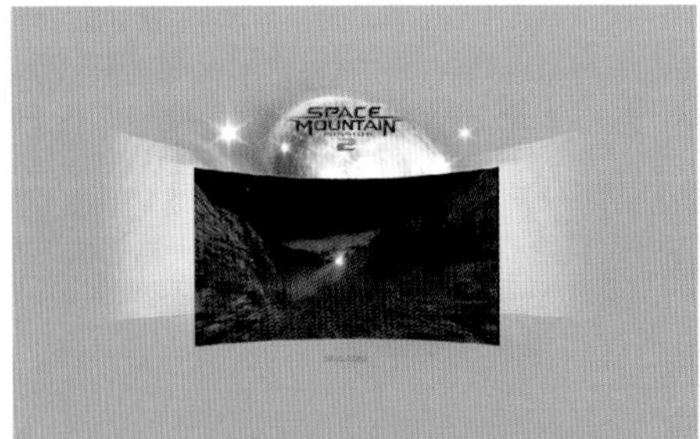

Info

**DESIGN:** Les Chinois <www.leschinois.com>: Ludovic Roudy (Creative Director). /// **PROGRAMMING:** Julien Bennamias (Lead Developer). /// **CLIENT:** Disneyland Resort Paris. /// **TOOLS:** Flash, Photoshop, After Effects. /// **AWARDS:** Silver Clic. /// **COST:** 3 months.

SPACE MOUNTAIN
MISSION
2
LAUNCH PAD :
DISNEYLAND RESORT PARIS
© Disney - All rights reserved

SPACE MOUNTAIN
MISSION
2
LAUNCH PAD :
DISNEYLAND RESORT PARIS
© Disney - All rights reserved

# SPOOKS GRID OPS

UK

http://spooksmi5.info

2004

Concept

To accompany the third series of BBC One's espionage drama Spooks, Preloaded developed an interactive experience set at the center of MI5 counter-terrorism operations, the GRID. /// Als Begleitung der dritten Staffel der Spionageserie *Spooks* von BBC One entwickelte Preloaded eine interaktive Erfahrung, die im GRID angesiedelt ist, der zentralen Terrorismusbekämpfung des MI5. /// **Pour accompagner la troisième saison de Spooks, une série d'espionnage de BBC One, Preloaded a créé une expérience interactive dont l'action se déroule au centre des opérations antiterrorisme du MI5, le GRID.**

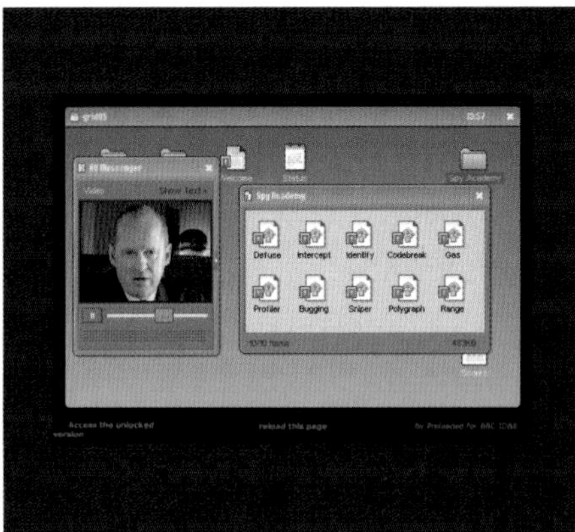


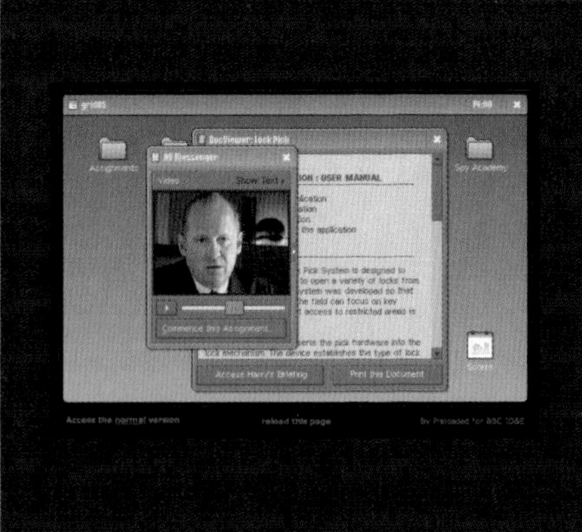


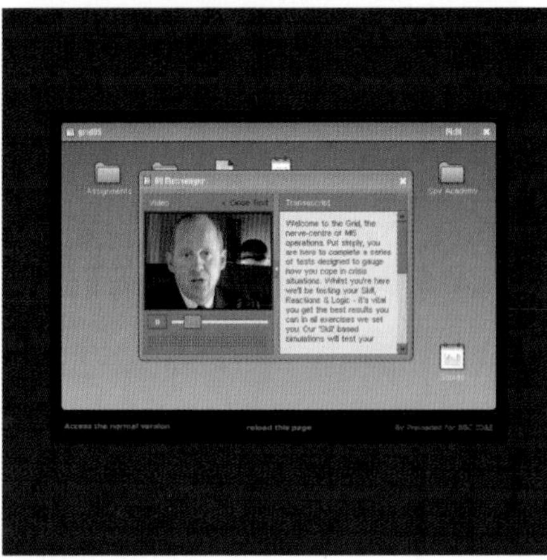


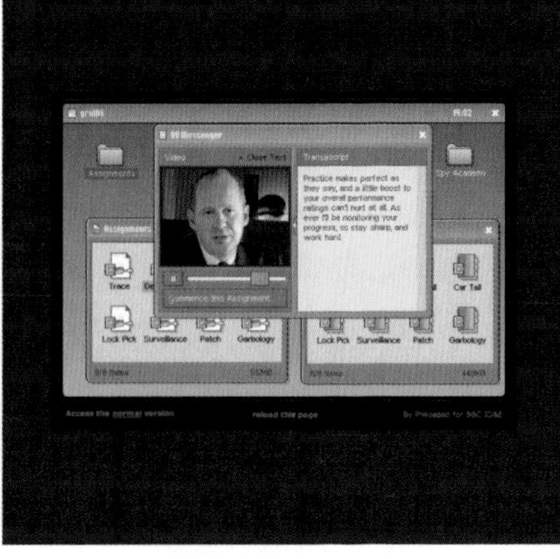


Info

**Design:** Preloaded <www.preloaded.com>. /// **Programming:** Preloaded. /// **Video:** BBC, Preloaded. /// **Client:** BBC. /// **Tools:** Flash, XML, Photoshop, Illustrator, After Effects, 3D Studio Max. /// **Awards:** BIMA (Entertainment and Games), SXSW (Games), W3 Awards (Entertainment/Silver), D&AD (In-book status), Creative Review (Annual), FWA (Site of the Day). /// **Cost:** 900 hours.

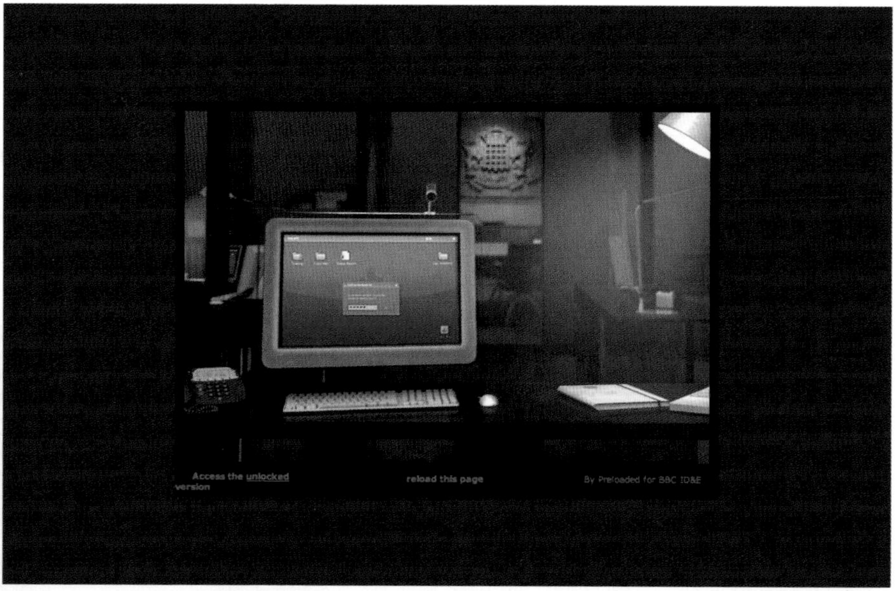

Access the unlocked version
reload this page
By Preloaded for BBC ID&E

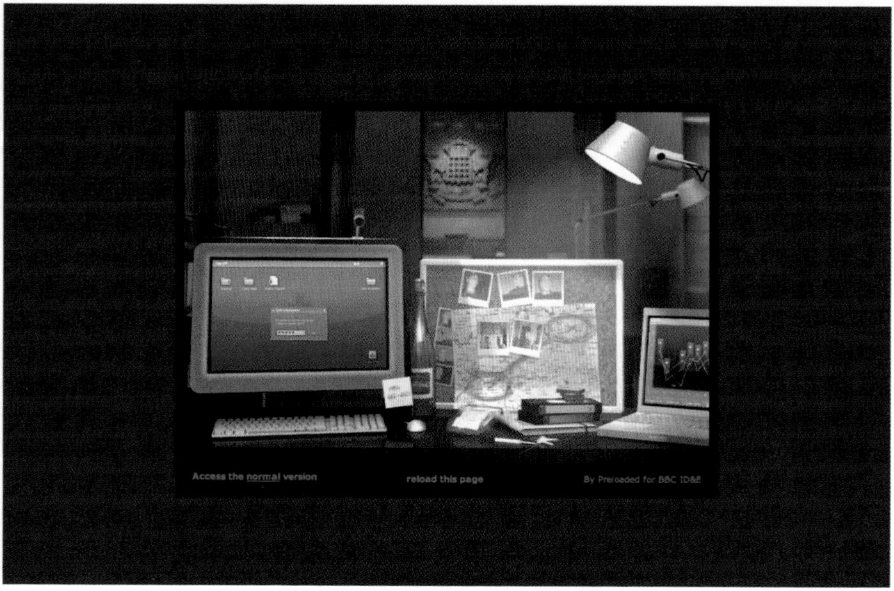

Access the normal version
reload this page
By Preloaded for BBC ID&E

# STOP SMOKING

SWEDEN

http://demo.fb.se/e/apoteket/stop_smoking

2007

Concept

Stop Smoking is a complete talk show about all the positive things that await you if you stop smoking. You can either view the entire program from beginning to end, or jump about in the menu between topics. /// Stop Smoking ist eine komplette Talkshow über all die positiven Dinge, die einen erwarten, wenn man mit dem Rauchen aufhört. Sie können sich entweder die gesamte Sendung von Anfang bis Ende anschauen oder themenbezogen bestimmte Stellen anspringen. /// Stop Smoking est un véritable « talk-show » sur toutes les bonnes choses qui vous attendent si vous arrêtez de fumer. Vous pouvez voir le programme dans sa totalité, du début à la fin, ou bien passer directement aux sujets qui vous intéressent grâce au menu.

Info

**DESIGN:** B-Reel <www.b-reel.com>; Forsman & Bodenfors <www.fb.se>. /// **PROGRAMMING:** B-Reel. /// **CLIENT:** Apoteket (Swedish Pharmacy). /// **AWARDS:** One Show.

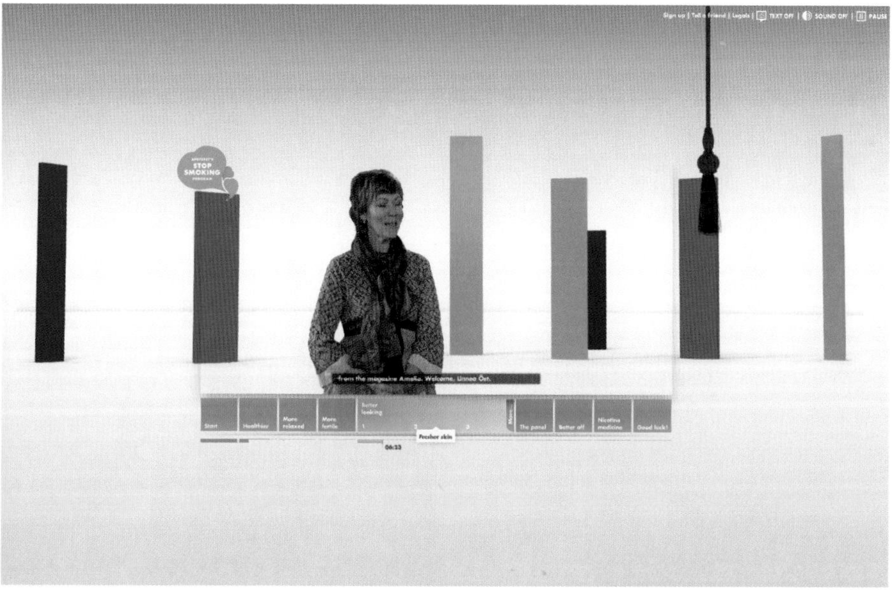
Sign up | Tell a friend | Legals | TEXT OFF | SOUND OFF | PAUSE
STOP SMOKING
from the magazine Amelia. Welcome, Linnea Öst.
Start
Healthier
More relaxed
More fertile
Better looking
Fresher skin
The panel
Better off
Nicotine medicine
Good luck!
06:23

Sign up | Tell a friend | Legals | TEXT OFF | SOUND OFF | PAUSE
STOP SMOKING
I can have longer walks, I feel clean.
10:06

# TERRANOVA KIDS

ITALY

www.terranovakids.it

2008

Concept

For this kids' brand, video is employed to show the happy atmosphere of the photo-shootings with the children. /// Diese Marke für Kinder setzt Videos ein, um die lockere Atmosphäre bei den Foto-Shootings mit den Kindern zu zeigen. /// Pour cette marque pour enfants, la vidéo sert à transmettre la joyeuse ambiance des sessions de photo avec les enfants.

Info

**Design:** Extera <www.extera.com>. /// **Programming:** Extera. /// **Video:** pingpot <www.pingpot.com>. /// **Client:** Teddy. /// **Tools:** Flash, Javascript, ASP, CSS.

COLLEZIONE DOWNLOAD BACKSTAGE PREZZI SHOPS

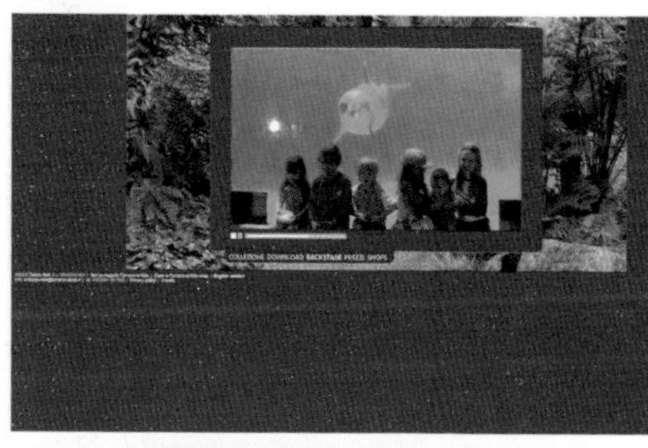

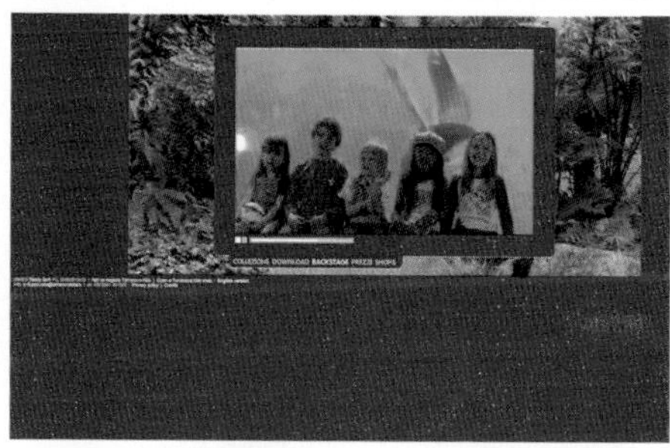

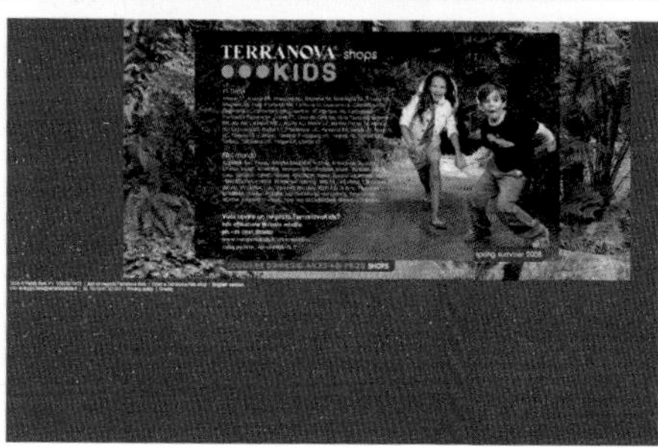


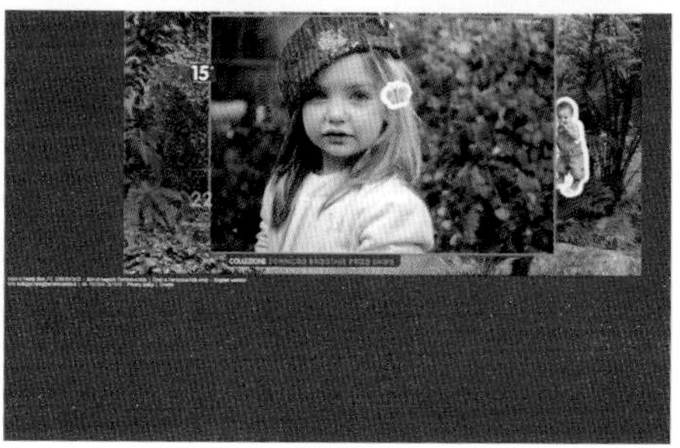

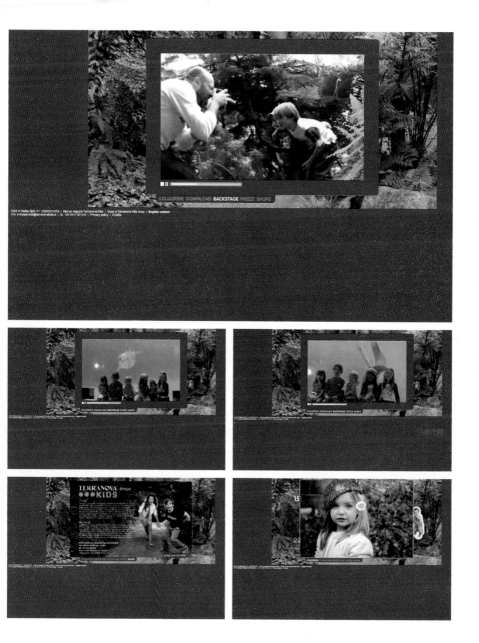

# TERRANOVA: SPIRITO ITALIANO

ITALY

www.terranova-on-line.com

2008

Concept

**For the Backstage part of the site, many videos have been combined to portray the fashion show and the making of the photo shootings.** /// Für den Backstage-Bereich dieser Site wurden viele Videos kombiniert, um die Fashion-Show und das *Making of* der Fotoshootings zu porträtieren. /// **Pour la partie Backstage du site, plusieurs vidéos ont été combinées pour donner une idée du défilé et du déroulement des sessions de photo.**

Info

**Design:** Extera <www.extera.com>. /// **Programming:** Extera. /// **Video:** pingpot <www.pingpot.com>. /// **Client:** Teddy. /// **Tools:** Flash, Javascript, ASP, CSS.

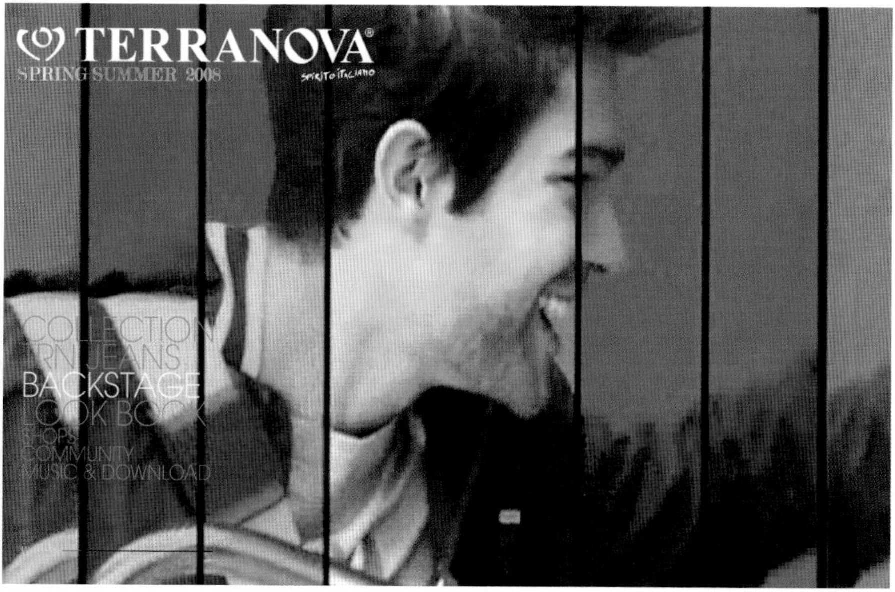

TERRANOVA®
SPRING SUMMER 2008
spirito italiano

COLLECTION
TRN JEANS
BACKSTAGE
LOOK BOOK
SHOPS
COMMUNITY
MUSIC & DOWNLOAD

TERRANOVA
SPRING SUMMER 2008

COLLECTION
TRN JEANS
BACKSTAGE
LOOK BOOK
SHOPS
COMMUNITY
MUSIC & DOWNLOAD

# TIGER BEER

UK

www.tigerbeer.co.uk

2008

Concept

This website is the home of Tiger Beer online, and video animations spread throughout the site aim to enhance the fluidity of the user experience. /// Die Website von Tiger Beer arbeitet mit Videoanimationen, um das Besuchserlebnis für die User möglichst flüssig zu gestalten. /// Ce site web est le quartier général de Tiger Beer sur Internet, et les animations vidéo qui le parsèment ont pour objectif de rendre la visite plus fluide.

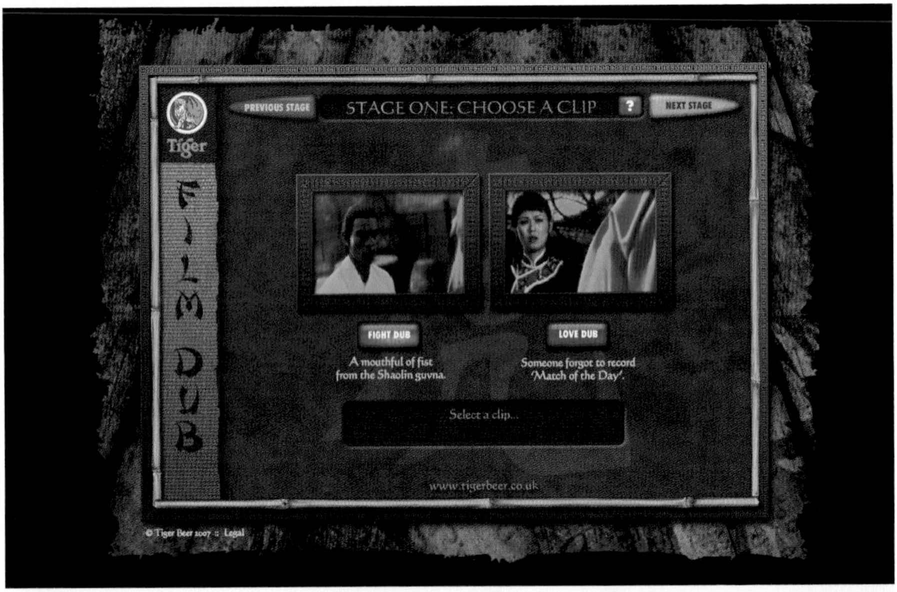

Info

**Design:** Onscreen Creative <www.onscreencreative.com>: Tim Dillon. /// **Programming:** Rob Thomson, Marotori. /// **Video:** Tim Dillon (Animation). /// **Client:** Tiger Beer. /// **Tools:** After Effects, Flash, HTML, Photoshop, Illustrator. /// **Cost:** 6 weeks, ongoing management.

STAGE FOUR PREVIEW & SEND
Tiger
FIGHT DUB
TASCHEN

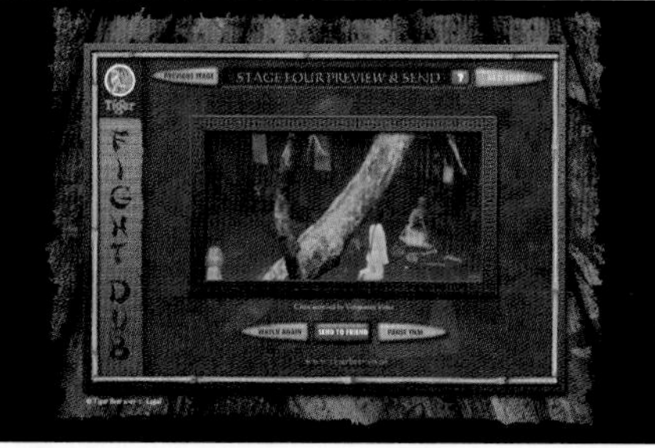
STAGE FOUR PREVIEW & SEND
Tiger
FIGHT DUB

STAGE FOUR PREVIEW & SEND
Tiger
FIGHT DUB

STAGE FOUR PREVIEW & SEND
Tiger
FIGHT DUB

PREVIOUS STAGE
STAGE FOUR PREVIEW & SEND
?
NEXT STAGE
Tiger
FIGHT DUB
Clips supplied by Vengeance Video
WATCH AGAIN
SEND TO FRIEND
PAUSE FILM
www.tigerbeer.co.uk
© Tiger Beer 2007 :: Legal

# VETOR ZERO

BRAZIL

www.vetorzero.com.br

1996

Concept

Vetor Zero, a film production company, had a large collection of excellent films to showcase, so this website helps the user to find and access them with a sleek interface. /// Die Filmproduktionsfirma Vetor Zero präsentiert eine große Sammlung ausgezeichneter Filme. Mit einem pfiffigen Interface kann der User diese Filme finden. /// Vetor Zero, une société de production de films, voulait présenter sa vaste collection d'excellents films. Ce site web aide le visiteur à les trouver et à les visionner grâce à une interface élégante.

Info

**Design:** 14bits <http://14bits.com.br>: Rico Villas Boas. /// **Programming:** Jayme Cavalcanti Neto, Rico Villas Boas. /// **Video:** Vetor Zero. /// **Client:** Vetor Zero. /// **Tools:** Flash. /// **Cost:** 500 hours.

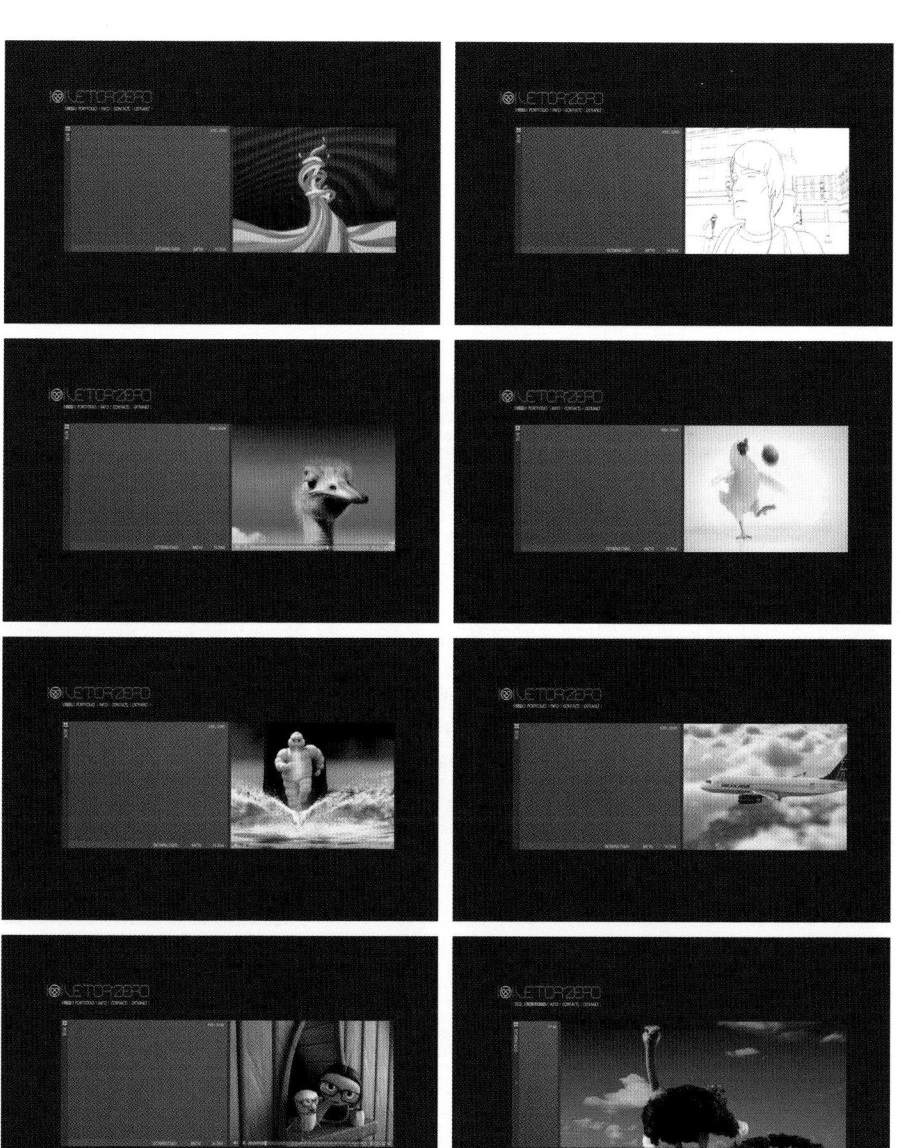

# VIRGIN RECORDS

USA

www.virginrecords.com

2006

Concept

Virgin Records wanted a powerfully branded showcase for muscular acts like The Rolling Stones, Ben Harper & Joss Stone. The challenge was to organize the artists into an easy-to-navigate portal, creating a framework for a broad range of musical styles. /// Virgin Records wollte für Top-Acts wie die Rolling Stones, Ben Harper oder Joss Stone ein kraftvolles Marken-Showcase. Die Herausforderung bestand darin, die Künstler in einem leicht zu bedienenden Portal zu versammeln und darin einen Rahmen für eine große Bandbreite von Musikstilen zu schaffen. /// Virgin Records voulait une vitrine possédant une identité de marque solide pour des géants tels que les Rolling Stones, Ben Harper et Joss Stone. Le défi consistait à organiser les artistes dans un portail à la navigation simple, et de créer un cadre général pour un vaste éventail de styles musicaux.

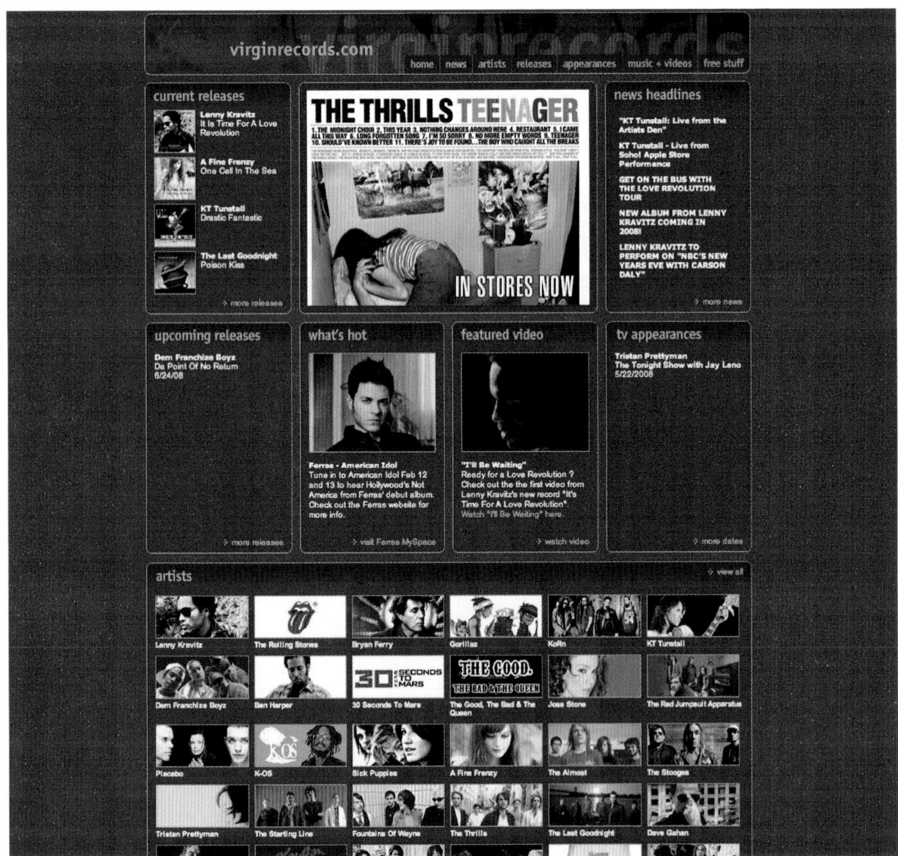


Info

**Design:** Fahrenheit Studio <www.fahrenheit.com>: Dylan Tran, Robert Weitz. /// **Programming:** Hillary Safarik, Heather Elliott, Dylan Tran. /// **Others:** Jesse Kanner (Senior Director Digital Strategy). /// **Client:** Virgin Records/Capitol Music Group. /// **Tools:** XHTML, Photoshop, Illustrator, Flash. /// **Awards:** Horizon Interactive Awards, Summit Creative Awards, Creativity Awards. /// **Cost:** 300 hours.

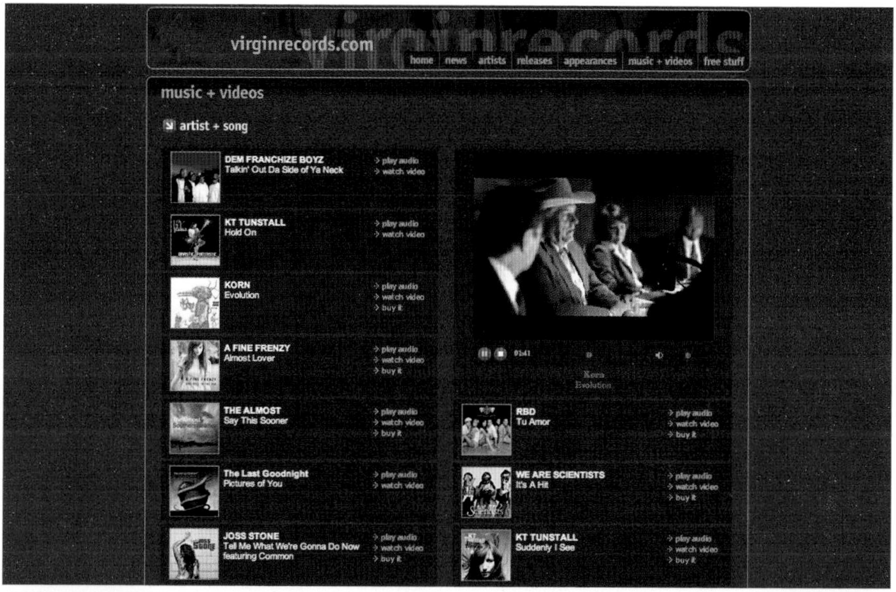

virginrecords.com

home | news | artists | releases | appearances | music + videos | free stuff

## music + videos

### artist + song

**DEM FRANCHIZE BOYZ**
Talkin' Out Da Side of Ya Neck
> play audio
> watch video

**KT TUNSTALL**
Hold On
> play audio
> watch video

**KORN**
Evolution
> play audio
> watch video
> buy it

**A FINE FRENZY**
Almost Lover
> play audio
> watch video
> buy it

**THE ALMOST**
Say This Sooner
> play audio
> watch video
> buy it

**The Last Goodnight**
Pictures of You
> play audio
> watch video

**JOSS STONE**
Tell Me What We're Gonna Do Now featuring Common
> play audio
> watch video
> buy it

01:41

Korn
Evolution

**RBD**
Tu Amor
> play audio
> watch video
> buy it

**WE ARE SCIENTISTS**
It's A Hit
> play audio
> watch video
> buy it

**KT TUNSTALL**
Suddenly I See
> play audio
> watch video
> buy it

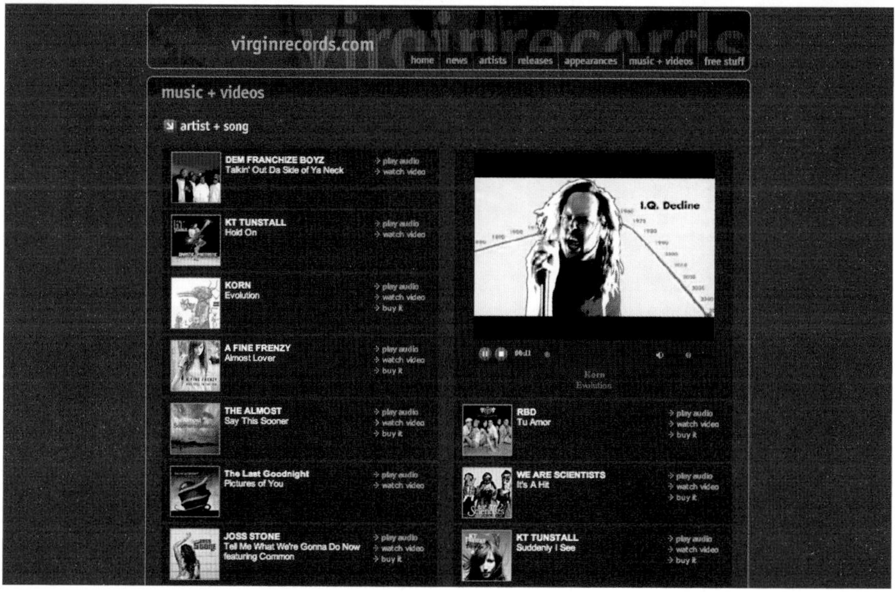

virginrecords.com

home | news | artists | releases | appearances | music + videos | free stuff

music + videos

artist + song

DEM FRANCHIZE BOYZ
Talkin' Out Da Side of Ya Neck
> play audio
> watch video

KT TUNSTALL
Hold On
> play audio
> watch video

KORN
Evolution
> play audio
> watch video
> buy it

A FINE FRENZY
Almost Lover
> play audio
> watch video
> buy it

THE ALMOST
Say This Sooner
> play audio
> watch video
> buy it

The Last Goodnight
Pictures of You
> play audio
> watch video

JOSS STONE
Tell Me What We're Gonna Do Now featuring Common
> play audio
> watch video
> buy it

I.Q. Decline

Korn
Evolution

RBD
Tu Amor
> play audio
> watch video
> buy it

WE ARE SCIENTISTS
It's A Hit
> play audio
> watch video
> buy it

KT TUNSTALL
Suddenly I See
> play audio
> watch video
> buy it

# VOLVO C30

SWEDEN

http://demo.fb.se/e/volvo/c30

2007

Concept

The Volvo C30 is a very different kind of Volvo and a different kind of small car. The "Think Outside the Box" website includes a creative workshop and an extremely colorful, interactive test-drive. /// Der Volvo C30 ist als sehr außergewöhnlicher Volvo eine ganz andere Art von Kleinwagen. Die Website „Think Outside the Box" enthält einen Kreativworkshop und eine ungewöhnlich farbenprächtige interaktive Testfahrt. /// La Volvo C30 est un cas à part chez Volvo, et un cas à part chez les petites voitures. Le site web « Think Outside the Box » comprend un atelier de création et un test de conduite extrêmement coloré et interactif.

Info

**Design:** Forsman & Bodenfors <www.fb.se>. /// **Programming:** Kokokaka Entertainment. /// **Video:** Stylewar. /// **Client:** Volvo. /// **Tools:** Flash, Illustrator, Photoshop, After Effects, Cinema 4D, Maya. /// **Awards:** 100w, Cannes Lions, Clio, D&AD, One Show.

C30

C30

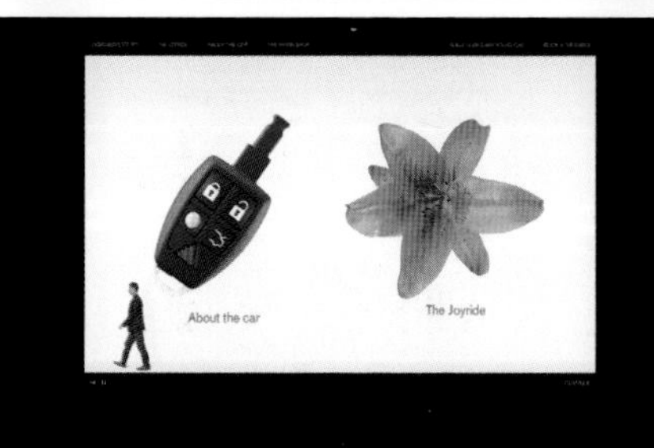
About the car
The Joyride

The Joyride

# WANDA

FRANCE

www.wanda.fr

2007

Concept

**A simple and effective online video portfolio of film directors.** /// Ein einfaches und effektives Video-Portfolio von Filmregisseuren. /// **Un portfolio de réalisateurs simple et efficace.**

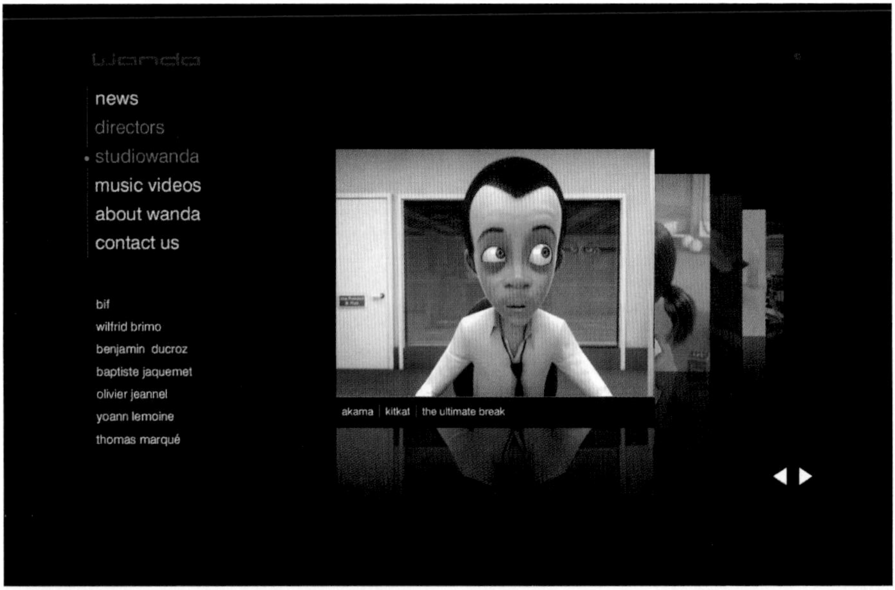

wanda
news
directors
studiowanda
music videos
about wanda
contact us
bif
wilfrid brimo
benjamin ducroz
baptiste jaquemet
olivier jeannel
yoann lemoine
thomas marqué
akama | kitkat | the ultimate break


news
directors
studiowanda
music videos
about wanda
contact us


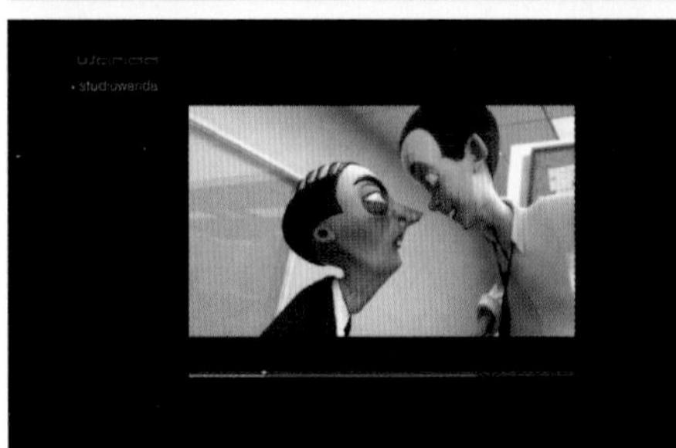

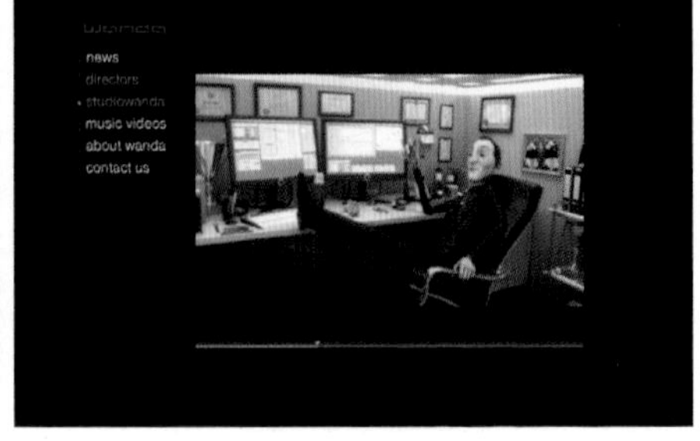

Info

**Design:** Spill <www.spill.net>: Liz Stirling, Nicholas Mir Chaikin, Virginie Nguyen Tan Hon, Adela Senous. /// **Programming:** Christophe Le Bars, Morgan Legal, Jonathan Da Costa, François Chay. /// **Video:** Wanda Productions. /// **Others:** Patrick Barbier (Executive Producer); Juliette Mage for Spill with Claire Potel, and Clementine Buren for Wanda (Design Coordination/Producer). /// **Client:** Wanda Productions. /// **Tools:** Flash, PHP, MySQL. /// **Cost:** 700 hours.

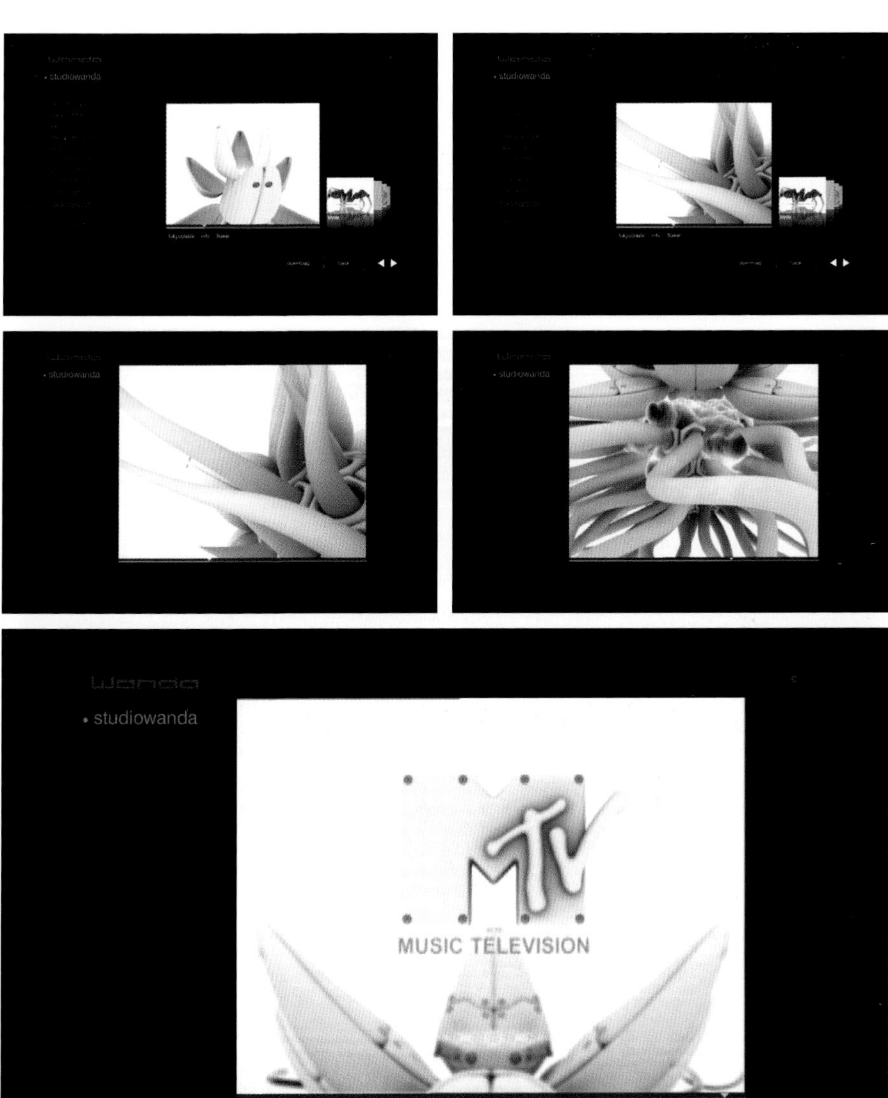
• studiowanda
• studiowanda
• studiowanda
• studiowanda
• studiowanda
MTV
MUSIC TELEVISION

# WHALEFOOTAGE

GERMANY

www.whalefootage.org

2007

Concept

The Okeanos Foundation is committed to the protection of the seas. This website serves as a platform for making the foundation's comprehensive film archive accessible free of charge. /// Die Okeanos Foundation setzt sich für den Schutz der Weltmeere ein. Die Website dient als Plattform, auf der das umfangreiche Filmarchiv der Stiftung kostenlos online gestellt wird. /// La Fondation Okeanos s'occupe de la préservation des océans. Ce site web lui sert de plateforme pour présenter gratuitement ses archives de films très complètes.

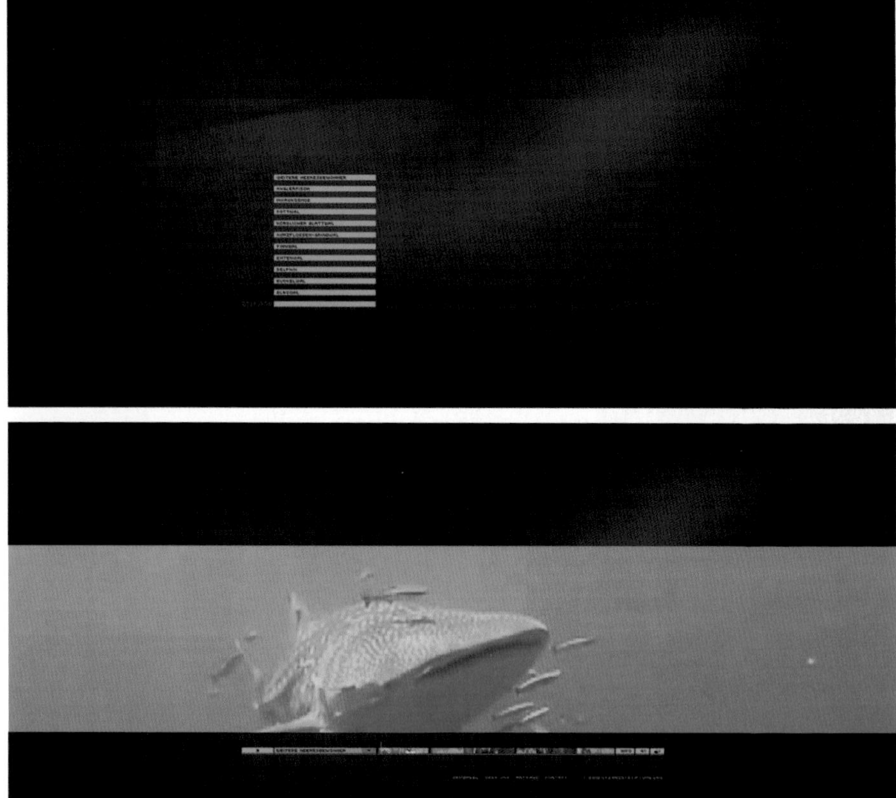

Info

**Design:** Scholz & Volkmer <www.s-v.de>: Heike Brockmann (Executive Creative Direction); Philipp Bareiss (Art Direction); Philipp Bareiss (Screen Design). /// **Programming:** Peter Reichard (Executive Technical Direction); Florian Finke (Programming). /// **Video:** Dieter Paulmann – Okeanos (Foundation for the Sea). /// **Others:** Peter Reichard (Project Management); Peter Reichard, Philipp Bareiss, Duc-Thuan Bui (Concept); Dieter Paulmann, Tanja Winkler (Copy); Jörg Remy (Sound). /// **Client:** Okeanos (Foundation for the Sea). /// **Tools:** Flash. /// **Awards:** FWA (Site of the Day), New York Festivals (Innovative Advertising Awards/Finalist).

# WOULD YOU LIKE A WEBSITE? USA

www.wouldyoulikeawebsite.com 2006

Concept

**Self-promotional website which contains eight 30-second spots that feature Freedom's staff hitting the streets of Manhattan in a modern-day twist on the traditional sandwich-board advertising method.** /// Eine Website zur Eigenwerbung, auf der acht 30-Sekunden-Spots enthalten sind, in denen Mitarbeiter von Freedom in den Straßen Manhattans als moderne Variante des Reklametafelmannes herumlaufen. /// **Site web d'autopromotion, avec des spots de 30 secondes où l'on voit l'équipe de Freedom arpenter les rues de Manhattan dans une réinterprétation moderne de l'homme-sandwich traditionnel.**

Info

**DESIGN:** Freedom Interactive Design <www.freedominteractivedesign.com>: Mark Ferdman (Creative Director); Matt Sundstrom (Senior Art Director); Sabina Hahn (Illustration/Animation). /// **PROGRAMMING:** Shea Gonyo (Tech Director); Josh Ott (Senior Action Script Developer). /// **VIDEO:** Shea Gonyo (Director, Editor, Post-production Effects); Josh Ott (Editor, Post-production Effects). /// **TOOLS:** After Effects, Flash. /// **AWARDS:** 11th Webby Awards (Corporate Communications/Nominee); FWA (Site of the Day); FWA (Top 50 Sites 2006); Adobe Design Center Feature. /// **COST:** 600 hours.

FREEDOM
INTERACTIVE DESIGN

We've been nominated for The Webby Awards Best Corporate Communications Website of 2007! **Vote for us** to win the People's Choice Award. Interested in more? Read about the making of this site and view outtakes at The FWA.

**Would You Like A Website?**

created for Design Center Adobe

# YOGA SCHELTER

CANADA

www.yogaschelter.com

2007

Concept

**Presents an engaging and calming experience for visitors to this site. The use of video throughout helps to unite the various sections of the site and provides a window into the yoga teachings of Jennifer Schelter.** /// Diese Site präsentiert den Besuchern eine bezaubernde und beruhigende Erfahrung. Der Einsatz von Videos eint die verschiedenen Bereiche der Site und bietet Einblicke in den Yoga-Unterricht von Jennifer Schelter. /// **Présente une expérience captivante et apaisante pour les visiteurs. La vidéo aide à relier les différentes parties du site et ouvre une fenêtre sur les enseignements de yoga de Jennifer Schelter.**

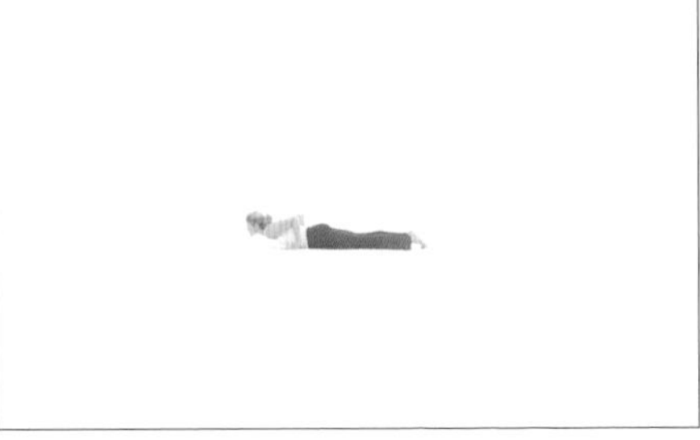

Info

**Design:** Analogue <www.analogue.ca>: Jory Kruspe, Craig Hooper. /// **Programming:** Jory Kruspe, Craig Hooper. /// **Video:** Weymouth Design, Inc. /// **Client:** Yoga Schelter. /// **Tools:** Flash, Photoshop, Dreamweaver, Quicktime, XML, HTML. /// **Cost:** 1 month.

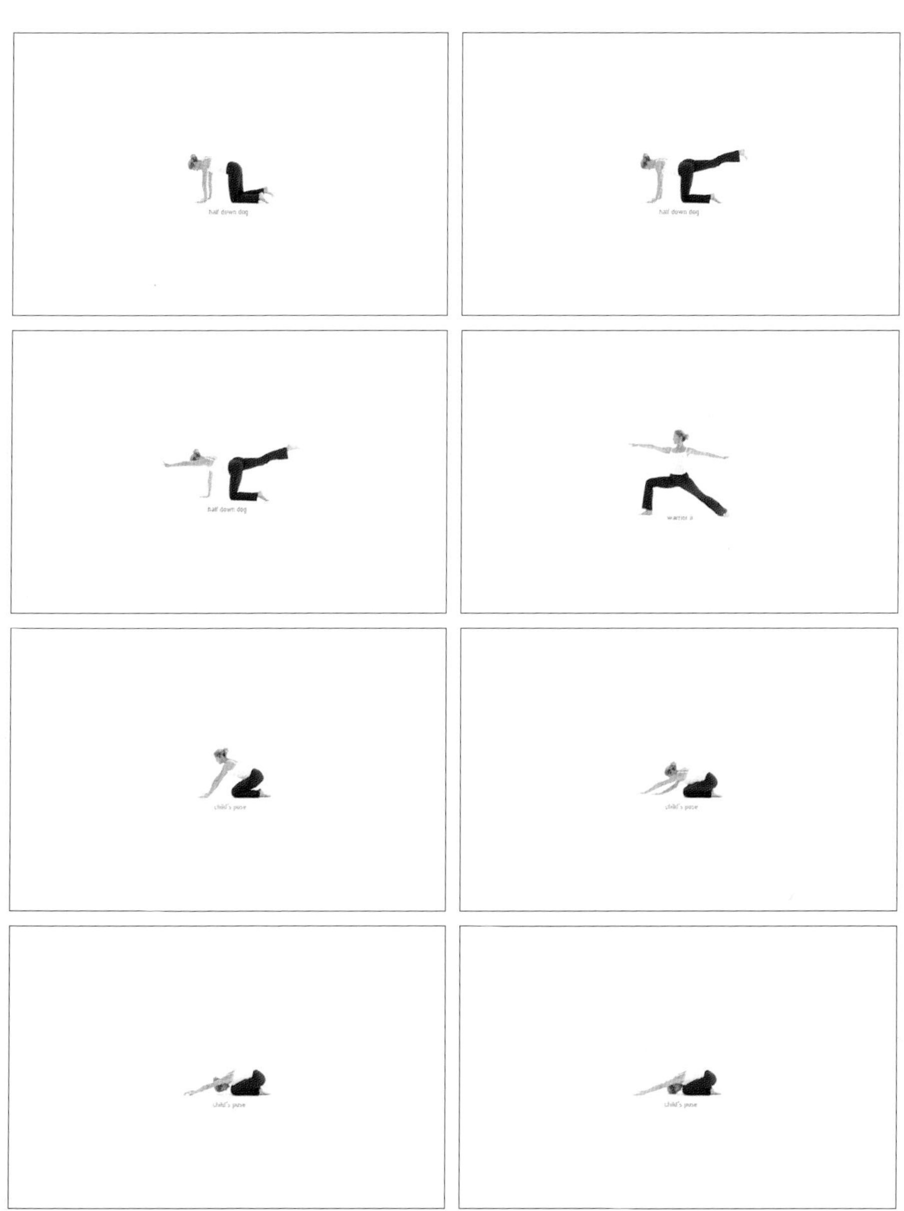
half down dog
half down dog
half down dog
child's pose
child's pose
child's pose
child's pose

# YOU NEED A QUIET SPACE

SWEDEN

http://demo.fb.se/e/ikea/calmbedrooms

2007

Concept

In this campaign IKEA invites you to look at your bedroom in a new way. Not just as a room to sleep in, but also as an oasis of calm where you can read, relax and recharge after a hectic day full of work and household chores. /// In dieser Kampagne lädt IKEA die Besucher ein, das eigene Schlafzimmer aus einem neuen Blickwinkel zu betrachten. Nicht bloß als Raum zum Schlafen, sondern auch als Oase der Ruhe, in der man nach einem hektischen Tag voller Arbeit und Haushalt endlich lesen, entspannen und Kräfte sammeln kann. /// Avec cette campagne, IKEA vous invite à voir votre chambre autrement. Pas seulement comme une pièce pour dormir, mais aussi comme une oasis de paix où vous pouvez lire, vous détendre et recharger vos batteries après une folle journée de travail et de corvées ménagères.

Info

**DESIGN:** Forsman & Bodenfors <www.fb.se>. /// **PROGRAMMING:** Thomson Interactive. /// **VIDEO:** St Paul. /// **CLIENT:** IKEA. /// **TOOLS:** Flash, Illustrator, Photoshop, After Effects, Cinema 4D, Maya. /// **AWARDS:** Art Directors Club (New York), D&AD, Eurobest, Guldägget, New York Festival, One Show.

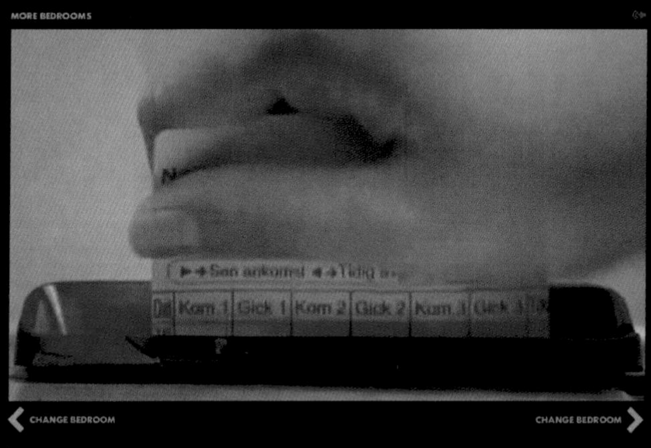
MORE BEDROOMS
Kom 1
Gick 1
Kom 2
Gick 2
CHANGE BEDROOM
CHANGE BEDROOM

MORE BEDROOMS
1.535:–
STOLMEN
storage system ›
545:– /each
ANEBODA
chest with 3 drawers ›
895:–
ANEBODA
bed frame ›
CHANGE BEDROOM
CHANGE BEDROOM

# ZARTOFON (JOKEPHONE)

POLAND

www.zartofon.pl

2008

Concept

**Demonstrations of a new service offered by leading Polish cell-phone provider Polkomtel that allows users to joke around with their friends by mobile phone. Includes several video spots and funny animations.** /// Demonstration eines neuen Dienstes, der vom führenden polnischen Handyanbieter Polkomtel angeboten wird. Hier können die User per Handy mit ihren Freunden herumalbern. Enthält mehrere Videospots und lustige Trickfilme. /// **Des démonstrations d'un nouveau service proposé par le premier fournisseur polonais de téléphonie mobile, Polkomtel, qui permet aux visiteurs de faire des farces à leurs amis par téléphone mobile. Comprend plusieurs clips vidéo et des animations amusantes.**

Info

**DESIGN:** Opcom Grupa Eskadra <www.opcom.pl>: Tomasz Marc, Grzegorz Gracz, Krzysztof Kochmanski. /// **PROGRAMMING:** Rafal Szemraj. /// **CLIENT:** Polkomtel. /// **TOOLS:** Flash, HTML, PHP. /// **COST:** 400 hours.

Zobacz, komu już wyrósł kaloryfer!
1. Wybierz numer *7-177 i naciśnij przycisk zadzwoń.
2. Żartofon poinformuje Cię, co nacisnąć, by wybrać jeden z trzech sposobów wkręcania. Wciskasz "1", jeśli chcesz wkręcić znajomego, "2", jeśli chcesz rozmawiać zmienionym głosem, a "3", jeśli chcesz zapewnić sobie alibi.
3. Żartofon poinformuje Cię o dostępnych odmianach danego sposobu, które wybierasz klawiszami 1, 2 lub 3. Podajesz numer telefonu osoby, z którą chcesz się połączyć, i wciskasz #.
4. Wkręcasz! Za minutę połączenia płacąc tylko 1 zł bez VAT*.
* opłata z VAT wynosi 1,22 zł; opłata za minutę połączenia nie zależy od wykorzystywanej taryfy osoby inicjującej połączenie; opłaty są naliczane za każde rozpoczęte 60 sekund połączenia.
ŻARTOFON
Plus.pl
REKLAMA
KONKURS
TO DZIAŁA
ZAPEWNIJ SOBIE ALIBI
ZMIEŃ GŁOS
WKRĘĆ ZNAJOMEGO
Created by Opcom

ŻARTOFON
Plus.pl
REKLAMA
KONKURS
TO DZIAŁA
ZAPEWNIJ SOBIE ALIBI
ZMIEŃ GŁOS
WKRĘĆ ZNAJOMEGO
Created by Opcom

# CREDITS

For reasons which became clear when putting together TASCHEN's recently published Web Design Interactive & Games, a book about the use of video on the web encounters similar difficulties when it comes to representing what is most current or most vital in web design today. As with all new tools which become popular, design companies as well as individuals have taken to using video and its new possibilities in their concepts for websites to express their own style and to make the sites they have worked on more engaging to users. Amongst the larger group of designers working in this field though there are those who stand out for their interest in extending the medium's possibilities still further, and who work as well with the technology involved to develop ever newer and fresher experiences for website users. Any list of such professional designers should not exclude the following, whose contributions to this book have been invaluable and to whom I wish to offer deep thanks, to Nicholas Mir Chaikin from Paris for the foreword, to Leo Prestes from Porto Alegre, Brazil, for the introduction, and for the two Case Studies at the beginning of the book I would like to thank Michael Lebowitz from New York, and Junichi Saito from Tokyo, respectively. My gratitude extends as well to the host of various programmers and creative talents across the world working in this exciting field and helping to take us all into unimagined futures.

Once again I would like to restate my huge thanks to Daniel Siciliano Brêtas, for his general overview in designing this series in the first place, and for his continued energy in seeking to make each new title an improvement on the last in terms of its overall quality. This guy is my right and left hand. To our production man, Stefan Klatte, my thanks are also due for his work in making this series look better and better, and for being able to work at almost the speed of light. With this series now arriving at its eighth title, we hope our readers share in the enthusiasm and excitement we feel each new part brings.

Julius Wiedemann

IMPRINT

## Web Design: Video Sites

To stay informed about upcoming TASCHEN titles, please request our magazine at www.taschen.com/magazine or write to TASCHEN, Hohenzollernring 53, D-50672 Cologne, Germany, contact@taschen.com, Fax: +49-221-254919. We will be happy to send you a free copy of our magazine which is filled with information about all of our books.

**Design & layout**: Daniel Siciliano Brêtas
**Production**: Stefan Klatte
**Editor**: Julius Wiedemann
**Editorial coordination**: Daniel Siciliano Brêtas

**German translation**: Katrin Kügler for Equipo de Edición, Barcelona
**French translation**: Aurélie Daniel for Equipo de Edición, Barcelona

Printed in Italy
ISBN: 978-3-8365-0494-2

**Guidelines for Online Success** Eds. Rob Ford, Julius Wiedemann / Softcover, 336 pp. / € 29.99 / $ 39.99 / £ 24.99 / ¥ 5.900

**Web Design: Interactive & Games**
Ed. Julius Wiedemann
Flexi-cover, 192 pp. / € 6.99 / $ 9.99 / £ 5.99 / ¥ 1.500

**Web Design: Studios 2**
Ed. Julius Wiedemann
Flexi-cover, 192 pp. / € 6.99 / $ 9.99 / £ 5.99 / ¥ 1.500

## "These books are beautiful objects, well-designed and lucid." —*Le Monde*, Paris, on the ICONS series

---

## "Buy them all and add some pleasure to your life."

**60s Fashion**
Ed. Jim Heimann
**70s Fashion**
Ed. Jim Heimann
**African Style**
Ed. Angelika Taschen
**Alchemy & Mysticism**
Alexander Roob
**Architecture Now!**
Ed. Philip Jodidio
**Art Now**
Eds. Burkhard Riemschneider, Uta Grosenick
**Atget's Paris**
Ed. Hans Christian Adam
**Bamboo Style**
Ed. Angelika Taschen
**Barcelona, Restaurants & More**
Ed. Angelika Taschen
**Barcelona, Shops & More**
Ed. Angelika Taschen
**Ingrid Bergman**
Ed. Paul Duncan, Scott Eyman
**Berlin Style**
Ed. Angelika Taschen
**Humphrey Bogart**
Ed. Paul Duncan, James Ursini
**Marlon Brando**
Ed. Paul Duncan, F.X. Feeney
**Brussels Style**
Ed. Angelika Taschen
**Cars of the 70s**
Ed. Jim Heimann, Tony Thacker
**Charlie Chaplin**
Ed. Paul Duncan, David Robinson
**China Style**
Ed. Angelika Taschen
**Christmas**
Ed. Jim Heimann, Steven Heller
**James Dean**
Ed. Paul Duncan, F.X. Feeney
**Design Handbook**
Charlotte & Peter Fiell
**Design for the 21st Century**
Eds. Charlotte & Peter Fiell
**Design of the 20th Century**
Eds. Charlotte & Peter Fiell
**Devils**
Gilles Néret
**Marlene Dietrich**
Ed. Paul Duncan, James Ursini
**Robert Doisneau**
Jean-Claude Gautrand
**East German Design**
Ralf Ulrich/Photos: Ernst Hedler
**Clint Eastwood**
Ed. Paul Duncan, Douglas Keesey
**Egypt Style**
Ed. Angelika Taschen
**Encyclopaedia Anatomica**
Ed. Museo La Specola Florence
**M.C. Escher**
**Fashion**
Ed. The Kyoto Costume Institute
**Fashion Now!**
Eds. Terry Jones, Susie Rushton
**Fruit**
Ed. George Brookshaw, Uta Pellgrü-Gagel
**Greta Garbo**
Ed. Paul Duncan, David Robinson
**HR Giger**
HR Giger
**Grand Tour**
Harry Seidler
**Cary Grant**
Ed. Paul Duncan, F.X. Feeney
**Graphic Design**
Eds. Charlotte & Peter Fiell
**Greece Style**
Ed. Angelika Taschen
**Halloween**
Ed. Jim Heimann, Steven Heller
**Havana Style**
Ed. Angelika Taschen
**Audrey Hepburn**
Ed. Paul Duncan, F.X. Feeney
**Katharine Hepburn**
Ed. Paul Duncan, Alain Silver
**Homo Art**
Gilles Néret
**Hot Rods**
Ed. Coco Shinomiya, Tony Thacker
**Grace Kelly**
Ed. Paul Duncan, Glenn Hopp
**London, Restaurants & More**
Ed. Angelika Taschen
**London, Shops & More**
Ed. Angelika Taschen
**London Style**
Ed. Angelika Taschen
**Marx Brothers**
Ed. Paul Duncan, Douglas Keesey
**Steve McQueen**
Ed. Paul Duncan, Alain Silver
**Mexico Style**
Ed. Angelika Taschen
**Miami Style**
Ed. Angelika Taschen
**Minimal Style**
Ed. Angelika Taschen
**Marilyn Monroe**
Ed. Paul Duncan, F.X. Feeney
**Morocco Style**
Ed. Angelika Taschen
**New York Style**
Ed. Angelika Taschen
**Paris Style**
Ed. Angelika Taschen
**Penguin**
Frans Lanting
**Pierre et Gilles**
Eric Troncy
**Provence Style**
Ed. Angelika Taschen
**Safari Style**
Ed. Angelika Taschen
**Seaside Style**
Ed. Angelika Taschen
**Signs**
Ed. Julius Wiedeman
**South African Style**
Ed. Angelika Taschen
**Starck**
Philippe Starck
**Surfing**
Ed. Jim Heimann
**Sweden Style**
Ed. Angelika Taschen
**Tattoos**
Ed. Henk Schiffmacher
**Tokyo Style**
Ed. Angelika Taschen
**Tuscany Style**
Ed. Angelika Taschen
**Valentines**
Ed. Jim Heimann, Steven Heller
**Web Design: Best Studios**
Ed. Julius Wiedemann
**Web Design: Best Studios 2**
Ed. Julius Wiedemann
**Web Design: E-Commerce**
Ed. Julius Wiedemann
**Web Design: Flash Sites**
Ed. Julius Wiedemann
**Web Design: Interactive & Games**
Ed. Julius Wiedemann
**Web Design: Music Sites**
Ed. Julius Wiedemann
**Web Design: Video Sites**
Ed. Julius Wiedemann
**Web Design: Portfolios**
Ed. Julius Wiedemann
**Orson Welles**
Ed. Paul Duncan, F.X. Feeney
**Women Artists 20th & 21st Cent.**
Ed. Uta Grosenick

ICONS